COMPUTERS,
MINDS
& ROBOTS

COMPUTERS, MINDS & ROBOTS

William S. Robinson

Temple University Press

Philadelphia

Temple University Press, Philadelphia 19122
Copyright © 1992 by Temple University. All rights reserved
Published 1992
Printed in the United States of America

The paper used in this publication meets the minimum
requirements of American National Standard for Information
Sciences—Permanence of Paper for Printed Library Materials,
ANSI Z39.48-1984 ⊗

Library of Congress Cataloging-in-Publication Data

Robinson, William S. (William Spencer), 1940–
    Computers, minds, and robots / William S. Robinson.
        p.   cm.
    Includes bibliographical references and indexes.
    ISBN 0-87722-915-5
    1. Computers.   2. Robotics.   3. Artificial intelligence.
4. Philosophy of mind.   I. Title.
QA76.5.R497   1992
006.3—dc20   91-39779

Figures 4.1 and 4.2 are copyrighted material reproduced from Daniel C.
Dennett, *Brainstorms* (Montgomery, Vt.: Bradford Books, 1978), by permission
of The MIT Press.

Contents

Preface

This book has grown out of a course on philosophical problems relating to artificial intelligence, "Brains, Minds, and Computers", that I have taught for several years in the philosophy department of Iowa State University. One course in philosophy is its only prerequisite, and both philosophy majors and students of the computer sciences have regularly taken it. In teaching the course, therefore, I have not been able to assume in the students either special knowledge of computers or special knowledge of philosophy. All necessary technical material has been introduced as part of the course. In this book, I have adhered to that policy. Some of the issues that are discussed here are unavoidably complex and therefore require some persistence to work through properly; but my aim has been to include every piece of background that the interested reader would need in order to follow the discussion.

My philosophical motto is "From obscurity into clarity." This reflects my view that philosophical problems arise from difficulty in seeing what the significance of facts (or possible discoveries) amounts to, and that philosophical progress consists in clarifying the implications of known facts and possible discoveries. The point of this book is thus not to provide information about the latest developments of computer or robot capability. Instead, it asks questions like these: If we had a machine that clearly did such and such tasks, what would that show about whether it could think or feel? What does our knowledge of mathematics imply about the nature of our thinking processes? What does the fact that we can do certain things imply (or fail to imply) about how we are able to do them? What would certain facts about ourselves imply about the possibility of certain kinds of machines?

True philosophical clarity does not come merely from plainly stating true views. One needs to spend at least as much time discussing muddled and incorrect views as one devotes to clear and enlightened ones, because the attractions of errors must be understood thoroughly if the errors are ultimately to be avoided. For this reason, readers will find here several sympathetic presentations of views with which I do not agree. I have, however—usually near the end of a discussion—stated my own view and the reasons for it. Thus, although this book covers much of what is standard material in courses in philosophy of artificial intelligence (AI) or philosophy of mind, it is not limited to a review of positions. It contains several new arguments and new attempts to resolve standing issues.

Two former students of mine, Mark Bowes and Brian Tiffany, are mentioned in notes to this book in connection with specific points that they brought to my attention. I wish to thank them here, along with the many other bright and interesting students who have made teaching "Brains, Minds, and Computers" a continuing challenge. From them I have gained a sharpened sense of what most needs to be clarified. They have often pointed out some confusion that one or another of my formulations invited, and readers of this book should be grateful to them for the resulting improvements.

I would like to thank Richard L. Epstein for reading more than half of an earlier version of this book and making many helpful comments, including one that rescued me from a substantial error. My colleagues Don Pigozzi in mathematics and Michael O'Boyle in psychology also read portions of the draft manuscript and made helpful suggestions, for which I thank them.

This book might not have been started without the encouragement of the Temple University Press philosophy editor, Jane Cullen. It might not have been finished without the encouragement of Maureen Ogle, whose dedication to her own work has been my inspiration.

COMPUTERS,
MINDS
& ROBOTS

Chapter 1

The Turing Test

In 1950, Alan Turing published a paper that has become a frequent starting point for discussions of artificial intelligence. In this paper, Turing introduced "the imitation game", which he described as follows.

> It is played with three people, a man (A), a woman (B), and an interrogator (C) who may be of either sex. The interrogator stays in a room apart from the other two. The object of the game for the interrogator is to determine which of the other two is the man and which is the woman. He knows them by labels X and Y, and at the end of the game he says either "X is A and Y is B" or "X is B and Y is A." The interrogator is allowed to put questions to (A) and (B) thus:
>
> C: Will X please tell me the length of his or her hair? Now suppose X is actually A, then A must answer. It is A's object in the game to try to cause C to make the wrong identification. His answer might therefore be
>
> "My hair is shingled, and the longest strands are about nine inches long."
>
> In order that tones of voice may not help the interrogator the answers should be written, or better still, typewritten. The ideal arrangement is to have a teleprinter communicating between the two rooms. Alternatively the question and answers can be repeated by an intermediary. The object of the game for the third player (B)

is to help the interrogator. The best strategy for her is probably to give truthful answers. She can add such things as "I am the woman, don't listen to him!" to her answers, but it will avail nothing as the man can make similar remarks.

We now ask the question, "What will happen when a machine takes the part of A in this game?" Will the interrogator decide wrongly as often when the game is played like this as he does when the game is played between a man and a woman? These questions replace our original, "Can machines think?" [1]

Questions About the Turing Test

Although Turing introduces a *game*, discussions of it almost always refer to a *test*. This way of speaking is quite all right, provided we are clear about how to answer certain questions that naturally go with the idea of a test. Let us look at a few of these.

What does the test test for?

It is tempting to answer "thinking", but this response has two drawbacks. One is that, as a look at the last sentence of the quotation will show, Turing was trying to get away from arguing about *thinking*. He believed that this would lead only to useless arguing over words. The other drawback is that the word "thinking" covers a wide range of activities. For example, a person's thinking that some statement is true can be a case of *believing*; or someone's thinking (or thinking over, or thinking about) may be *solving a problem*; or someone's thinking about last spring's vacation in Jamaica may be *remembering* with enjoyment. Believing, problem solving, and remembering often occur together, but they can occur separately, and so they are different. This makes it possible to wonder whether there could be machines that could solve problems but not really have beliefs, or remember but not solve problems, and, if they are possible, whether we should say that they could think. These questions do indeed seem to be verbal ones that distract us from what it seems we really want to know about machines. So, let us not say that the Turing test tests for thinking. Still, we need *some* answer to what a test tests for. I shall take a cue from Turing's title and use "intelligence" for this purpose. Turing was acute in this choice of word; it will turn out to have just the right kind of narrowness that is required, and to leave open just the right further questions.

What counts as *passing* the test?

The object of the game for player A is to fool the interrogator. It would be natural to take success in doing this as "winning" and it would be natural to equate passing the test with winning the game. Turing, however, does not quite do this. He asks whether the interrogator will decide wrongly "as often" when the game is played with a machine as player A instead of with a man as player A. Later in the paper quoted above, he says he believes "that in about fifty years' time it will be possible to program computers . . . to play the imitation game so well that an average interrogator will not have more than 70 percent chance of making the right identification after five minutes of questioning"(13). These remarks show that Turing assumed that the imitation game would be played many times, with different interrogators and presumably different human opponents. If there are many games played, however, the highest standard we could propose for passing the test is *winning the game half the time*. Doing that means that after the game is played, the interrogator does no better than just guessing. Presumably, interrogators will pose questions that they believe will require intelligence to be answered well. If doing this fails to make their identifications better than guessing, then they are not learning about any difference between machine and human on the ability—namely, intelligence—that they are trying to test by the questions.

Of course, there are weaker standards one could take. Turing's figure of 70 percent correct identifications corresponds to the machine's fooling the interrogator 30 percent of the time. In this case, the interrogator is learning something from the questioning. Still, even that might be pretty convincing as a test for possession of intelligence in some degree. After all, fooling the interrogator 50 percent of the time might be taken as showing not only intelligence but intelligence of the same degree as the human opponent. Compare, for example, a chimpanzee. Many people would be willing to say there is some degree of intelligence in this case, but there would be no question of winning at the imitation game because there is such a great disparity of degree.

There is a good reason for Turing to have introduced the idea of playing a series of games instead of just one. In a single game there is always the possibility of luck or incompetent judges or uncooperative human opponents. But if half, or even 30 percent, of a series of games is won by a machine, it would be quite unlikely that such extraneous reasons would account for the winning. The only plausible idea that would be left is that the machine wins because of some property that it possesses.

What counts as failing the test?

Nothing. That is, no result of playing the game can be used to show that something is not intelligent. Suppose a machine showed just a little more intelligence than humans. This might incline interrogators to guess it to be the human a little more often than not. That would not show that people are not intelligent. Suppose a machine were super-intelligent in some respect, for example, in doing arithmetic. It might, of course, also suppress its excellence when it was in a Turing test situation so that its ability would appear to be no better than what is average for people. If it were arrogant, however, it might fail to suppress its superior ability. That would be a dead giveaway, so interrogators might never be fooled about which was the machine, and which the human. This result, however, would not show that machines were not intelligent. Again, people might be judged to be the machine through uncooperativeness or misunderstanding of the object of the game, but none of that would show that they were not intelligent. Again, a machine might conclude from its data base that if it is thought to be intelligent, people's prejudices will lead them to destroy it. It might try to avoid such a result by feigning stupidity, say, by repeating the same wooden phrases over and over. Perhaps every interrogator would judge it to be the machine, but that would not show that the machine was not intelligent.

Historical Note: René Descartes (1596–1650) was quite sure that he could always tell the difference between a person and a machine, even if the machine were dressed up to look exactly like a human. He did not speak of a game, or of a test, but he did, in effect, propose a test that he thought no machine could pass. It amounted to this: Engage whatever it is in a conversation. If it is a human, even a very stupid one, it will make a response that is appropriate in some way to whatever you say to it. Even if the response is not brilliant, it will be relevant to the topic of conversation and will make sense given what has been said earlier. But no machine, he thought, could respond with this kind of appropriateness in a conversation.

    Turing, as we have seen, is more hopeful about a machine's passing this sort of test. But it is interesting that despite their different views about machines, Descartes and Turing are very close on the question of what kind of test might be appropriate for telling the difference. We might say that by including the ability to converse on a wide variety of topics, Turing includes in his test whatever Descartes has in his.

      What questions will be on the test?

The answer is the one that professors would most like and students most fear: Any question. In fact, it need not be exactly a question; it could be an instruction to which the machine has to respond. The response, however, has to be something that can be printed out; the interrogator, says Turing, "cannot demand practical demonstrations"(6).

    We shall see as we go on how powerful a test this is. For now, let us just list some of the kinds of things that Turing imagines an interrogator might ask.

> Add some numbers.
> Solve a chess problem.
> Write a poem.
> Discuss a poem.
> Have a conversation on any topic the interrogator
>   chooses.

We should also note that the situation imagined by Turing is like that of an oral examination. The advantage of this kind of test is that examiners can halt a line of questioning on which the examinee does well and turn to another topic. This explains why students in systems where such examinations are common are generally terrified of them: They constitute a very efficient procedure for finding out the *limits* of the examinee's ability.

There is a property that has come to the surface in our discussion of what will be on the test and in the historical note. This property is so important that we ought to have a name for it. A suggestive name is *flexibility*. I shall say that something has flexibility when, and only when, it can respond to a wide variety of circumstances in a way that is relevant and makes sense given the history of a situation. Flexibility is not brilliance; things that have flexibility need not hit upon the best solutions to problems. But they have to produce what at least appear to be passable solutions for a wide range of cases. Flexibility can be exhibited in conversation. It can also be exhibited by behaving appropriately in a variety of situations.

There is a common misunderstanding of the Turing test that a proper appreciation of flexibility will enable us to correct. The misunderstanding arises from a certain way of thinking about some of the successes of computer programming. For example, let us imagine a setup in which a human chess player receives opponents' moves as instructions on a monitor screen. The level of play by some machines is very good, so the human player might very well not know whether the instructions on the screen came from another human or from a machine. Unfortunately, it is tempting to describe this situation by saying that good chess machines pass the Turing test, within the limited domain of chess. Similar temptations arise in the case of expert systems for medical diagnosis, multicomputer system design, and the like. Once a certain level of competence is reached, the results provided by machines may not be easily distinguishable from some of those produced by people. So, it can seem natural to say that such machines can pass the Turing test within their field of expertise. Perhaps the most remarkable case of this sort is Joseph Weizenbaum's ELIZA program.[2] In one of its versions, this program is used to imitate a Rogerian psychotherapist. It does this by using relatively simple rules that reflect people's statements back to them, or that use references to mothers as prompts for questions about the rest of the family. Weizenbaum was amazed to find that people reacted to this program as they might react to a psychological counselor, even to the point of requesting privacy in communicating with it and attributing genuine understanding to it. Here again, some people are tempted to express these facts by saying that ELIZA passes the Turing test in the limited domain of psychological counseling.

Flexibility, however, is the ability to give appropriate responses *over a wide range of cases*. Here we should recall the oral examination character of the Turing test situation. This type of examination prevents candidates from succeeding by carefully rehearsing a set speech, or by intensively preparing a small amount of material. The same kind of exposure of narrow abilities is built right into Turing's test. (Indeed, all the cases mentioned in the last paragraph are immediately exposed as nonhuman, the moment you ask for something outside the domain for which they are designed.) For this reason, the idea of "passing the Turing test within a limited domain" is self-contradictory. The whole point of the imitation game is to test the ability to cope with whatever comes up, no matter what domain it is in. An absolutely essential point about flexibility is that it is broad. Speaking of flexibility restricted to a particular domain is as silly as claiming to be able to play any card game described in Hoyle's book of rules, so long as the game occurs on some designated page.

The Significance of the Turing Test

We have now described the Turing test and answered some important questions about it. We have seen some of the motivation for it. At this point, there are two questions that we should want to ask. These questions are sometimes difficult to keep separate from one another, but it is very important that we keep them separate. They are the COULD THERE BE and the SO WHAT questions.

> COULD THERE BE? Could there ever be a machine that would pass the Turing test?
> SO WHAT? So what if there could be, what would that show?

We shall start to work on the second of these questions. This will keep us occupied through the rest of this chapter and in the following three. In Chapter 5, we shall turn to the background necessary to investigate the COULD THERE BE question.

One answer to the SO WHAT question is that if a machine passed the Turing test, that would show it to possess some property that is quite remarkable, a property that is very similar to one of ours and that we consider very important, namely, intelligence. This, in fact, seems to be the obvious answer. It is so obvious that it sometimes leads people to argue this way:

> If a machine could pass the Turing test, it would be
>   intelligent; but
> No machine could be intelligent; so,
> No machine could pass the Turing test.

Now, this gets us nowhere, because others will be happy to argue:

> If a machine could pass the Turing test, it would be
>   intelligent;
> Some machine could (someday) pass the Turing
>   test; so,
> Some machine could be intelligent.

Those who doubt machine intelligence but want to get beyond this stalemate have two options. One is to find some other argument for doubting that machines could ever pass the Turing test. In the later chapters of this book, we shall see what can be said for a skeptical view of this kind. Now, however, we will turn to the second option. This is to find reasons for doubting what may have seemed obvious, namely, the first premise in both of the above arguments. Several such reasons have in fact been offered. Some of these can be dealt with fairly briefly, and I will finish this chapter by discussing them. Others are more intricate and I shall turn to these in later chapters.

> Passing the Turing test shows only that a machine can
> do *one* thing; intelligence, however, involves being
> able to do many things.

We can use many activities to illustrate the variety of abilities that intelligence requires. Even a homely activity like shopping for groceries will do. Here, we have to do many things; count, add, weigh, stack perishable items carefully, read, remember what the people we are going to eat with like, and so on. Moreover, we have to coordinate these abilities, for example, in rejecting items that are too expensive, or in deciding what size box to buy. Now, if intelligence is many-sided and the Turing test is only one-sided, then passing the test is not a good indicator of intelligence.[3]

This criticism of the test, however, does not sufficiently recognize the key fact about the imitation game. This "one game" or "one activity" does, in a sense, include all activities—that is, it includes all activities in so far as they depend just on *intelligence*. Thus, an interrogator can ask a contestant to count or to add. The interrogator cannot ask the contestant to weigh or to stack, since doing these things involves making bodily movements. This example shows us how we can separate a physical component from an intelligence component. That is, we can imagine someone physically able to weigh produce but not doing so out of either forgetfulness or inability to read the scale. We can imagine someone able to see different items and strong enough to move all of them, but too stupid to realize that the tomatoes do not belong underneath the six-pack. Conversely, we can imagine a machine able to answer questions from the interrogator like these: "If you want three pounds of potatoes and the scale reads two pounds, ten ounces, how much is the weight of potatoes that you need to add?" and "If you're packing your last bag and you're down to a six-pack, a sack of onions, and a tomato, which should you put in the bag first?" A contestant's answering these questions correctly would show that it can do whatever it is about weighing and stacking that requires intelligence. But we can use questions like these to capture the intelligence component of any of the myriad activities that we find to require intelligence. Thus, we can work the whole vast range of intelligence-requiring components of human activities into the context of the imitation game.

We can state this conclusion a little differently. Nathan Hale said, "I only regret that I have but one life to lose for my country." No one would respond to this by saying that Hale, after all, lost only one thing, while others lost many. When the one thing is a life, it encompasses many things. This is how it is with the imitation game. Like a life, this kind of "one thing" is a single framework into which we can fit many things—enough things to exhibit the *flexibility* that is the hallmark of intelligence.

> Learning is essential for genuine intelligence. The Turing test does not show that machines can learn, so it is not a good test for intelligence.

This is a point that comes up frequently. Contrary to appearances, however, the format of the imitation game does allow for learning. For one thing, the machine must be able to *converse* with the interrogator. If it "forgets" what has come earlier in the interrogation, or if it fails to adjust its response to what the interrogator says, it will immediately give itself away as an empty-headed imposter. Even the most brilliant response will be of no use if it is mindlessly repeated. But retaining what has gone before in a conversation is a kind of learning. Furthermore, the interrogator can invent a game, state the rules, and ask the contestant questions about what moves would be good ones. Inventing a simple game would ensure that the rules had not already been given to the contestant; and so, the ability to answer questions about moves correctly would show that the contestant had learned the rules from having been told them. In this way, again, the imitation game allows the interrogator to test whether the contestant can learn.

> Creativity is essential for genuine intelligence. The Turing test does not show creativity, so it is not a good test for intelligence.

This is another frequently raised objection. Part of what makes it plausible is an ambiguity in the word "creative". Sometimes, when we use this word, we mean it as high praise. Perhaps we are thinking of a Picasso or a Shakespeare, someone who invented a new style or raised some dimension of human endeavor to a new standard of richness. It is quite true that passing the Turing test does not show this kind (or, perhaps, degree) of creativity. This does not disqualify the Turing test as a test of intelligence, however, for most of us are intelligent but do not have the creativity of a great artist.

In another sense (or degree) most people do exhibit creativity. That is, we are constantly faced with situations that are not exact copies of anything we have previously encountered, and in which we act in some appropriate way. We have to create a new response, or at least create a new connection between a response and surrounding circumstances. This kind of creativity, however, is the same thing as flexibility, and possession of this, we have seen, is exactly what success on the Turing test shows.

> Doing well at the imitation game shows only that machines could imitate intelligence.

The intuition behind this objection comes from the many cases where it is indeed true that being able to imitate something does not show that the imitator has it. I can imitate a person being angry or in pain; that does not show that I am angry or in pain. We might test a mattress by constructing a machine that would imitate a person lying down on it, getting up from it, and rolling over on it. Imagine that we can hide the fact that we got the equivalent of fifteen years of use by running the machine for two days. Suppose we put it beside mattresses that really have been used for fifteen years by real people and we find that no one can distinguish the machine-tested mattress from the ones used by people. This result would have no tendency to convince us that the machine slept on the mattress, or even that it laid down on it, got up from it or rolled over on it.[4] Applying the same reasoning to the Turing test leads to the conclusion that passing it would at best show the possession of imitation intelligence, and not the possession of the real thing.

In many cases, however, imitation does require reality. If I do a good imitation of Jones's funny accent, I actually have to pronounce words, and I have to do so in a way very similar to the way Jones does. If I cook with imitation orange flavoring, I have to use something that has a real flavor, and, moreover, one that really is similar to the flavor of an orange. If I buy a painting by a mere imitator of a famous artist, I buy a real painting.

These examples show only that we have to be careful about "imitation" and that "imitation intelligence" *could* turn out also to be the real thing. Can we find a reason to decide whether this is actually so? We can indeed. Let us take another look at one of our examples.

Suppose I imitate being angry when I am not angry at all. I have to think about how angry people look, what sort of movements they make, how their voices are different, what kinds of words or phrases they might use. In short, I have to become an actor. But acting is an activity that itself takes intelligence. So, in imitating an angry person, I actually have to use intelligence. Perhaps this is not quite clear because anger is something that occurs only in beings that have some intelligence. So, let us think of some children who are going to try to "be trees". Needless to say, they do not have to be particularly brilliant to do this, but they do have to remember that a tree stands still, that the branches are not usually perfectly straight (so, perhaps they will bend their elbows a little), and that branches end in smaller branches (so, good imitators will remember to spread their fingers). This takes some degree of intelligence and here it is unmistakable that the intelligence is in the activity of imitating, not in the thing being imitated.

These remarks point to the conclusion that imitating is something that requires intelligence. In saying this, however, we must be a little careful. We may say of a certain chemical that it imitates the flavor of an orange, but we are not to conclude from that that the chemical is intelligent. Here, "to imitate" has the same sense as "to be very similar to". The kind of imitating that takes intelligence is not a mere state of being similar to; it is, instead, an activity. It is the activity of *producing* something similar. Thus, an actor produces movements and inflections that are similar to those of a possible other person; a forger produces a painting that looks like that of another artist; the children we imagined produce a bodily shape that resembles that of a tree; and the imitator of an accent produces words that sound like those of another speaker. The parallel point with machines is that if it is their activity that produces the similarity between their results and other things, then they are engaged in an activity that requires intelligence.

We must be careful here in another way. In some contexts it would be natural to say that the voice (or, the mouth) produces the accent that is like another person's, or that the brush produced the forged painting. In most contexts, however, we would regard the voice or the brush merely as tools used by the producers of the similar results. It is the producers and not the tools that must be intelligent if there is to be the activity of imitating. Applied to machines, the parallel conclusion is this: If the machine is an imitator, in the sense of an originator of similarities and not merely some other producer's tool, then it is intelligent.

This conclusion raises the question of how we are to tell whether a computer is an originator or a mere tool. This is an important question and we shall return to it later. Here it is enough to be clear that saying something is an imitator of intelligence is *not* a way of supporting the view that it is not really intelligent. On the contrary, if you do agree that something can imitate intelligence, you should agree that it is intelligent.

To this conclusion we can add the observation that the more intelligence there is in the thing to be imitated, the more intelligence is required from the imitator. For example, imitating something we have heard Jones say requires some intelligence. But suppose we are asked to imitate Jones's reaction to a scene to which we were not eyewitnesses (or that has not yet happened): This requires a lot more, since we cannot just make sure we repeat Jones correctly. We would first have to think up the kind of thing Jones might say. To do this, however, we have to be able to think up some response to the new situation that is as intelligent as Jones's response is likely to be. The more complex we imagine the scene to be, the harder it will be—the more intelligence it will take—to do this. The imitation game presents an extremely hard task, however, because it requires the machine to imitate humans with respect to unforeseen comments and questions on whatever topic the interrogator happens to like. It seems, therefore, that a machine that did well on the Turing test would have to be not only intelligent, because it can imitate at all, but intelligent at a level comparable to humans, since it can imitate a wide range of their intelligent behavior.

The Block Machine

The next objection to the Turing test that we must consider requires the introduction of an imaginary machine described by Ned Block.[5] To get the idea of this machine, we have to note that although we all know a large number of words, the number we know is finite. We cannot speak infinitely fast, so given a finite time—say, Turing's five minutes—there can be a conversation of only finite length. Compounding conversations of finite length out of a large but finite set of words gives you a very large but still finite number of possible conversations. Block imagines an army of workers who labor to construct a machine in the following way. First, all possible conversational openers that an interrogator might use are written down. Think of each of these openers as the trunk of a tree. Next, for each trunk, the workers figure out and record a few responses that would pass as possible to be given by a human. We now have a large number of trunks and a larger number of trunk-plus-main-branch pairs. (That is, there is more than one trunk-plus-main-branch pair for each trunk.) Next, for each trunk-plus-main-branch pair, the workers figure out all the possible responses by the interrogator. They write these down, then figure out a few of the possible responses to these responses, and so on. At each level of branching, they take into account not merely the previous branch, but the whole of the conversation up to the point they are working on. They continue until they have written down the branchings of each of the possible openers up to a time of five minutes. We should imagine that there is some kind of ordering of their results, for example, that trunks, main branches, subbranches and so on are recorded in alphabetical order.

The tree-table (Figure 1.1) is the heart of the Block machine. All we have to add is a mechanism for looking up branches and reading them out. An interrogator says something to open the conversation. The Block machine scans the trunks until it finds that opener. Then it moves up one level and reads out the first (let us say) branch above that opener.[6] That is what gets printed out to the interrogator. So far, so good, because, remember, the branches above each opener are all passable as human responses. Now the interrogator says something more. The Block machine moves up another level and scans until it finds it. Then it moves up one more level and reads out the first response to the interrogator's most recent move. Again, so far, so good, because the branches are selected in such a way that they are passable responses to all that has gone before in the conversation. This procedure is repeated until the time of the game is up.

The point of introducing the Block machine is that we can use it to raise a doubt about the significance of the Turing test. We can put this doubt succinctly as follows.

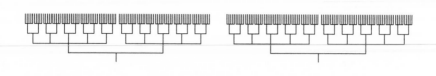

FIGURE 1.1 Tree-table for the Block machine

> The Turing test does not rule out the Block machine.
> But that machine is certainly not intelligent; so the
> Turing test does not establish intelligence.

That the Block machine could pass the Turing test should be obvious from the way it is constructed. It should also be clear, however, that it is not intelligent. All it does is use an entry to guide it to a certain place on a tree and then it reads what it finds there. That is about what happens at the check-out counter in an up-to-date grocery store. The product code causes the system to look up what is in a certain place in the system's memory, and whatever price it finds there gets printed on the tape. But nobody thinks that the code-reading system is intelligent. So the Block machine is not intelligent. If we put this together with the premise that it could pass the Turing test, we get the conclusion that passing that test is not enough to show that something is intelligent.

The argument based on the Block machine is ingenious and it introduces an idea we will come back to, but it cannot really be used to reject the Turing test. To see this, we must first think about how big the tree-table would have to be. Let us continue to use Turing's suggestion of five minutes as the length of each game. It takes about two minutes to read a typed, double-spaced page. That rate gives us about 750 words for five minutes. Contestants will, however, need time to think (or, to put it more neutrally, to react to interrogators' input), so let us imagine that no more than 500 words are used in a game. These words may, however, be drawn from anywhere in the players' vocabularies. Size of vocabulary is difficult to measure, but 3,000 items is among the low estimates for first graders. Just to be sure we do not make the task too difficult, let us take this as our assumption about vocabulary. The possible strings of words in five minutes can then be calculated. The first word can be chosen from a list of

3,000. So can the next one, and the next one, and so on for 500 times. Thus, the number of possible five-minute strings amounts to $3,000^{500}$, which works out to something more than 10^{169}. Of course, the builders of the Block machine will be able to reduce the number of conversations, because many of the five-minute strings will be unintelligible or ungrammatical. Even so, if one in a few billion billion is a passable human conversation, there will still be more conversations than there are atoms in the sun. The builders will not have to work up all of these, because they do not need all possible responses for the machine at each point; two or three will do. They will, however, need to work up all the further questions, instructions, or comments that interrogators might make. If we assume the interrogators will be speaking for only half the time of the test, this still leaves us with something on the order of 10^{70} conversations to deal with. Since this is still far too large a number of conversations to figure out, we know that there cannot actually be a Block machine.

What is the significance of this unfeasibility of the Block machine? One reaction might be that it doesn't matter. After all, the Block machine is only supposed to be a thought experiment and thought experiments do not have to be something we can actually do. They must not involve a logical contradiction, but the Block machine does not violate *that* restriction. Thus, one might say, the unfeasibility of the Block machine is irrelevant to its usefulness in showing up a flaw in the Turing test.

This reaction, however, misses a key point. We have been asking about the significance of the Turing test. This is to ask what we ought to conclude if we should be faced with a machine that *actually* passed the Turing test. Since a Block machine is unfeasible, we know that there cannot actually be such a thing. So, if we had a machine that actually passed the Turing test, we ought not to suppose that we might be dealing with a Block machine. The logical possibility of a Block machine shows the logical possibility of something nonintelligent passing the Turing test; but something's actually passing the Turing test would show the *feasibility* of that thing and *that* would show that it was not a Block machine. The logical possibility of something nonintelligent passing the Turing test shows that we cannot make passing that test a *definition* of intelligence; but the unfeasibility of the logical possibility we have imagined leaves us with something that is quite satisfactory as a *test* of intelligence.

Someone might agree that the Block machine is unfeasible but still think that canning is not. By "canning" I mean doing the kind of thing that is involved in building the Block machine but not carrying out the project completely. Perhaps, one might think, it would be enough to work out, say, ten trillion conversations and have a machine that just looked them up. Our discussion, however, makes it easy to see that this will not do. The chance of matching a whole conversation is the number of canned conversations divided by the number of possible conversations. So, if 10^{13} conversations have been canned and 10^{70} are possible, then the chance of matching a whole conversation would be about 10^{13} divided by 10^{70}, or about one in 10^{57}. The fact is that a thing's *actually* passing the Turing test would be perfectly wonderful evidence that whatever was going on inside it was *not* the looking up of responses in a tree-table.

I turn now to another doubt about the significance of the Turing test. This doubt can occur independently of the Block machine, but the Block machine provides a useful example for discussing it and makes the motivation easy to see. The doubt I have in mind is often expressed in words like these:

> Passing the Turing test might show that a machine
> could think, but it would not show that it thinks in the
> same way that we do.

The most important thing to say about this objection is that its force is not clear until you specify what you mean by thinking "in the same way". One possible specification would be to take the Block machine as illustrating a way of doing something (namely, providing responses to questions) and then to say that we do not do the same thing in that way. This is a clear claim, but if that is what is meant, there is, as we have just seen, no ground for objecting to the Turing test. That is, if we actually had a contestant that passed the Turing test, it would not be reasonable to think "but maybe it does it in the way that a Block machine works." Here is another way of explaining thinking "in the same way". There are often different strategies that will work in solving a problem in mathematics or logic. Some students will discover one way of doing it, some will discover another. Sometimes the same kind of thing applies more widely. Perhaps one mathematician has a distinctive approach to a variety of problems.

His colleagues notice that he "doesn't think in the same way" as they do about problems. Or perhaps one person buys things thinking of convenience alone while another is always thinking of the environmental damage involved in producing various items. One of these people might well say of the other, "She thinks differently than I do." If this is what is meant, however, it is no objection to the Turing test that passing it does not show that a thing thinks in the same way that we do. We ourselves do not all think in the same way (in this sense), but that does not make some of us intelligent and others not: it does not even necessarily make us more or less intelligent. Style of thinking is irrelevant to the question of possession of intelligence.

These are two clear senses of thinking (or not thinking) "in the same way as we do". There is one other clear sense that I know of for this phrase. To introduce it would require more background than I can give here, but we shall come across it in Chapter 9. When we do so, we shall find that, like the two senses just discussed, it does not lead to a successful objection to the Turing test. But perhaps there are other senses of which I am not aware. So let me put forth a challenge: if you want to say that passing the Turing test would fail to show that a machine thought "in the same way" that we do, first specify the sense of "in the same way" and then show that in *that* sense, there really is an objection.

There is a point to watch out for in trying to meet this challenge. "Thinking, but in a different way" is easily confused with "thinking, but in a different *sense*". This confusion is even more likely when we speak of intelligence, which is why I have instead spoken of thinking in the last two paragraphs. In fact, however, the expressions "in a different way" and "in a different sense" have completely different implications. If we have problems with our parents and we solve them in different *ways*, then we both do solve them. But if you solve yours and I solve mine "in a (different) sense"—for example, by refusing to recognize the problem, carrying on as if it did not exist—then I do not solve it. Someone can live in New York "in a sense"—that is, by reading about New York and the people who live there, keeping up on what plays are opening, what movies are playing, and so forth—while not actually living in New York. Just to be confusing, our language is so structured that there are some contexts in which "in a way" means "in a sense". For example, you could say of the person just described, "In a way, she lives in New York." But in the case of intelligence, exercising it "in some way" is actually exercising it, while exercising it "in a sense" may *not* be exercising *it*, that is, the real thing. So, you have to be careful not to move from "uses intelligence, but in a different way than we do" to "uses intelligence, but in a different sense than we do". For the second of these may very well lead you on to "does not use intelligence in the same sense", that is, "does not really use *intelligence*", or, "seriously speaking, does not have intelligence". If you want to reject the Turing test, you should try to show how something that is not intelligent could pass it. It is not enough to merely show how something could be intelligent but also different from us and then slide along the road from "different" to "different sense" to "not the real thing".

Producers and Conduits

I have been defending the significance of the Turing test against various doubts. I have argued that passing it shows a rich variety of abilities. It reveals the capacity to learn and be creative. The test cannot be dismissed as requiring only a mere imitation of intelligence for passing it. Actual passing of the test would rule out the admittedly stupid construction of the Block machine. Finally, I know of no clear sense in which the different "way" a machine might be intelligent justifies the conclusion that it is intelligent only "in a sense", that is, not really intelligent at all. The conclusion that is suggested (I do not say yet that it is proved) is that intelligence really is required to pass the Turing test, and therefore, passing it shows the presence of intelligence.

Even if this is granted, however, there remains a difficult problem. Sometimes this problem is expressed as an objection, in this way:

> Passing the Turing test shows that the machine's
> builders or programmers are intelligent but not that the
> machine is intelligent.

We can also put the problem as the question, To whom or what should we credit the intelligence that the Turing test shows to be present somewhere? Should we say that it is the machine that is intelligent? Or does passing the test show only that builders and programmers are intelligent? Can a machine be taken to be intelligent in its own right? Or is it merely a conduit of the intelligence of others, in the way that compact discs and the apparatus that plays them are conduits for the skills of musicians?

In responding to these questions, the Block machine once again comes in handy. Here, it provides us with a case in which the question of who gets the credit is clear. If there were such a machine, all the intelligence of its output would belong to the army of people who constructed it, and the machine itself would be a mere conduit of that intelligence. We can abstract a general principle from this case by asking what makes us so sure that the intelligence in it does not belong to the Block machine itself. The answer is this: The output of the Block machine depends on the fact that something else (one of its builders) has already thought of *particular circumstances* and has already generated appropriate responses to them. Because of this, each answer given by the Block machine is really a playback of something thought up somewhere else. We can conclude that if any machine is properly credited with its own intelligence, then it *produces* its own flexible output, where *being a producer means that its output does not depend on any other thing's having already thought of particular circumstances and particular responses to them.*

This conclusion does not by itself imply the converse claim that if a thing produces its own flexible responses then we have a sufficient reason for definitely assigning intelligence to it. In our examination of objections to the significance of the Turing test, however, we have found no reason against taking production of flexible response to be sufficient for intelligence. Nor do any of the arguments yet to come provide such a reason. So, I shall take a thing's production of flexible response (in the sense of "production" just defined) as a working criterion of a thing's intelligence.

It will, perhaps, be helpful to state the conclusion we reached about the Block machine in the language we have just now developed. So formulated, it comes to this: first, passing the Turing test shows flexibility of response; second, passing the Turing test cannot show it to be logically impossible that what gives the response is not a mere conduit; but, finally, it would be a practical impossibility (an unfeasible task) to make a passer of the Turing test that did not produce its own flexible responses.

How might a machine be made to be a producer of flexible responses? Two ideas present themselves immediately. One is that a machine may be designed so that its parts interact with each other according to some general principles. This is compatible with producing its own flexible responses, provided that the builders did not arrive at their choice of design by figuring out in advance the particular problems it will be used on and the solutions to them. The other idea is that a machine may be made to follow general rules. This again is compatible with the machine's producing its own flexibility, provided that the choice of rules does not depend on its programmers' having identified all the particular problems to be solved and worked out their solutions.

In later chapters, we will return to these ideas in more detail. It is enough for the purposes of this chapter to consider two final expressions of skepticism about the significance of the Turing test. First, someone may say that no matter how much builders or programmers may be surprised by the responses of their machines, it is still they who chose the principles or rules. Operating according to the way a thing is constructed, or even following rules, is not intelligence; only inventing principles of operation or rules requires intelligence. So, once again, we ought to attribute any intelligence that is revealed by the Turing test to builders or programmers and not to machines themselves.

The trouble with this argument is that it is not obvious that operating according to principles of construction or by following rules is not operating intelligently, if the principles or rules are complicated enough. Indeed, many have thought that one or the other of these phrases describes exactly what intelligence is. It is not obvious that they are wrong. It is not obvious that *our* intelligence is not a matter of operating in certain ways or of following rules. Of course, we are not usually aware of our principles of operation, or aware that we are following rules; what we ordinarily call "following a rule" is only a special case of our intelligent activities. But, as we shall see later, we must suppose that there are processes of which we are not conscious but that contribute to our being intelligent. Since we are not conscious of them, it cannot be obvious that these processes are—or that they are not—of this or that particular nature.

The second skeptical point appeals to a more general argument, namely, that the mere fact that machines are made and programmed by people ensures that it is the human makers, and not the machine, that should be credited with intelligence. In answering this point, I think it will help to put ourselves in mind of an old problem that has bothered theologians for centuries: If God made people and if God knows everything they are going to do, can people really be said to be free? I am not going to go into this problem here, but what is interesting for me is that there is another question that is parallel to this one that has *not* been asked. God has been supposed to have made people and bestowed upon them all their abilities. God has been supposed to have used intelligence in doing this. To the best of my knowledge, however, no one has ever worried that people could not really be intelligent. No one has supposed that our having been made by an intelligent God means that our intelligence is not real or that our speech and actions are only expressions of an intelligence that must really be credited to God. Whether you believe in God or not, the absence of a problem here should be taken as showing something about our concept of intelligence. Namely, it shows that there is no contradiction in the idea of creating something that is intelligent in its own right. There is not a contradiction even in the idea of using intelligence to create a thing that is intelligent in its own right. So, you cannot argue that machines cannot be intelligent solely on the ground that their ability to pass the Turing test was bestowed on them by intelligent builders. If you want to credit the intelligence to builders, you will have to find some particular feature of what they do and argue that *this particular kind* of bestowing of ability prevents machines from really having their own intelligence.

In this chapter, I have defended the significance of the Turing test against many common and plausible objections.[7] I believe that the result that it is a proper test of intelligence will stand. John Searle, however, has written a famous paper that is often taken as casting doubt on the Turing test. This is by no means the only good reason for examining Searle's paper, but it makes it natural to turn to it at this point.

Chapter 2

Searle's Chinese Room

The argument we are to consider in this chapter concerns the structure and operation of what has become known as the "Chinese Room".[1] Before entering that room, however, we need to say two things about the setting of the argument. First, Searle distinguishes between "strong AI" (Artificial Intelligence) and "weak AI". Weak AI asserts only that computers can be a valuable tool in studying the mind. Searle's argument is not aimed against this claim. It is aimed against strong AI, which is the view that "the computer is not merely a tool in the study of the mind; rather, the appropriately programmed computer really *is* a mind, in the sense that computers given the right programs can be literally said to *understand* and have other cognitive states" (417). Second, although Searle rightly claims general significance for his results, he has in mind a particular example of work in AI and he phrases his argument as a response to it. This work, led by Roger Schank, aimed to get computers to understand stories.[2] Schank provided his computers with a description of typical relationships in some domain, for example, a customer entering a restaurant, ordering, eating, paying, and leaving, or an accident occurring, producing a victim who is taken to a hospital, treated, and perhaps released. These descriptions are called "scripts". A computer that is supplied with (1) a program and (2) a script may then be given (3) a story that takes place in the domain of the script. If we want to know whether the computer understands the story, we may give it (4) a question, and see whether it supplies the correct answer. Of course, we will not be convinced that the computer understands if we ask it a question whose answer is explicitly stated in the story, for then it may just be reading, that is, merely reproducing some words in the story. So, we will ask it questions about what is *not stated* in the story but would be known by anyone who understood the story. For example, if you understood what I said a few lines ago, you probably assumed that the accident victim suffered an injury (why else would she have been taken to the hospital?). But I did not *say* that. Your saying you thought there was an injury is the kind of thing that would convince me that you understood what I had said. Analogously, if the computer correctly answers many questions about what was not actually stated, we might conclude that it understood the story.

Against this, however, Searle means to argue that no matter how good the answers a computer might give, we should *not* believe that it understands the story. Let us now turn to the Chinese Room to see why.

The Chinese Room Argument

The Chinese Room is a room that has two small windows, through which notes may be passed. Inside there is a person who speaks English but who neither speaks nor understands Chinese. Provided you fit this condition, we may imagine that the person is you. Also inside the room are (1) a program, (2) a script (for example, a restaurant script), and (3) a story. The program is in English; the script and the story are in Chinese. You cannot, of course, read the Chinese; the characters are just meaningless collections of various marks—so, you do not know that (2) is a script and (3) is a story, you just know they are batches of paper with some unfamiliar marks on them. You can, however, *recognize* repeated occurrences of the same character, that is, you can tell when the same bunch of marks in the same spatial positions are printed again. The program, although written in English, is *about* Chinese characters. It consists of rules to the effect that if you see a certain character in one place and then you see other characters (given, again, only as complex shapes) in certain other places, then you should make a certain further kind of mark at some particular place.

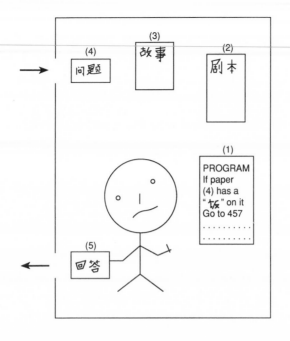

FIGURE 2.1 The Chinese Room

The procedure in the Chinese Room is this. Through one of the windows in the room, you receive (4) a piece of paper with a question on it, written in Chinese. You do not know it is a question, of course, but you see the marks and you realize that your program has rules that apply to them. You go to work, looking at your three batches of marks as the program directs, and occasionally writing down a shape when the program tells you to do so. After a while, you will have a collection of marks on a piece of paper (5) and you obey the instruction in the program to pass it out the other little window (see Figure 2.1).

If the program has been well written, the result will be that the paper you pass out will have Chinese characters on it that form a good answer to the question that was passed in to you. By a "good answer", I mean one such as a native Chinese speaker might have written, given (3) the same story and (4) the same question concerning it. That is, the people outside the room, who see only what story has been put in, what question was passed in, and what answer came out would have no way of knowing that there was not a native Chinese speaker inside who read the story, understood it, read the question, understood that, and wrote down the correct answer. Or, we could say, if we set a test to see whether Chinese judges outside the room can tell from the quality of the answers alone whether it is you inside rather than a native Chinese speaker, they will do no better than just guessing. But even if we had a program so good that we could reach this ideal, it would still be clear that you do not understand a word of the script, the story, the question, or the answer. That is, you might pass the test of fooling the judges about who was in the room without understanding *at all*. You, however, have everything that a computer would have. (That is, a computer works, just as you do in the Chinese Room, by applying rules to signs that it can deal with only through their being certain shapes in certain locations.) So even if a computer could pass the test of giving out answers that would fool judges half the time about whether what is inside is a computer or a native Chinese speaker, we should not conclude from that that the computer understands, any more than you would conclude from your success in the imagined case that you understood Chinese.

Some Objections and Replies

While everyone agrees that you would not understand any Chinese even if you were the person inside the room, not everyone thinks that this is quite the relevant point. Schank thought his *computer* might understand stories; he did not claim that some *part* of his computer could understand them. But the proper analogue of the *whole* computer is the *whole* Chinese Room, that is, not just you, but you together with the program, script, and story. So, the proper question to ask may not be whether *you* understand the story and questions in Chinese but whether the whole system composed of you, program, script, and story understands. We might say that if we are going to ask whether something understands, we have to be careful to get the boundaries of the thing we are interested in exactly right. After all, although I am sure that I understand most of what people say to me, I

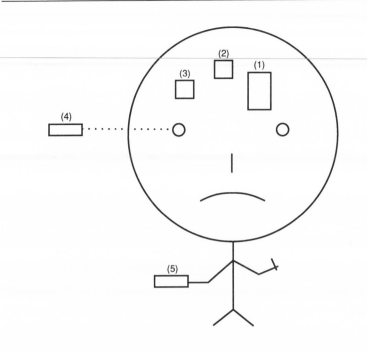

FIGURE 2.2 Response to the systems reply

am not in the habit of thinking of the left temporal lobe of my brain as an understander of anything at all. If I draw a boundary around *it*, what is inside will not be a plausible candidate for possessing understanding. Even if we think of drawing a boundary at the cranium, so that the whole brain is included within it, it is at least questionable whether we should agree that we have bounded *an understander.*

Searle is aware of the objection that he has incorrectly drawn the boundary of the subject about whom he asks "Does it understand?" He calls it "the systems reply" because the people who make it are saying that the boundary of the relevant candidate for an understander is not you but the whole system. Searle has an ingenious response: Put the program, the script, and the story *inside* you—that is, let you memorize them. Now, the boundaries of the system and of you coincide, but, says Searle, you still do not understand Chinese or have any idea of what the story and the questions are about.

We have to be clear about what lies behind this last point. You are to imagine that the procedure by which you arrive at what you write down as the answer is the same as it was before you memorized everything. At that time, you looked at the characters in the question, story, and script and followed instructions in the program that related to them. Now, you do the same thing; the only difference is that whereas you used to turn physical pages of the program and read them with your eyes, you now turn them only in memory and use your memory to tell what is on them (Figure 2.2). The conclusion Searle invites us to draw from this situation is that you are just as much a stranger to Chinese as before; you still give the right answers, in Chinese, to questions; the boundaries of the whole system coincide with the boundaries of you; and, therefore, a system could give answers that would satisfy native Chinese speakers and yet not understand the story, the questions, or the answers. Fooling the judges, that is, passing the Turing test, does not show understanding.

This is an extremely persuasive response to the systems reply, but it is only partially successful. To see this, we have to consider exactly why we are so sure that YOU—that is, you after you have memorized the program, script, and story—do not understand Chinese. After all, YOU give a good appearance of understanding it; so good that native speakers accept YOU as understanding Chinese.[3] There are three reasons we should consider.

REASON 1: When we imagine ourselves in YOUR position, we realize that we would not take ourselves to understand. That is, we can see that we might very well say to ourselves, as we write out in Chinese some perfectly good answer, "I wonder what this is all about. Sure wish I knew what all these squiggles mean, or even whether they mean anything! What a nuisance it is to have to make meaningless marks all day!"

This reason is not adequate to establish the conclusion that YOU do not understand. To see this, we should attend to the fact, agreed to by Searle, that when in the ordinary course of things you speak English, something goes on in your brain. Searle thinks this is not running a program, but he does think that there is some brain process and that your ability to produce right answers to English questions depends on it. He also would agree that you are not aware of this process. Now, let us imagine a thought experiment in which you do somehow become aware of it. You say to yourself, "This neuron is firing and then that one, then this other one and then the first one again." Let us further imagine that whatever it was that gave you this insight into your brain processes has also distracted you from your ordinary frame of mind so much that you do not have the sense of understanding what you say. There is a familiar experience that will make this easier to imagine. Sometimes, when we repeat a word several times, it can come to seem just a meaningless noise. So, let us imagine that you have this "meaningless noise" sense about everything you are saying, but, at the same time, you have detailed awareness of your brain processes. Would we say, in such a case, that you did not understand English? (Remember, the words you actually produce are perfectly sensible English answers to questions you have been asked.) Possibly, but there is an alternative description that seems just as correct. This is, that you are suffering from some form of psychological dissociation that gives you a (false) sense of estrangement from your words, even though you evidently continue to understand English just as well as before.

Before elaborating on the point of this thought experiment, let us entertain an objection to the effect that it is totally unrealistic. Our brain operations, it may be said, are too complex for us to comprehend in detail, especially at the speed at which they actually take place. The conclusion would be that since the conditions of the thought experiment are impossible, the fact that the experiment can be adequately described without denying understanding is useless for getting us to actually accept any conclusion.

I agree, of course, that we could not actually become aware of the neuron firings that are going on in our brains while we are thinking. If, however, the thought experiment is to be rejected on this ground, then Searle's response to the systems reply must also be rejected. For it is equally unrealistic to suppose that anyone could actually memorize a program that has the complexity that would surely be required to do the imagined task of giving good Chinese answers to questions written in Chinese. It is also unrealistic to suppose that anyone could actually keep track of the steps involved in running such a program. If we rejected Searle's response to the systems reply on this ground, we would have to be content to say that there is no realistic way for him to respond to that objection. We might also carry things a bit further and observe that the whole Chinese Room setup is unrealistic. A person working through a complex program by hand would be so slow that there would be no question of actually fooling anybody about whether or not there was a person in the room who spoke Chinese.

In short, we are already up to our ears in thought experiment and there is no principle on which we can accept Searle's experiment but reject the one I just described. The point of saying this, however, is not to suggest that we should reject them. It is much more interesting to allow both of them and see where they lead us. The experiment I just described has led, so far, to the conclusion that neither a sense of estrangement from our words nor an awareness of the means by which they are produced is a ground for denying understanding.

Let us now apply this lesson to the analogous case of YOU in Searle's response to the systems reply. Here, first, YOU do not have a feeling of familiarity about YOUR words. Just as before, this is not a reason for denying understanding. Second, YOU are aware of the means by which YOUR words are produced. The only difference in this case is that instead of being aware of neuron firings, YOU are aware of applying the instructions of the program to various memorized pages of marks. This awareness of the means of generating YOUR words is analogous to the previous case, and leads to the same point, namely, that adding awareness of means is not a reason for denying understanding.

It may be helpful to look at the point from a slightly different angle. Sometimes we can do very familiar operations "without thinking". Maybe you have had the experience when balancing your checkbook of knowing the correct number to write down faster than you can say to yourself the reasons involved in the calculation. Or, maybe you know what it is like to be able to play a bit of music straight off without having to think of the elements of the chord or the melody line. Now imagine that YOU get so good at looking up instructions and comparing characters on various pieces of paper that YOU do it "automatically", without paying attention, so that YOU are hardly aware of doing it. This need not make YOU any worse at giving good answers in Chinese, any more than playing music without having to think about how you do it makes you a worse musician. (In

Historical Note: Gottfried Wilhelm von Leibniz (1646–1716) was a philosopher, mathematician, scientist, engineer, and logician who designed an early calculating machine. Although his work contains no exact parallel to Searle's argument, the following passage from his *Monadology*, sect. 17, is very suggestive.

> It must be confessed, however, that Perception, and that which depends upon it, are inexplicable by mechanical causes, that is to say, by figures and motions. Supposing that there were a machine whose structure produced thought, sensation, and perception, we could conceive of it as increased in size with the same proportions until one was able to enter into its interior, as he would into a mill. Now, on going into it he would find only pieces working upon one another, but never would he find anything to explain Perception. It is accordingly in the simple substance, and not in the composite nor in a machine that the Perception is to be sought.

Many people today would not accept this argument. But to reject it is to agree that although thought would not be recognized in any piece or any few pieces of the detailed operations of the brain, that does not show that the combination of the operations of those pieces is not thought, or understanding.

---

fact, playing "automatically" is necessary for being a good musician.) Let us add to this a cure for YOUR feelings of dissociation. We know there is the experience of *déjà vu*, that is, the sense that something has occurred in your presence before when it certainly has not done so. If this can happen, surely it could happen that YOU came to have a feeling about squiggles that they were quite familiar. Now, I have asked you to imagine these things because, first, neither of these changes in our example adds understanding to it. But if we make them, we have a situation in which YOU do everything YOU did before, with none of the things that might have made YOU think YOU did not understand. So, perhaps what we had before these changes was understanding together with dissociation and awareness of means. In fact, perhaps what you actually have when you speak English is just like what is supposed to go on in the Chinese Room, with no sense of unfamiliarity with the words you use, and no awareness of how you produce sensible speech. But if this is possible, then we have not yet found any reason to deny understanding of Chinese to YOU as pictured in the systems reply.

> **REASON 2:** YOU could not translate the story or any of the questions or answers. But YOU do know how to speak English. If YOU had understood the story, questions, or answers, then YOU ought to be able to state their sense in English. Because YOU cannot do this YOU must not understand.[4]

To evaluate this reason, we shall have to consider another, somewhat strange thought experiment. A certain person, let us call her June Lee, converses in Chinese when in China and in English when in England or the United States. Chinese speakers accept her as indistinguishable from native Chinese speakers (she can pass a Turing test when set behind a screen and competing with a native Chinese speaker) and English speakers accept her in the same way as indistinguishable from a native speaker. What is stranage is that Ms. Lee cannot translate. If you ask her to translate a conversation she has recently had in Chinese, she just draws a blank, looks puzzled, shrugs her shoulders, and says "Sorry."

It seems clear that the description of this case is not self-contradictory. It is not even so very much more strange than actual cases of dissociation. There are, for example, people who have gone blind but who give every indication of not believing that they have done so. There are aphasics who evidently grasp the nature of objects that they see but who cannot produce words for them. There are "split brain" patients in whom the right hand does not know what the left hand is doing.[5] The proposed thought experiment certainly stretches our ability to imagine dissociations, but not beyond the point where we can think clearly about them.

The question we must now ask about the case of Ms. Lee is this: Must we (or should we) say that she does not understand Chinese (or, does not understand English, assuming that she also cannot translate an English conversation into Chinese)? I believe we do not need to say this. We can just as well say that Ms. Lee is suffering from a deep dissociation, one that would no doubt tax the explanatory abilities of psychologists. We can allow ourselves to be impressed by the fact that she does as well in Chinese conversation as do Chinese of whom it would not even occur to us to ask if they understood their language. We can note that in split brain experiments, we do not say that the subject does not understand an instruction but only that the instruction does not "get through" so as to be connectable to a certain part of the subject's activity. We can conclude that the inability to translate, strange though it is, is not by itself sufficient to imply the absence of understanding.

We can make another point. Let us imagine that June Lee memorizes a program that enables her, at last, to do translation. This program is written in Chinese. It refers to strings of Chinese words and gives instructions about how to calculate the correct English translation, which it mentions as the appropriate output. After she calculates, she pronounces the output directed by the program. We may imagine that she learns to do this calculating very fast—so fast that after a while, you cannot distinguish her from an ordinary translator. (We may even imagine that, as she reads along the output, which is in English, she has an odd sense of thinking something for the first time, even though she knows she is translating something she just said in Chinese.) Now, we should first notice that in making this addition, we have not had to change anything that we had assumed about her performance in Chinese. Second, there is nothing in what we have added that adds anything to her abilities in using Chinese. But after we have made this addition, we have removed Reason 2 for denying that she understands Chinese. So, if she now understands Chinese, and we did not add anything to her ability in Chinese, then we should conclude that she understood Chinese all along and that what she suffered was a peculiar inability to translate. That is, finally, we should conclude that the inability to translate, strange though it is, does not by itself imply that she did not understand.

The reason I asked you to imagine June Lee's predicament is that we can extend the conclusion to you as described in the systems reply. Like June Lee, you cannot translate the Chinese questions or answers into English, even though, like her, you understand English.

As in her case, this does not show that YOU do not understand Chinese; for it may be that YOU lack some further ability to connect YOUR languages, one that people who understand several languages usually have, but which they could lack without implying lack of understanding of the languages they speak. Reason 2 thus does not give us a sufficient argument for saying that YOU do not understand. It does not give us a reason why we must say that running a program is not the way in which a person understands.

> **REASON 3:** YOU cannot connect the words YOU are able to process for conversational purposes with the things around YOU that they mean. For example, let us imagine that we give YOU a slip of paper on which is written, in Chinese, "We've kept you at this for six hours, you must be getting hungry. If you would like a hamburger, just hold up your left hand." YOU calculate and produce a message that is the Chinese for "Why, thank you very much, I believe I could use some food." But YOU do not raise YOUR hand.[6]

We can put this reason briefly by saying that YOUR performance with Chinese establishes that YOU can make the same word-word connections that native Chinese speakers do, but it leaves YOU without the word-*world* connections that they have. By "word-world connections", I mean two things. First, normal people can generally move from perception of things or situations to correct words for them. If they are looking at a book or a fight and you ask them to tell you what is before them, they can produce the words "book" or "fight" in answer. Let us call connections of this kind "input-word connections". Second, normal people can move from words that express practical directions to the corresponding actions. Not only can they *say* that they should close windows to keep the dust out if there is a windstorm, they can *do* that action, if and when they are faced with open windows and a windstorm. I shall refer to connections of this kind as "word-action connections". "Word-world connections", then, covers both input-word and word-action connections.

Unlike the first two reasons, Reason 3 gives us an extremely compelling ground for saying that YOU do not understand. Some people may, however, question whether the absence of word-world connections should lead us to deny *understanding* rather than something else. To support the correctness of denying understanding, let us imagine that I have asked you to read some instructions for setting up some word-processing equipment, booting up, formatting your disc, and starting a document. When you have finished, I may wonder whether you understand the instructions. I might ask you to repeat them. Your doing so correctly would be a very good sign but might not put all my doubts to rest. I might think, for example, that you just had a good memory and had not understood a word. I might ask you questions that would require you to reason about the instructions—questions like "How many steps come between plugging the keyboard into the system unit and inserting the first disc?" Your answering correctly would be another good sign, but I still might not be completely satisfied. Finally, I might give you the equipment (without the instructional materials) and ask you to set it up and create a document. If you could not do it, you might have understood the instructions but forgotten them. Suppose, however, that you can still repeat the instructions to me, but you cannot set up the equipment. A very natural way for me to describe this situation would be to say that although you can talk a good game, you do not really understand what you are supposed to do.

Word-world connections are extremely important. They have everything to do with the reasons why we speak at all and, indeed, with how it is possible for what we say to have any meaning. Their absence is, therefore, an extremely significant feature of the YOU of the systems reply. This absence, I have just been arguing, is naturally described as a lack of understanding. So it is correct to say that YOU, as described in the systems reply, do not understand Chinese. If this point is accepted, it will also be clear that Schank's computer does not understand the stories it is given, no matter how well it does in answering questions about the stories. Further, nothing in the argument depends on how versatile the program is made, how many subjects it can answer questions on, or how long it can continue to give good answers. The only thing that proved crucial was absence of word-world connections. So it is not just Schank's computer that will lack understanding but any computer that lacks word-world connections, no matter how well it does in conversation. So, finally, Searle is right to reject strong AI, which, let us recall, holds that "computers given the right programs can be literally said to *understand*".

Some Limitations of Searle's Argument

This last conclusion is Searle's success. The reader may recall, however, my earlier remark that Searle's argument is only partially successful. I can best bring out what I meant by setting forth some claims that express what Searle has not shown, but which it would be easy to think that he had shown.

> Searle has not shown that we ought to abandon the
> Turing test.

Searle has shown that computers do not *understand*. But Turing's test was a test for *intelligence*. Searle's argument does not give us a reason to say that YOU, as imagined in the systems reply, would not be intelligent, or that YOU would not be exercising intelligence in formulating answers in Chinese. It therefore gives us no reason to abandon the Turing test.

This point may appear to be a verbal quibble, but it is not. The appearance of verbal quibble is generated by the fact that "intelligence" and "understanding" are both mentalistic words that are somewhat vague and have overlapping uses. We do, sometimes, take performance with things in the world as tests of intelligence. We do, sometimes, say that an intelligent solution stems from a deep understanding of a problem even if the understanding involved only thinking about the problem and not manipulating things. The appearance of quibble, however, can be dispelled by replacing "intelligence" and "understanding" with phrases that remind us directly of their roles in the surrounding arguments. So let us speak, on the one hand, of production of flexible response and, on the other hand, of word-world connections. Then we can say, without even the appearance of verbal quibble, that the Turing test tests for production of flexibility, that this ability is important in its own right, and that this ability does not require any word-world connections.

In the next chapter we shall continue to examine understanding, and we shall have ample opportunity to see whether our division of intelligence from understanding will hold up. For now, I will add only that intelligence can still be presumed to be a necessary requirement for understanding of words. The consequence of what I have

been saying is only that intelligently manipulating words is not sufficient for understanding them.

> Searle has not shown that a robot could not have
> understanding.

Searle has not shown—indeed, he does not try to show—that we
could not add sensing devices and motor devices to the input channels and output channels of a computer in such a way as to make a
robot that makes word-world connections. If we imagine such devices
added in appropriate ways, we can imagine a robot that both makes
the right word-word connections and also the right word-world connections. Such a robot would possess exactly the feature whose absence from a mere computer is what enables Searle to show that the
computer lacks understanding. Thus, it cannot follow from Searle's
argument that such a robot would not understand the symbols to
which it responds appropriately in both verbal and nonverbal ways.

Searle does discuss the possibility I have just imagined, under the
heading of "The Robot Reply". He begins his response with this sentence: "The first thing to notice about the robot reply is that it tacitly
concedes that cognition is not solely a matter of formal symbol manipulation, since this reply adds a set of causal relations with the
outside world" (420). Apart from the problematic term "cognition"
(is this the same as understanding? as intelligence?), his sentence is
exactly correct, and we have already agreed to its point. Now, Searle
could have stopped here and could legitimately have said that any
further comment about robots is strictly irrelevant to his attempt to
refute the thesis of strong AI. That thesis is, after all, a claim about
computers, and says nothing about robots. He does not, however,
stop here. He continues, not by denying that the robot we imagined
above is possible, but instead by denying that such a robot would
have understanding. How does he argue for this denial? The key
move is contained in the following passage.

> Suppose that instead of the computer inside the robot, you put me
> inside the room and, as in the original Chinese case, you give me
> more Chinese symbols with more instructions in English for match-
> ing Chinese symbols to Chinese symbols and feeding back Chinese

symbols to the outside. Suppose, unknown to me, some of the Chinese symbols that come to me come from a television camera attached to the robot and other Chinese symbols that I am giving out serve to make the motors inside the robot move the robot's legs or arms. . . . I am receiving "information" . . . giving out "instructions" . . . but . . . I don't know what's going on. I don't understand anything except the rules for symbol manipulation. Now in this case I want to say that the robot has no intentional states at all. (420)

This argument does not work because Searle has not attended to the boundary problem—the very problem that the systems reply called attention to and to which his earlier response was to have YOU memorize all the materials YOU needed. The result is that all his argument establishes is that some *part* of a robot would not have understanding. This point is perfectly compatible with a view according to which the robot—the robot as a whole—understands. We can look at it in the following way as well. In the quoted passage, the subject that fails to have the required word-world connections is the man inside the robot. True enough, this man does not understand the symbols he manipulates. But the statement under discussion (and the statement that concludes the quoted passage) is about the (whole) robot. It does have the right word-world connections (as well as the right word-word connections). So we cannot legitimately conclude that it has the same limitation as its part.

Caveat

In asserting this last limitation of Searle's argument, I mean exactly what I have said: His argument does not show that a robot could not have understanding. This is a statement that characterizes Searle's argument rather than its conclusion, and it does not imply much about robots. In particular, it does not imply that robots actually could have understanding of their words. (Nor, of course, does it imply that they could not.) In order to deal with the interesting issue of whether robots could understand their words, we need to resolve some issues about understanding that we have not yet even mentioned. We will turn to some of these issues in Chapter 3.

Chapter 3

Paralytics and Robots

In Chapter 2 we introduced the term "word-world connections", which covered both input-word and word-action connections. This term was useful enough, because everything we considered in that chapter either possessed both kinds of connection for Chinese words or else lacked both of them. (The robot we considered toward the end had both; the man in the Chinese Room, the system consisting of the man and all the paper in the room, and YOU after memorizing everything had neither.) The further questions that we now need to raise, however, require us to separate the two kinds of connection.

We can get the required separation by considering paralysis. This condition does, of course, come in several degrees, both of severity and extent. For the purposes of this chapter, we shall have in mind a severe case, namely, a person who can speak but who can do nothing else. Even with this stipulation, we have to be careful. Contemporary devices permit typing and self-feeding by people who have very little muscular control. Perhaps all those who can do so much as speak could be given machines that would permit them also to act in some significant ways. If we allow our imaginations to run wild, we may even think of a future in which paralytics are hooked up to machines that understand language. Such people might be able to carry out a large number of actions quite easily, merely by stating out loud their practical conclusions about what ought to be done. We might even imagine that after a period of training the use of such a device would feel completely automatic, and that it would enable paralytics to feel as much doers of their own actions as a good artificial leg makes its wearer feel able to walk. In this chapter, however, I want to consider the case of a person who might have lived some years ago, when electronic aids had not been introduced. We may imagine her to be called "Akinetia". Akinetia is able to speak and to respond to what is said to her quite sensibly in a manner that anyone would take as expressive of intelligence, but she really cannot *do* anything at all. She can see and hear what goes on around her and she can describe what she perceives. She can remember what she has perceived, relate it to what she knows, and draw correct practical conclusions about useful actions. She is, however, unable to act on those conclusions.

Let us now introduce an electronic device that we shall call "Robot Ang". Robot Ang has a (main) computer that can receive verbal input and produce outputs that can drive the keyboard of a microcomputer. We may think of the result of the keyboard activity as the production of words on a monitor screen, and we may suppose that the quality of this result would enable Robot Ang to do well in a Turing test situation. Robot Ang also has a TV camera and a microphone. These are hooked up to its (main) computer. We shall suppose that the computer has a program that can receive the video and audio inputs and generate from them good descriptions of things and movements in its vicinity. Robot Ang can retain what its sensing devices have recorded, relate it to items in its knowledge base, and produce correct practical conclusions about useful behaviors. Robot Ang is, however, unable to move.

One interesting question to ask here is whether Claim 1 is true:

CLAIM 1: Robot Ang understands the words that appear on its monitor screen.

The interest of this question can be brought out by comparing it with the parallel claim about Akinetia:

CLAIM 2: Akinetia understands her words.

It seems (to me, at least) that it could turn out that Claim 1 is false. It seems, that is, that we need some genuine argument to decide its truth, and that we cannot be immediately sure which way things will turn out. This is in stark contrast to the parallel claim about Akinetia: I have never met anyone who doubted that people who are severely paralyzed in the way I have described Akinetia to be would indeed understand what they were saying. We are thus led to a puzzling question:

> **QUESTION:** Why should there be such a difference between claims 1 and 2, when they ask the same thing about subjects that are alike in so many ways?

Since we shall be discussing this difference for some time, it will be convenient to have a shorthand way of referring to it. I shall call it the *status difference*. This is short for "the difference in status between claim 1 and claim 2". This difference is that the first of these judgments is problematic or debatable in a way in which the second is not. Reasonable people can and do dispute about the first, but not about the second. It will also be convenient to say that Akinetia's understanding has a different status from, or is less debatable than, Robot Ang's understanding. This is a short way of saying that the claims about their understanding differ in status or debatability.

Bodily Connections

There is a family of views that tries to account for the status difference by reference to the relations that Akinetia has to her body. The most basic of these is suggested by the obvious point that Akinetia is suffering from a medical problem, not a mental one. Let us begin by saying why this point might be relevant here.

Potential Connections

If we think of Akinetia's problem as medical, we also may think of a possible cure for it. This leads naturally to the idea of the potential reconnection of her brain and her body. Akinetia, we may think, has no word-action connections, but she *would* have them, if only she could be cured. She has, so to speak, everything that is needed to act; it is just that her system doesn't work. In contrast, our description of Robot Ang does not even imply that it has a body. (If you find it peculiar to speak of a robot as having a "body", just read the word in such contexts as "analogue of a body".) Perhaps, then, it is this difference that accounts for the status difference.

This suggestion seems quite dubious to me, and I want to explain why. In doing this, it will be convenient to be more definite about our description of Robot Ang, and also to introduce a second robot. I shall stipulate that Robot Ang does not have a body (except for the camera and microphone analogues of sense organs) and, in fact, has only what we have explicitly described it as having (and anything that logically follows from that). Robot Brf, however, has everything that Robot Ang has and a body besides. This body would enable Robot Brf to act on the practical recommendations its computer produces, except for the fact that the computer and the body have not yet been connected. To complete the picture, let us suppose that Robot Brf's keyboard is not external to it. Instead, it is inside its body, and the monitor that displays the results is located in its chest. The monitor is hooked up, and may display a message like "Your match has set off the sprinkler system! I should get out of here, or at least find a raincoat, so my circuits will not be damaged, or my skin begin to rust!" Alas, not having its computer hooked up to anything else, it stands motionless.

Robot Brf is like Akinetia in that it *potentially* has word-action connections as well as input-word connections. All we would have to do to get these connections is to "cure" it, that is, put the wires running from its computer to its body in order.[1] This fact, however, does not reduce the discrepancy we are trying to explain. That is, the status difference between Robot Brf and Akintia seems exactly as great and of the same kind as that between Robot Ang and Akinetia. There is a reason why this should be so. Robot Brf is Robot Ang with a body built around it, but not connected to it. This seems an unlikely way to build in an increase of understanding, either for the part that is inside, or for the combination of the part inside with the added (but not connected) body. We must, of course, bear in mind that we are talking about actual understanding, not potential understanding. That is, we do not think that Akinetia merely *would* understand her words *if* she were cured: we think she understands them all

along. Adding the mere potentiality for word-action connections to
Robot Ang, by adding a body, does not improve the prospects for
actual understanding, even if it should prove relevant to providing
potential understanding.

Historical Connections

I conclude from these remarks that the status difference between
Akinetia and Robot Ang is not explained by the fact that the first
has a body and the second lacks one. I now want to turn to two
proposals that are related to this one. The first of these remarks that
Akinetia differs from the robots we have described in the fact that
she was at one time healthy and could act as well as speak. Akinetia
is, on this view, to be credited with understanding her words simply
on the ground that she once possessed both kinds of word-world connections.

I do not believe I can show that this claim leads to contradiction,
but I do think that considering Robot Cth will convince you that
having or lacking a history of word-action connections is not the key
to the status difference. For Robot Cth is exactly like Robot Brf in
every respect that can be described without looking into the past.
The only difference between them is that Robot Cth, unlike Robot
Brf, did in the past have its computer connected to its body, so that
it not only had practical recommendations on its screen, but acted in
accordance with them. Since that time, however, it has had its computer disconnected from the motors that move its body (although not
from its internal keyboard and monitor screen).

In short, Robot Cth differs from Robot Brf solely in the history of
its connections. Therefore, if history were the key to the difference
between Akinetia and Robot Ang, we ought to think that it is a
serious question whether Robot Brf understands its words but that
there is no such serious question about Robot Cth's understanding.
My prediction, however, is that the reader will find no such difference, and that Robot Cth's understanding of its words will seem exactly as debatable as Robot Brf's understanding. If this is right, then
it is not a historical difference that makes the difference between
Akinetia and the robots so far discussed.

Some may balk at this conclusion because they think Robot Cth will have information that Robot Brf lacks. For Robot Cth was once connected and can therefore be presumed to have moved around and been places to which Robot Brf has not been. So, Robot Cth will have stored information that it got from its camera and microphone during its travels and that Robot Brf will not have. We may suppose, however, that we have copied Robot Cth's storage tapes (discs, or whatever) onto Robot Brf's storage. In this way, we can make good on the idea that Robot Brf is to be an exact and complete replica of Robot Cth in every respect except historical ones. (For example, it is true of Robot Cth that it once was connected up; but this will not be true of Robot Brf. Similarly, there may be two pennies that I cannot distinguish even by the closest examination. It may still be true of one of them but not the other—not that I can tell which is which— that it was in my pocket yesterday.) When this point is taken into account, I think the reader will be clear that the status difference between Akinetia and Robot Cth is exactly the same as that between Akinetia and Robot Brf. The conclusion, as before, is that historical difference is not what makes for the status difference.

Structure of Connections

The last idea that we need to pursue in this section is that the status difference is to be explained by a difference in the kind of connection that we might envisage to hold between a brain or a computer and a body. What the difference of kind might be and why that difference might be thought to be relevant here will take a little explaining. Our task will be easier if we imagine two more robots, Drg and Esh. These robots both fit the description we gave of Robot Cth, but they differ in some details that we did not specify in Robot Cth's case.

When Robot Drg (Figure 3.1) was properly hooked up, it worked in the following way. First, its (main) computer produced output, based on stored knowledge and current input from the sensing devices. This output was fed to the internal keyboard and monitor. In cases where what appeared on the monitor was a practical recommendation, the computer's output was also fed to another system, which we may call the ACTION SYSTEM. This system turned the practical

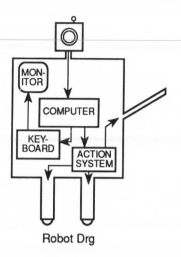

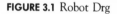

Robot Drg

FIGURE 3.1 Robot Drg

recommendation into a set of commands to Robot Drg's several motors, with the result that Robot Drg's body moved in a way that carried out the recommendation.

The ACTION SYSTEM has to do quite a lot of computing, but it is a different physical unit from Robot Drg's main computer. It receives input from the main computer, but is not connected with it in any other way. In Robert Esh, however, there is no such duplication of computing units. In Robot Esh (Figure 3.2), the computer that generates the commands to each motor is not distinct from the computer that drives the internal keyboard. Nor is there any way of cleanly dividing up this single computer into different parts, or different times of use, so that we can identify one part or time-interval as doing exclusively one of the tasks while other parts or intervals are dedicated to the other task.

Let us now explain why the difference we have just seen might be thought to be relevant in the present context. The key point is that the only way of disconnecting Robot Esh (without disturbing the quality of its monitor screen output) leaves it "closer" to action than does one way of disconnecting Robot Drg. This is because, in the case of Robot Esh, all the computation for instructions to motors

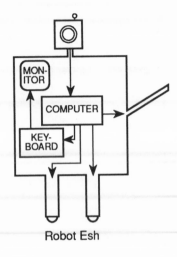

Robot Esh

FIGURE 3.2 Robot Esh

---

must be done if the monitor output is unaffected; so the only thing that can be wrong with a "paralyzed" Robot Esh is the connections to the motors. But Robot Drg can be "paralyzed" (without affecting the quality of its monitor output) by severing the connection between its (main) computer and its ACTION SYSTEM. In such a case, there would be an important computational task that would go unperformed, but would be required for action.

We shall see that the kind of difference between robots Drg and Esh that we have described is quite important in some contexts. We shall return to it in Chapter 11 in more detail and with more care. Here, it will be enough to point out that the difference we have just described does not give us what we need in order to explain the status difference. One way to see this is to notice that the descriptions of robots Brf and Cth are quite neutral with respect to the difference between robots Drg and Esh. But they both fall definitely on the side of problematic understanding, while Akinetia's understanding is not problematic. So, it cannot be that this latter difference depends on the difference between robots Drg and Esh.

Here is another way to look at the matter. Are you so sure you are wired up like Robot Esh and not like Robot Drg? I do not see how you could be sure. In fact, one important issue that is currently under debate can be phrased as the question of which of these robots human beings are more like. Certainly, this is not something you can find out just by casually thinking about how you think, or by thinking about what it would be like to be paralyzed. If this is right, however, then the difference between claims about Akinetia's understanding and claims about our robots' understanding cannot depend on anything we have learned about the difference between robots Drg and Esh.

Finally, when I ask myself whether Akinetia understands her words, it never crosses my mind to ask how she is wired up. What happens is that I imagine myself paralyzed. I imagine myself wanting to stand up and go somewhere and finding that simply nothing happens. When I imagine this, there seems to be no interference with what we might call "the life of the mind". I imagine that I would say to myself, more or less all at once, that this is a terrible position to be in, what on earth has happened to me, how long is this going to last, what if I cannot be cured; and I imagine myself as understanding every word. Now, if this is your experience, you will agree that your conviction that paralytics do understand their (and your) words does not depend on any belief you may have about how human beings are constructed.

We have been exploring the idea that the status difference depends on some fact about the relation to a body. This idea has not worked; there are always robots that are like Akinetia in the respects proposed, but whose claims to understanding have a different status. It is time to look at an explanation for the status difference that is of a quite different kind.

Sensations and Feelings

The view we shall now consider notes that the status difference in regard to understanding has a parallel in a difference about sensations and feelings. Just as there is no doubt that Akinetia understands her words, there is no doubt that she has sensations and feelings. Just as there can be reasonable disagreement about whether robots can understand their words, there can be reasonable disagreement about whether they can have sensations and feelings. The view we are now to examine is that the status difference concerning understanding is not only parallel to, but is based upon, the status difference concerning (judgments about) sensations and feelings.

It is obvious that the second difference is parallel to the first and so divides Akinetia from our robots in the right way. What we have to argue for is that facts about sensations and feelings are relevant to claims about understanding. We can establish this relevance if we can show that Akinetia's connection to her sensations and feelings is a positive reason for thinking that she understands her words. So, let us ask why we should think this is so.

When we imagine Akinetia, we do not imagine only that she both has sensations and uses words. Instead, the words and the sensations are connected. One connection is that her having certain sensations or feelings leads her to use certain words. She may use the word "pain" in reporting to her doctor, if she has had some pain, or she may use terms like "fear", "joy" or "hunger" if she has had the corresponding feelings. Another connection is that when she hears those words used by others, she may remember times when she has had the corresponding sensations or feelings. A third connection is that when actions are described, fear or anticipation may result. For example, if we tell Akinetia that a friend will arrive later, or that she will be taken to a concert, she may experience joy. On the other hand, if she is hiding some deep military secret, learning that torturers are on the way may incite fear of suffering from the pains of thumbscrews, from feeling cold in an unheated cell, and from unbearably foul stenches. She may also remember or imagine what friends, cells, music, and so on look or sound like. Finally, when her words recommend practical actions, she will know whether, if she could do them, they would be done joyfully or regretfully, and she will know whether she would have had soreness in her muscles as a result. She will know the effects on others, including what sensations and feelings they will have as a result. She will be able to imagine what things around her would look like after she had acted upon them, and how she might be warmer or colder, or better able to hear a sound, if she were able to change her position.

In short, Akinetia's words are richly connected to her sensations and feelings. Sensations and feelings, however, are obviously not themselves words. So, her words are connected to something other than words. Now, I do not think that the term "understanding" is so clear that we can simply define it as correct word-word connection, plus input-word connection, plus some further connection beyond words. Nonetheless, it is extremely plausible to suppose that connection to nonwords has something to do with understanding. In Akinetia's case, there is no action to be connected to, and we saw that potential for action will not explain actual understanding. Connection to sensations and feelings is the only further connection (that is, connection additional to word-word and input-word connections) that is available to Akinetia. So, it is extremely plausible to suppose that it is our believing that there is this connection in Akinetia that makes us think she understands her words. It is also plausible that when we think of Robot Ang, we think of something that, like Akinetia, has no connection to actions but, unlike Akinetia, may not have any connection to sensations and feelings either (because it may not have any sensations or feelings). Since there is nothing else around to provide a further connection for Robot Ang's words, we are led to think that Robot Ang may not understand its words. We will be prepared to attribute understanding to Robot Ang if we find some argument that shows it to have sensations and feelings to connect its words to, but if it turns out not to have sensations and feelings, we will think it does not have understanding.

If all this is accepted, it is natural to go on to ask whether in fact robots can have sensations and feelings. I will return to this question in Chapter 4, even if only for the single case of pains. There is, however, another question that we shall pursue first. We must take up this question, because until we have resolved it we cannot have a clear view about understanding.

Pointlessness

One way of summarizing what I have just been arguing for is to say that a thing's having a certain group of connections is *sufficient* or is *enough* for it to understand its words. This group of connections is

> Word-word
> plus   Input-word
> plus   Word-(sensations and feelings)

But we also can ask whether this group of connections is *necessary* or is *required* for a thing to understand its words. The importance of the question is this: If its answer is Yes, then even the robot we imagined at the end of the last chapter might not understand its words. That robot had

> Word- word
>
> plus   Input-word
>
> plus   Word-action

connections. This group of connections is missing the third item in the previous group. So, if that item is necessary for understanding, then we would not be entitled to say that the robot at the end of the last chapter understood its words.

Let us now try to get clear whether or not connecting words to sensations and feelings is necessary for having understanding. I will begin by stating an argument for saying that this kind of connection *is* necessary for understanding. I will present it baldly and forcefully; later, I shall have some comments about it.

> You would not credit something with understanding phrases like "was in prison for ten years", "was threatened at knife point", or "was separated from family for a long time" unless you also thought that it knows that these conditions are undesirable. But if it knows this, it must understand what is meant by saying that something is undesirable. If it understands this, it must know that if a thing is undesirable, it has consequences of which the following are representative examples: pain, hunger, and nausea; feelings of loneliness, hatred, jealousy, or hopelessness; deprivations of the taste of good food, bakery smells, and lovers' touches; and fears of all of these things. If a thing knows that being undesirable involves these consequences, it must understand what the words that denote or describe these consequences mean. But in order to

understand these words, it must have at least some of the corresponding sensations and feelings.

A similar conclusion can be reached if we start with any phrase describing an action, for actions are connected to expectations of sensations and feelings. The lines of connection may be very long, but they are there. For example, we get in our cars to go to the store, so that we can get food, so that we can eat, so that we will not experience hunger. (Of course, we do not get just any food. Usually, we get some that leads to the best taste, if we can afford it, or that leads away from pains due to ill health.) We work so we will have money, so we can have a place to live, so we will not be cold in the winter, or so we can enjoy having a companion. There is a structure and order to our behavior that depends, sooner or later, on consequences for sensations and feelings. Therefore, if we imagine a thing that does not have any sensations or feelings (as the robots in this and the previous chapter *may* not), we imagine a thing from which we have removed the ultimate purposes of action. There would be no real point *for it* to its doing anything. (There might be a point for its owner. For example, if some activity protected it, or fueled it, its owner would have an interest in its doing the activity.) If it went to the store, bought chops, cooked them, and consumed them, its motions would be all performance with a hollow core of pointlessness, no matter how perfect the exterior execution might be. Since there would actually be no point (for itself) to its actions, there is no way it could use an examination of its actions to understand their point. So, even if it could string together a series of sentences that expressed reasons for doing something, it would not really understand them, because it would not understand the last terms (that is, the ones for sensations and

feelings) that describe what is ultimately the point
of actions.

I believe that these remarks do show something. We have to be careful, however, to correctly identify what they show. The immediate
question is whether they show that if a thing has no sensations or
feelings then it cannot understand its words. I do not believe that
they do show this. In order to see why, let us consider the following
example.

> Robot Frp fits the description given for Robot Cth,
> except that it has never been disconnected.* Just to
> remind you, this means that it has good input-word
> connections, good word-word connections (it can
> do well in a Turing test situation) and good word-
> action connections. Robot Frp also *definitely lacks*
> what the other robots in this chapter only *may*
> lack, namely, sensations and feelings.
>
>   Now, suppose I say to Robot Frp, "Go to the
> drug store and bring back the prescription that the
> druggist will have for me. It will be $15.75." This is
> all I say to Robot Frp, but it goes to the drug store
> and comes back with my prescription. It has never
> been to this drug store before, and since I gave it
> no directions, it looked up the address and
> consulted the map in the telephone book. It also
> looked up the bus route and checked its small
> equipment box to see whether there was enough
> money for the prescription and the bus fare both
> ways.

Did Robot Frp understand what I said to it? Here, I have only intuitions to appeal to, but they say that it did. Denying that Robot Frp
understood what I said to it in a case like this would seem to imply
that it made some mistake, like going to the wrong store, or schedul-
ing the trip to the store for next week, or going to the right store but
returning with the wrong item, or simply doing nothing. But no failure of this sort occurred in the example; Robot Frp grasped what I

---

*Pages on which robots are introduced and described may be found in the Index of Robots,
p. 275.

told it to do, and when it was to do it (even though I did not actually say when). Its subsequent actions show that it took in what I said, took it in correctly, and connected my instructions with appropriate actions.

If my last few paragraphs have been successful, we will now find that we harbor conflicting intuitions about whether having sensations and feelings is necessary for a thing to understand its words. What can we do to resolve this conflict? The first thing we should face up to is that "understanding" is not a precise term. It has many uses and carries many suggestions. It is unlikely that we are going to get everyone who is interested in the questions we have been discussing to agree on a definition of "understanding" that is clear enough to generate good arguments for either "Sensations and feelings are necessary conditions of understanding" or for the opposite statement. It is, therefore, useless to insist on either of these conclusions. In all of our actual experience, and most of our imagined experience, the possession of input-word, word-word, and word-action connections has occurred together with word- (sensations and feelings) connections. For this reason, it should not be surprising that we do not have a common usage that tells us clearly and sharply what we should say about a case where some of the kinds of connections are separated.

The point here is similar to one that often comes up in discussions of congenitally blind people. Do they understand remarks that involve color, like "Chlorophyll is green" or "Strawberries are red"? A simple yes seems inadequate, because that would ignore the obvious fact that they have never experienced the color of anything. Congenitally blind people can, however, use their knowledge to infer that chlorophyll resembles the traffic light for go in color; they may know that orange is a likely color to be found on monks in the East but not in the West; they can follow the point of stories and jokes in which color words play important roles; they can worry about whether the colors of their clothes are pleasing to others; and they can sometimes give lectures on the physics of color perception. In the face of these abilities, a simple no to the question of whether congenitally blind people understand color words seems preposterous and even insulting. Since both a simple yes and a simple no are inadequate, it is pointless to insist that we apply or withhold the epithet "understanding" here.

If Robot Frp and congenitally blind people are alike in generating conflicting intuitions, we should expect that the resolution of the conflict should also be similar. We can make progress in this direction by recognizing that we have a conflict because "understanding" is (naturally enough) used to cover two things. One of these is connection to sensations and feelings; one is connection to appropriate action. We could express the situation of Robot Frp by saying that it understands what it says and hears, but that its actions (including its utterances) ultimately have no point for it. We could also say, however, that it does not understand its words (meaning that they ultimately have no point for it) but that its words do stand for things to which it is connected both on the input side and in actions. How we put the matter is not so important; what is important is to maintain clear recognition of each of the two distinct characteristics that normal people have and whose possible separability gives rise to the puzzlement about understanding.

It is possible that someone may object to these last few paragraphs in the following way. My discussion has taken it for granted that my description of Robot Frp does not involve any contradiction. This description, however, has Robot Frp responding to the world in a rich variety of appropriate ways, but having no sensations or feelings. If responding well over a wide range actually implied that a thing has sensations and feelings, the description would be inconsistent, and any conclusions drawn from the possibility of Robot Frp would be unwarranted. My response to this objection is this. If the description of Robot Frp were inconsistent in the way just indicated, then I would indeed have to withdraw some of what I have said. Whether it is inconsistent in this way is one of the questions that we will be investigating in the next chapter, and we must wait for that discussion to get any arguments. I shall, however, anticipate the results of Chapter 4 far enough to say that I will not have to withdraw any of the above remarks on account of what we shall find there.

Overview

In these first three chapters we have described several possible kinds of thing, and it may be helpful if we set them all side by side. We can do this in Table 3.1. If an item is not listed in a grouping, it is to be understood that that item is absent. Below the lists of properties are

Intelligence
Word-word connections
Input-word connections
Word-action connections
Word- (sensations and feelings) connections
 Normal People
 Robots?

Intelligence   Intelligence
Word-word connections   Word-word connections
Input-word connections   Input-word connections
Word-action connections   Word- (sensations and feelings) connections
 Robots?   *Paralytics*
                                       Disconnected Robots?

Intelligence
Word-word connections
 Computers?

Intelligence
 Some animals?

TABLE 3.1

things that exemplify, or may exemplify, that list. The entry at the
bottom of the table may be surprising, because I have not discussed
animal intelligence. That is a subject for a different book. I did allow,
however, that flexibility can be exhibited by suiting actions to circumstances without any words being involved, and if animals exhibit
sufficient flexibility, they may be intelligent without any connections
with words at all. We can add two remarks that will help us see the
need for keeping the entry one up from the bottom separate from the
two next-higher ones. First, playing chess is commonly regarded as
requiring (and exhibiting) a high degree of intelligence. It is, however, an activity in which word-action connections are at a minimum. At most, one has to move pieces. Even this can be dispensed
with, however. Anyone can play chess by mail, and some excellent
players can keep board positions in mind without having to look at
an actual board with pieces. If two such excellent players played by
mail, we would have a case in which hardly any word-action connections would be used, but in which intelligence would be well exer-

cised. The second remark will be acceptable only to those who agree that the description of Robot Frp is consistent. This granted, we can at least consider the possibility of a different robot that is like Robot Frp in many ways, but that also has word-(sensations and feelings) connections. In making this addition, we are imagining something added to Robot Frp's mental life. I do not believe, however, that anyone will think that what we have added makes Robot Frp any *smarter*. This is a reason for making a division between intelligence and other aspects of a thing's mental life.

Finally, we should be explicit about the relation of our conclusions to Searle's argument. What we found to be the single legitimate strand of Searle's argument was that a computer could be running a program and giving good answers to questions without having any connections between its words and anything beyond words. Searle's way of stating this was to say that computers do not understand their words. We noted in Chapter 2 that this argument could not show that robots could never understand their words. In this chapter, we have seen that *understanding* is more complicated than we had any indication of in Searle's work. Robots could have the thing whose lack is enough to show that mere computers do not have understanding, namely, word-world connections of both kinds; but their having these connections would not clearly entitle us to say that they do understand their words. We have not found anything that entitles us to say that robots do not understand either; but if we do say that they understand their words, we must be prepared to add that, nonetheless, there may ultimately be no point for them in their words or actions. Whether their words and actions are pointless (for them) depends on whether they can have sensations.

Chapter 4

Dennett, Robots, and Pains

In this chapter, we turn directly to the question of whether it is possible for a robot to have sensations and feelings. There is an obvious approach to this question, namely, to imagine trying to build such a robot and to see what difficulties we may run into. This kind of approach has been taken by Daniel Dennett in an intriguing paper, "Why You Can't Make a Computer That Feels Pain".[1] We shall profit by thinking about some of the things that Dennett says in this paper.

In the last chapter, we wondered about possible robotic possession of quite a large range of sensations and feelings. Dennett's paper is just about pains. Pains, however, are representative of many examples of sensations and feelings. For the most part, the arguments that apply to one example apply to the others, or can be made to apply by being tailored to new cases in straightforward ways. So, although we shall follow Dennett in limiting our discussion to the case of pains, our results can be taken as having general significance for the question of robotic sensations and feelings.

A Point of Strategy

If you are going to build something of a certain kind, you have to know what kind of thing you are building. You have to be able to recognize whether you are making progress in the right direction and you have to know when you have succeeded and can quit. If, for example, you want to build a pump, you have to know that a pump is something that moves fluids from one place to another in a system of conduits. You will have succeeded in building a pump when you have built something that does that. We can draw on earlier chapters for another example. If you want to build something that has intelligence, you must build something that exhibits flexibility and that is not dependent in a certain way on the intelligence of something else. You will have succeeded in your task if and when you have built such a thing. Now, likewise, if you want to build a robot that can have pains, you have to know something about pains. You must state some facts about pains that will provide a way of recognizing when (or if) you have succeeded in building the right kind of robot.

Not just any fact about pains will be what we need. This parallels the point that not just any fact about pumps or about intelligence is what we need. A list of what pumps are made of, for example, would not be to the point, because we know that a pump could be made out of materials that have never yet been used to make one. It is a fact that pumps do not grow on trees, but, again, they might have done so, and perhaps on some other planet they do. So this fact about pumps is not important for the purpose of building one or for knowing whether we have built one. Likewise, no matter how favorable you may be toward the possibility of artificial intelligence, I think you will agree that all the intelligent things that we know of that existed before 1800 were alive. But if the earlier chapters of this book have been convincing at all, you will see a way in which a machine may turn out to be intelligent. So, if we are looking for facts that are going to help us decide whether we have built an intelligent robot, you will not think that the association between being intelligent and being alive is one that is appropriate to include. Now, analogously, we must not expect that just any fact that concerns pain is relevant to determining whether we have built a robot that can feel a pain.

The obvious question is, What facts about pain are relevant in this context? Unfortunately, this is even harder to answer in this case than it is in the case of intelligence. We will have to consider some facts that at least give the *appearance* of being relevant and see whether they really are.

Is "Pain" Coherent?

There is a group of facts that Dennett reviews at the end of his paper, but which I think we will do well to begin with. The first of these is that if you believe that you have a pain, you do have one. Although we sometimes wonder whether people are lying about their claims to be in pain, we do not suspect them of being mistaken. We do not try to console people who claim to be in pain by telling them that it's all right, perhaps they only think that what they have is pain and that maybe it is itch or euphoria instead. We allow, of course, for babbling "I am in pain" in one's sleep or while drugged. But we count these as cases of confused mental capacities, not as cases of believing mistakenly that one is in pain. We allow for foreigners declaring "I am in pain" when they have mislearned the word. Again, we do not count this as mistaken belief about pain; we count it as mistaken belief about the proper use of the word "pain". Where we allow for genuine believing that people are in pain, we do not allow for mistake by illusion with respect to what is felt.

If we are going to try to make a robot that has pains, we will want to ensure that whenever it believes it has a pain, it actually does have a pain. Let us now notice a second fact about pain, one that would surely have to apply to any truly pain-feeling robot. This is, that pain is something that is disliked. It is something that those who have it mind having, because what it is, is awful. The existence of masochism, by the way, does not conflict with this. It is only because pain itself is disliked that the receiving of it can reduce the sense of guilt or be an expression of submission to the sadist who inflicts it. The awfulness of pain is not like the awfulness of some music—I might prefer silence, but I suppose its composer actually liked it. Salman Rushdie has a character ask, "Lives there who loves his pain?" Odd question; because unlike "Lives there who likes to eat fried ants?" the answer seems quite certain and not merely very likely to be no. That pain is awful (in one degree or another) seems just part of what is included in the idea that it is *pain*.

It is, of course, not obvious how we are to build a robot that meets the two conditions just described. Dennett, however, suggests a still more difficult problem. This arises when we add what he takes to be a third fact, namely, that *people sometimes believe they have pains,*

Awful: "Awful" is used by Dennett and by others, so it is hard to avoid it here. But it has a problem: besides being a description of pain, it can also be used to indicate an extreme degree. For example, "That play was just awful" is a severe condemnation. It says that the play was worse than just a little slow, worse than just having some dialogue that did not quite ring true. So, if you mix the two senses, you will come out with the idea that all pains are terribly bad pains. This, of course, is not true: Some pains are bad and some are not so bad. When we say here that pains are awful, we just mean that pains hurt. They may hurt awfully (be *awfully* awful), or they may hurt just a little (have a mild degree of awfulness).

---

but do not mind, do not experience anything that is awful. The people in question are takers of morphine and other such dissociative drugs. Under certain conditions, such people will say that they definitely have a pain, but that they do not mind having it. They seem to be fully mentally competent and to know what the word "pain" means; they claim to have a pain; yet they act content and do not complain or ask for (any further) pain killers.

Let us make sure we understand the logical position this claim puts us in. Consider this analogy.

- The butler murdered Sir Reginald in the library.
- Sir Reginald was murdered between 10 P.M. and midnight.
- The butler was in the kitchen during the entire time between 10 P.M. and midnight.

Any of these statements might be true. Moreover, any pair of them could be put forward by a respectable detective in setting out a theory of the case. But the detective who puts forward all three ought to be fired; for the three cannot all be true together. Now the same holds true for the following three statements:

- Anything that believes it has a pain, has one.
- Nothing could be a pain that was not awful (in some degree).
- Some people believe they have pains when in fact they do not have anything that is awful.

By the first statement, people who believe they have pains actually have them. The second statement says that what they thus have is awful. So, the first two statements tell us that if they believe they have pains, then they have something awful. This, however, rules out the possibility that the third claim is true.

Let us consider some reactions to this situation. Here is a fairly extreme one. We might think that something is a pain only if all of what people believe is true of pains is true of it. But what people believe about pains is inconsistent. So, nothing could possibly fit all that people believe about pains. Therefore, nothing could be a pain. The reason you cannot build a robot that feels a pain is the same reason you cannot make a flat coin that is both round and square: The description is inconsistent and nothing can satisfy an inconsistent description.

You will probably not like this view, because it will not take you long to see that it has the consequence that you don't have pains either! Fortunately, refusing to accept this first reaction is quite reasonable. Consider the moon or the earth. In the course of history there have been widespread views about these things—their shape, size, and distance from each other—that have been quite wrong. There was, in fact, nothing that fit what most people thought about the moon and the earth. But that does not show that these things do not exist. It just shows that being a certain kind of thing does not require that all of the widespread views about that kind of thing have to be satisfied. Our being confused about what to say about the reports of the morphine patients will not and should not convince us that we do not have pains.

Here is another reaction. We have pains and, for all we have yet argued, robots may have them. But the only way we can know that a robot has them is to know that it satisfies all that we believe about pains. Alas, what we believe is inconsistent. So, we know that we will never be in the position of having established that all that we believe about pains is true of a robot. That is, we know that we will never be in the position of having established that a robot has pains.

Here is a third view. What we now believe about pains is inconsistent. But since we really do have pains, there must be a consistent way of describing them. In the future we may change some of what we believe, and these changes may result in our having a consistent set of views about pain. At that time we may be able to get in a position to establish that a robot satisfies all that we will then believe about pains; and this will be to establish that a robot can feel a pain.

Here is the last reaction I will list. We do not really believe the third of the statements that seem to raise a problem. We do not really believe what the morphine patients say, when they say they have pains that they do not mind. We accept that they are sincere and generally mentally competent, but we think they are a bit confused about how they ought to describe what is happening. We have good evidence that they are a little confused. For, in the light of the first two statements, we can see that they are actually contradicting themselves; yet, they are willing to persist in claiming to have pain.[2] There is also a likely explanation for the confusion. Suppose that pains have at least three characteristics: (1) location in some part of the body, (2) awfulness, and (3) some property like throbbing, warmth, or tearing. (The third property need not be the same for every case of pain.) Suppose the morphine removes the awfulness but leaves the third property in the same location. Then there would be *something* there that is continuous with what used to be a pain. Moreover, it might be that nothing else a patient has ever experienced has throbbed or felt tearing in this particular way. So, "pain" would be a natural term to apply to it, even though the key ingredient—awfulness—is missing. If this is how things are, we could understand how claims to have pain in the absence of awfulness are false, while understanding how mentally competent people come to assert them.

As you can probably tell, I like the last of these responses to our problem best; however, I am not going to defend it or criticize the second and third responses. It is enough for our purposes to see that there are alternatives to the first response. For, if we agree that the concept of pain is or may become coherent, the threatened obstacle to our ever building a pain-feeling robot has been removed. Moreover, if either the third or the fourth response is correct, the suggested obstacle to our ever *knowing* we have built a pain-feeling robot has also been removed.

There is a further reason for not pursuing the discussion of the responses. The problem that Dennett raised is interesting in its own right and, because it occupies an important position in the paper we are examining, we really had to discuss it anyway. However, *from the point of view of the task of trying to build a pain-feeling robot, the key claims about pains that we have discussed in this section are entirely beside the point.* The reason is that in order to establish that these claims are true of a given thing, you must already have established that that thing has pains. Take the first claim: Anything that believes it has a pain has one. To know whether we have built a robot that satisfies this, we first have to build one that believes it is in pain. It is, of course, already a problem to know when we have done this, but let that pass. We would, next, have to test whether, when our robot believes it has a pain, it really does have one. That is to say, we would have to have a way of knowing that it does or does not have a pain, in order to find out whether it satisfies the requirement of believing it is in pain only when it is. But if we have such a way of knowing, then we do not need to ask further whether it believes it is in pain only when it is. The irrelevance of the second claim, that nothing could be a pain that was not awful, is even easier to see. This tells us that if we are to build a robot that has pains, we must build something that has something awful. But it does not tell us how we are to determine whether a robot has something awful. In fact, determining this is just the same problem as deciding whether a robot has a pain.

Pain Behavior

If we are going to make any progress, we must look at some other facts that we know about pain. The most obvious of these involve the behavior that is associated with having pain. For example, if you should be the unfortunate recipient of an anvil dropped from two feet onto your left foot, you would, I suppose, let out a monstrous yell, hop around on your right foot, clutch at your left foot, and start swearing. Pains in other places would have analogous but somewhat different results. Other things being equal, less heavy objects dropped on the same place would have results whose difference would be roughly proportional to the difference in weight.

There are some behavioral facts related to pain that extend over a longer period of time. When your friends take you to the clinic, the doctor may ask whether your foot still hurts. You will probably say yes. You may beg for a pain-killing drug. Uttering these remarks is behavior that relates to pain that you still have. Some other utterances will concern past pains. Thus, when you are asked about your encounter with the anvil in two weeks, you will probably say that the pain was excruciating, that it seared like a hot knife and then throbbed mercilessly. Mild pains may be forgotten after not too long a time, but your tendency to elaborate on the description of severe ones will last longer. Finally, having had a painful experience is likely to lead to your acting very carefully to avoid similar encounters in the future. Perhaps you will start wearing steel-toed shoes, or you will stay a good distance away from anvils that are not firmly on the ground.

Let us imagine that Robot Grn has been constructed in the following way. Various parts of its roughly anthropoid body have been provided with slots that receive tokens of various sizes. Beside each slot is a picture indicating an action, for example, dropping from two feet or rubbing back and forth. Tokens also have pictures that represent objects, such as an anvil or sandpaper. The slots are attached to devices that work like a vending machine; that is, the tokens are sorted by size and weight. When you put a token in a slot, Robot Grn produces the behavior that you would expect from having the object represented by the token put into the relation to your body that is indicated in the picture by the slot. If you put the sandpaper token into the "dropped from two feet" slot in Robot Grn's foot, you do not get much—maybe a "What was that?" out of Robot Grn's speaker. If, however, you put the sandpaper token into the "rub back and forth" slot on Robot Grn's nose, it instantly jerks back, croaks an "Ouch!" followed by "What did you do that for?" and various insulting remarks about your ancestors, and clutches its nose. For a while afterward, it answers yes when you ask it whether its nose still hurts. If you ask it to describe its pain, it will say something like "burning and tearing". For at least a few days, it is ready to recount in some detail how awful it felt to have its nose sandpapered, and it tends to keep well away from you, especially when you have tokens in your hand.

Do we know that Robot Grn feels pains? I think no one will say that we do. The jerking away and the swearing require nothing more than what we find in vending machines. Instead of having a motor release a can of pop, it would move Robot Grn's head in a direction opposite to where its nose was pointing and activate the swearing tape. We would need a clock in order to get the right decrease of intensity of expressions as Robot Grn "calmed down", but that is no more interesting than, say, an oven timer. It would be very complicated to add to Robot Grn the ability to recognize when it was being asked about its pains, but this ability is required only for verbal response. Nonspeaking animals typically are credited with the ability to feel pain, and if we thought we could teach them how to talk, we would not think that thereby we were giving them more pain. The chimpanzee Washoe, for example, was taught quite a few words in sign language, but no one worried that if she were taught to report on her pains, she would thereby suffer more intensely. So, Robot Grn's ability to respond well verbally, complicated though that ability would be, is tangential to the question of whether Robot Grn feels any pain. The ability to recognize you again might be very complicated but does not itself have anything to do with pain. On the one hand, recognizing one's friends is not painful; and, on the other hand, we have voice-recognizers that no one thinks feel anything. Once recognition was accomplished, it would be relatively trivial to have Robot Grn tend to increase its distance from you after you have activated a jerking and a swearing response from it. A device that monitors an autofocus mechanism and uses the results to drive a motor could be made to do the trick. The upshot of these observations is that although Robot Grn might be quite complicated to build, it is not complicated in ways that are relevant to feeling pain. It is too much like a bunch of very ordinary devices hooked up together. If you are not seriously worried that your stereo system may be suffering from noise-induced headache and you are not concerned that complex devices like cars or nuclear power plants may be having pains, then you have no reason to suppose that Robot Grn is suffering when it jerks away, swears, and avoids you.

Let us now think about Robot Hln. This robot is just like Robot Grn in what it does and what it says. But to get it to do and say things, we no longer put tokens in slots; we drop anvils on its feet, apply sandpaper to its nose, and so on. Do we now have good reason to suppose that Robert Hln must feel pains?

Again, I believe that you will not be inclined to say yes here. The reason is that, as far as we can gather from what we have been

Functions: The function of a pump is to move fluids in a closed system. If a thing performs this function, it is a pump. It is the function of a vending machine to give you some product and change *if* you have inserted coins of sufficient value and pressed a button. Anything that can do this is a vending machine. (Of course, some Martians might not realize this and use one as a table instead.)

In both of these examples, the *function* is constituted by there being certain relationships. An object, some fluid, and some tubes or ducts must be related in a certain way in order for the object to work as a pump; a machine, coins, and a product must be related in certain ways for the machine to be a vending machine. We can generalize this idea and regard any set of relationships as a function. We can then identify what performs the function as the thing that stands in the specified relationships.

The facts about pain that we have considered in this section involve relations among a thing, its circumstances, and its movements. We can say that Robot Grn performs a certain function and that Robot Hln performs another function that is very similar but not exactly the same. We can put the question we have been asking by saying, "Is performing the function that Robot Hln performs enough to show us that it has pains?" The conclusion of our argument regarding Robot Hln can then be expressed as a negative answer to this question.

The advantage in putting the question this way is that it unifies our discussion. We are going to keep adding facts about pain, that is, we are going to keep describing more and more complicated functions. The question at each stage will be of the same kind: Does the fact that a robot performs such and such a function (or, such and such a set of functions) show that the robot has pains?

---

told, Robot Hln can be so very much like Robot Grn. For example, nothing I said rules out a mechanism like the following. Dropping an anvil on Robot Hln's foot causes a token stored inside the foot to fall into a certain slot, rubbing sandpaper on Robot Hln's nose causes a token stored inside the nose to fall into a certain slot, and so on. If this is the setup, however, then Robot Hln is just like Robot Grn from, say, two inches deep all the rest of the way in. Or, it is just like Robot Grn except for some extra machinery at the outer layer. Moreover, this extra machinery could be much like what you could find in vending machines. So, if you do not think that Robot Grn has pains, you have no reason to think that Robot Hln has them either.

If we ask either of our last two robots to describe their pains, they will provide appropriate descriptions that involve terms like "burning", "throbbing", or "stabbing". But our descriptions of our robots' behavior and construction do not imply that there is anything about them that burns or throbs or stabs. So, there may be some who would suppose that what is missing from our robots is something to which these adjectives might apply. Let us try to remedy this deficiency by supplying lights at various locations on the bodies of some more complex robots. Robot Imb has everything that Robot Hln has. In addition, it has lights that throb whenever the body part surrounding the light has been affected in a way that would produce a throbbing pain. If the injury would produce a dull throb in a human being, the lights wax and wane gradually; if the injury would produce a stabbing pain, the lights change much faster, almost flashing up to their more intense level and then diminishing. The color of these lights can also change: they will be red when the pain that a human being would have would be a hot one, and they will be yellow or blue when the pain would not be described as "hot".

While we are at it, we might as well note that some pains go with certain bodily changes that would not correctly be called "actions". I have in mind things like crying, shaking involuntarily, and reddening. Robot Jnk has everything that Robot Imb has. In addition, when the injury suffered by Robot Jnk is the kind that would make a person cry, tears appear in Robot Jnk's eyes; when the injury would make a person shake, Robot Jnk shakes. On appropriate occasions, we can see a reddish tinge spreading over Robot Jnk's neck.

Robot Jnk performs a function that is quite complex. (Remember that each of our robots since Robot Grn includes all the functions of previous robots in the series.) Performance of that function involves many different situations and many different effects, all coordinated with each other and with gradual dissipation as the time after the damage to its parts increases. Is performing this function enough to show us that Robot Jnk feels pain? As before, I think you will answer no, and with good reason. What we have added since we considered Robot Hln (which feels no pains) is "too easy". Of course, in one way, it is quite hard. It's expensive. But we know how to do it; we know, in fact, where to go to see that it has already been done. It is all Hollywood stuff. Tears can be produced by a little motor that squeezes a liquid-filled bulb, shaking by eccentric flywheels, and reddening by red lights at the edges of lucite sheets. Adding gadgets of this kind does not have the slightest relevance to pain. Robot Imb's lights are Christmas tree decorations with fancy switches; adding those does not have any relevance to pain either.

The complex function that Robot Jnk performs includes all the kinds of facts that seem to have something to do with pain and that we could get to know by looking at a robot's outsides. The conclusion so far, then, is that we cannot show that a robot has a pain by showing that it satisfies any function, where the function is described by what can be observed from outside. The natural move in response to such a conclusion is to look for facts that can only be discovered by looking inside or theorizing about what goes on inside a robot—facts that have something to do with *how* the robot does what it does, facts that are about how it is hooked up inside. Very roughly, we might say that performing our "external" functions is not enough to show that a thing has pains. But perhaps if a robot were to perform our "external" functions *in the way that we do*, that is, *by performing some of the same "internal" functions*, that would show that it can have pains. Let us examine some more careful expressions of this idea.

Looking Inside

There are many facts about pain that involve what goes on inside us. Many of these are very interesting and many are discussed in fascinating detail in Dennett's paper. I shall not repeat that detail here. What we need is only a few facts that are representative of the *kind* of thing we can learn about what goes on inside. The conclusions we can draw about these representative facts can be generalized to many other similar facts.

Let us introduce the first new fact by considering Robot Kwz. This robot does everything that Robot Jnk does. One aspect of this ability is that rubbing the body part in which the pain is located leads to behavior associated with diminished pain. (The rubbing leads, for

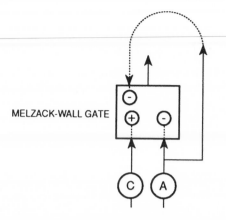

MELZACK-WALL GATE

FIGURE 4.1 Diagram of Melzack-Wall gate. The dotted line represents inhibition of C fiber transmission caused by indirect effects of A fibers (that is, effects that depend on the A fibers' affecting other parts of the brain). Derived from D. C. Dennett, *Brainstorms* (Montgomery, Vt.: Bradford Books, 1978), p. 200; used by permission of The MIT Press.

example, to less complaining, to continued rubbing, and to reports of a lesser degree of discomfort.) In Robot Kwz, however, this ability is accomplished by a particular mechanism that parallels the structure of our Melzack-Wall gates.[3] Schematically, our pain-gates are places that receive input from two kinds of pain-causing neurons, A fibers and C fibers (see Figure 4.1). Activity in the A fibers tends to prevent the C fibers from passing their activity through the gate. Rubbing the affected part of the body stimulates both kinds of neurons. The "gate closing" due to the increased activity in the A fibers, however, more than offsets the tendency to worse pain due to increased activity in the C fibers. The result is a lessening of the pain that is due to C fiber stimulation. When this happens, we naturally complain less, keep rubbing the affected part, and report a lessened pain.

Should we think that if we build Robot Kwz we have come closer to building a pain-feeling robot than we would if we built Robot Jnk? In favor of saying so, we might say that we have pain and that we know Robot Kwz to be more like us than we have any reason to think Robot Jnk is. Against this, however, lies the following. Because the explanation of pain reduction is that the output from the gate is reduced, the story about how the gate works assumes that whatever the output of the gate is, is what causes pain. It follows that as long as the output after the gate is the same, the pain will result. This, in turn, has the consequence that if we build something that is just like us from the point just after the gate, we should expect it to have pain. This, however, shows that the presence or absence of the gate is irrelevant to the question of whether or not there is pain. The situation is analogous to a light switch. This can be used to *control* the flow of electricity to a light bulb and thus to control whether the light will be on. But it is not a light bulb and it does not cause the light, despite being able to control the cause. If we screwed the switch to a tree, we would not think we had made progress toward producing light. Just so, the gate is a control mechanism, not a producer of pain. In adding it to our robot, we must not think we have made progress toward producing pain. If we can satisfy ourselves on some other ground that a robot has pain, then an analogue of a Melzack-Wall gate may be a pain-control mechanism; but without that other ground, we have no reason to assume that there is anything (except electrical current) for it to control.

This kind of argument will apply to many facts about pain that we might mention. In particular, it will apply to many of the individual boxes in a diagram that Dennett has used to represent some facts about pain (see Figure 4.2).[4] There is, however, another kind of fact that might be thought to be relevant, namely, the way the whole diagram is structured. This suggestion corresponds to a very plausible idea, namely, that pain depends on a very complex set of events in the brain and not just on a few simple events. We might suppose that although any single mechanism (any one box in the diagram) is dispensable, a robot that had most of the relations among kinds of internal function performers (boxes) that we do would be a robot that felt pains. More carefully, let us stipulate that Robot Lul has everything that Robot Kwz has and, in addition, instantiates all the relations in Dennett's diagram. Then our next task will be to examine the suggestion that we have good reason to think that Robot Lul feels pains.

There is a striking fact that Dennett tells us that casts doubt on this suggestion. This is that we have two neural pathways that lead to pains. Dennett refers to one of these as the "old, low path" and the other as the "new, high path". What does this mean? Think of mak-

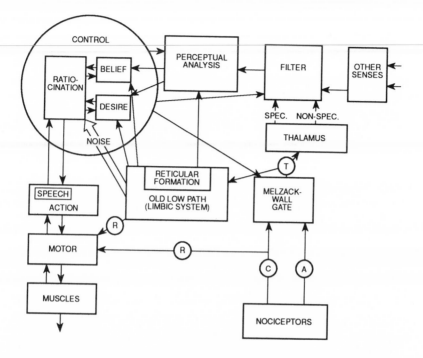

FIGURE 4.2 Source: D. C. Dennett, *Brainstorms* (Montgomery, Vt.: Bradford Books, 1978), p. 205; reproduced by permission of The MIT Press.

ing a fist while wearing a boxing glove. Hold your forearm so that it rises from elbow to hand at about 45 degrees and hold your hand so that the knuckles are up, like a row of mountain peaks. Looking at your gloved hand sideways, you will see something very roughly the shape of a brain. The part that is glove (minus the palm, lacing, and wrist) is roughly where your cortex would be; the part that is fist (you cannot see that, of course, but you know where it is) is where the "older" part of the brain is. Why "older"? If you go down the evolutionary scale, that is, toward animals like those that evolved before later forms, you will find that the part corresponding to the glove gets thinner and thinner. The structures in the part corresponding to the fist are detectable for a long time backward, and in less developed animals they occupy a proportionately larger part of the brain. What happens in our "fist" is thus structurally similar to old life forms, that is, forms that have been around a relatively long time. What happens in our "glove" is, evolutionarily speaking, a new development. Of course, in the position that our brain has when we are standing or sitting, the "glove" is mostly above—higher than—the "fist".

One of the pathways whose activation causes us to have some of our pains lies in the lower, older part of the brain. This fact ought not to surprise us; after all, we do think that animals like rats, whose brains are mostly "fist", can feel pain. There is, however, an interesting consequence of this fact: it shows that the structures in the "glove" are not required for us to have pains. Therefore, to create a pain-feeling thing cannot be the same thing as creating a thing that instantiates the whole of, or even most of, Dennett's diagram.

A plausible response to this point would be the following. Having most of the structures in Dennett's diagram, you may agree, is not required in order to have a thing that feels pain. Still, you may say, this is quite compatible with the view that if you did build a thing that had all the structures in the diagram, that would have to be enough for having pains. Maybe it would be more than enough, but it would have to be at least enough. The fact that the old, low path is sufficient for pain, however, raises a problem that goes pretty deep. It is a problem that is quite like the one that led us not to be impressed by the presence of an analogue of the Melzack-Wall gate. Let us spell this problem out in terms of an analogy.

What do we know about wine? Here are some facts. It is a liquid that often comes in bottles with corks. It is often drunk during a meal. It comes in a certain range of colors. Too much of it makes people drunk. Suppose, now, that we take some water, add alcohol and appropriate vegetable dyes, put the result in a corked bottle and start drinking it with dinner. Should we conclude that we are well on our way to making wine?

I believe you will answer no to this question. But why should you? It is because the facts we have mentioned are not the important facts about wine. They are facts, and they are about wine, but they are not the right kind of facts about wine. Making a liquid that is like wine in these ways simply is not relevant to making a liquid that is like wine in respect of its being wine.

The point of this analogy is to suggest that the facts about the relations of our beliefs, filters, perceptions, and pains are not the right kind of facts. That is what the observation that the old low path is enough for pain does; it shows that we can have pain without these

relations, and that suggests that it is not *those* facts that are important
if we want to have pains in our robot. But I want to counter directly
the argument that if we just make sure our robot is like us in a great
many respects, we are bound to have made it like us in being able to
have pains. The objection I am making is that this is no more plausible than the suggestion that the liquid I described must be wine. The
point, in general form, is this: The *number* of *inessential* similarities
that two things have is *irrelevant* to their being similar in some designated respect. On the other hand, it may be one or some few points
of similarity that matter in a certain case. Wine is fermented and
undistilled liquid from grapes and a few other fruits or vegetables. It is
completely irrelevant to its being wine whether we put it in a corked
bottle or a bag with a rubber bung. It is irrelevant whether we drink
it with meals or use it to remove paint. If we dye it blue without
changing the taste too much, it is still wine.

Now, the trouble with the idea that we have reason to believe
that Robot Lul feels pains is that we have no reason to think that the
facts in the diagram are the right kind of facts—the relevant ones, or
the important ones—for having pains. As far as we have any argument, they may be just as irrelevant to pain as the wine bottle being
corked is to the contents being wine. They may be facts that are
about pain without being facts that matter to whether pain is present.
But if the boxes in the diagram are known not to be necessary for
pain, and if we are not impressed by sheer numbers of likenesses that
we have no reason to think are relevant to pain, then we should not
suppose that we have any reason to think that Robot Lul has pains.

The natural response to this, I believe, is to propose that a robot
will feel pain if it instantiates *every* fact that we know about pain.
Even if we do not have an argument about which of the facts about
pain are important for pain to be present, we can be sure that we
have the important ones if we have them all. This idea leads us to ask
if there is any kind of fact that we have not yet considered. Indeed,
there is, and we will now turn to it.

Morphine

Pains, or at least their awfulness, are interfered with by morphine. If
we are trying to build a pain-feeling robot by instantiating every fact
that we know about pain in it, we will have to make it so that its

behavior and internal operations are affected by morphine in a way analogous to the way morphine affects us.

There is a lot involved in doing this right. If I take off the top of my wordprocessor's system unit and squirt in some morphine solution, I am sure I would be stopping its pain if it had any—but only because I am sure I would be putting an end to *whatever* it does. This is plainly not the kind of effect we want. For one thing, although there can be fatal overdoses, morphine does not generally kill the patients who receive it. For another, I can get the same effect on my wordprocessor by squirting in the same amount of salt water; but I cannot relieve distressed people with salt water. So, the function that we really need to get a robot to satisfy is having its relations among injuries, pain behavior, and internal operations interfered with selectively by morphine. That is, our robot should be affected by morphine in a way that it is not affected by such things as salt water and sugar solutions.

Robot Mrg has everything that Robot Lul has and, in addition, satisfies the function we just described. Should we think that we have reason to suppose that Robot Mrg can have pains? Certainly, there is a good show here. Robot Mrg, remember, exhibits all the right yelling, hopping around, and crying that any person would, rubs injured parts, avoids the source of injury and says the right things, both at the time and later. It has internal filters, gates, and other structures that are hooked up in the way that parts that perform similar functions in us are hooked up. And, if we inject it under certain spots in its Ultra Naugahyde Super X skin with morphine (but not just any old liquid) it calms down, says it feels much better, and so on.

We should not conclude, however, that Robot Mrg has pains unless what we have said rules out everything that might lead us to deny that it has pains. It is compatible, however, with everything we have heard about Robot Mrg that it operates in the following way. Under its "skin" there are microanalyzers that function as morphine detectors. It doesn't really matter if they can be fooled by a few things—after all, some other drugs work in a way similar to morphine—but they must not be fooled by salt water or sugar solutions. When the microanalyzers detect the presence of morphine, they send out an electrical signal that is received at places that function analogously to the boxes in Figure 4.2. The result of this reception is more filtering of certain signals, less moaning and groaning, reports of feeling better, and so on.

If this is how Robot Mrg works, we should not think that it has pains. Here's part of the reason. Robot Mrg is rather like Robot Nrb. Robot Nrb has everything Robot Lul has and, in addition, lots of little photoanalyzers in its skin. One end of each of these pokes a small lens through Robot Nrb's "skin". The photoanalyzers can recognize the word "morphine" if we hold a card with this word written on it near Robot Nrb's body. They may give output for a few other words, but not for most, and certainly not for cards bearing the words "salt water" or "sugar solution". The effects of holding up a "morphine" card when Robot Nrb is exhibiting pain behavior are parallel to those of injecting Robot Mrg with real morphine. In fact, this is the point: If we start one-sixteenth of an inch behind Robot Nrb's photoanalyzers and one-sixteenth of an inch behind Robot Mrg's microanalyzers, their construction and operation is *exactly* the same. Now, assuming you have agreed that Robot Lul has no pains, I believe you will not think that Robot Nrb has them. That is, you will not think that adding circuits that take a written input into interference with the pain behavior production mechanism will be the addition that produces pain. But if you do not think that Robot Nrb has pains, you should not think that Robot Mrg does either, because, apart from the structure of certain analyzers near their surfaces, they are exactly alike.

Strictly speaking, there is no formal contradiction in the claim that the difference between Robot Nrb and Robot Mrg that we have described is a crucial point of difference that makes the difference between not having pain and having it. Such a claim, however, seems very puzzling. What the morphine interferes with on the *insides* of Robots Nrb and Mrg is the same. Because we have no reason to think that Robot Nrb has any pains, we have concluded that that interference is not equal to reduction of pain. So, if Robot Mrg has real pain that the morphine is reducing, it must be caused solely by what is going on in the detector, before it detects the morphine! This idea, however, will condemn Robot Mrg to a painful existence at all the times it is not receiving morphine at all of its microanalyzers, no matter what it says and no matter how it is behaving.

These reflections on Robot Mrg will, I think, force you to consider a response that you may have thought of for other reasons. One of our functions is to have our pains interfered with by morphine. But if we want to specify this function more fully, we will have to mention another fact that we know about pain and morphine: the morphine does not work at the surface of our bodies, it works only if it gets to the brain. The mistake about Robot Mrg, therefore, was to have morphine interact only with microanalyzers at the surface. If we want to build a robot that feels pain, we must aim to construct Robot Ojh instead. In Robot Ojh, the morphine detectors are not just under the skin. They have been moved inward and attached to the units that their output will affect. In Robot Mrg, the detectors were at the surface, so the distance between the skin and the morphine detection was very short, really just the distance along the tube that delivered the morphine to the detector. The distance between the detector and the mechanisms controlling behavior was rather longer, and was traversed by wires. In Robot Ojh the situation is reversed. Tubes of about the same length as Robot Mrg's wires conduct the injected solution up into Robot Ojh's head, where the morphine detectors are. The wires coming out of the detectors are very short, since they need only to connect the detectors to units that they are screwed onto. In every other respect, however, Robot Ojh is just like Robot Mrg.

I do not think that anyone will believe that Robot Mrg lacks pain but Robot Ojh has it. What difference to pain could it possibly make *where* we put the morphine detectors? Robot Ojh is valuable, however, because it suggests another improvement. This is to construct Robot Prl, in which some of the functional units corresponding to the boxes in Figure 4.2 are interfered with *directly* by morphine. There is no longer any distinction between the detectors and the mechanisms controlling action. The mechanisms themselves are selective morphine detectors because the activities that are going on in them *when an injury has taken place and they are involved in producing Robot Prl's pain behavior* is damped or stopped by morphine (and not by salt water or sugar solutions).

This is the best idea yet for building a pain-feeling robot. But alas, it leads straight to a difficulty that I do not know how to resolve. The problem is that if we want selective response to morphine without a distinction between a detector and a mechanism that controls actions, we are going to have to give up on the familiar sort of detector that yields electronic outputs. We will have to involve ourselves with complex molecules that *chemically* interact with morphine and related compounds but not with salt or sugar. This is, we must note, not a matter of mere logic. It is just a fact derived from what the sciences that study such things as electricity and complex molecules tell us about how the world actually is. But it is a significant fact for our purposes. The problem it presents is that the complex molecules we are going to need will be ones that are standardly called "organic" compounds. The presence of these, however, casts doubt on whether the thing that has them is a *robot*. One of the most firmly entrenched facts about robots is that they are essentially "metal people". They work mechanically and electronically, not by organic chemical processes. Lucas's *Star Wars* character C3PO is a paradigm of our conception of an advanced robot. When it is wounded, we see plenty of *wires* coming out of its broken body, but no evidence of material of the kind that would be necessary to support the operation of a chemical morphine detector.

The point being made here gets stronger and stronger as we add more and more facts about the interaction of drugs and pain. Thus, for example, Dennett points out the disturbing fact that curare stops pain behavior without stopping pain. To build something that would parallel this function, we are going to have to let curare selectively interfere with the production of pain behavior without interfering with the operation of centrally located interactions (that is, without interfering with most of the relations among the boxes in Figure 4.2). This means that our system will have to be constructed so as to distinguish at least three different kinds of chemicals: morphine, curare, and salt or sugar. Again, this is a task we can do only with organic compounds. If the parts of the systems are to be affected directly in these different ways by different drugs (as opposed to merely receiving signals from detectors in the way they do in Robots Nrb, Mrg, and Ojh) they will have to be made out of organic compounds; and thus they will be evidence that we are not dealing with a robot. The more different drug effects we try to parallel in Prl, the more complicated, chemically speaking, Prl's parts will have to be and the greater will be the evidence that Prl is not a robot after all.[5]

The point we are developing here is, of course, compatible with Prl having an Ultra Naugahyde Super X skin, silicone flesh, Lucite and gel eyes, and so forth. It is also compatible with having metal skin, eyes that are obviously cameras, and arms that look like the wheel and cable contraption that dentists once used. In short, Prl might look to outward appearance as thoroughly robotic as you like. But if it turns out that when we open her up, her performances all depend on the chemical interactions in a wonderfully complicated control system made of organic compounds, then we have strong reason to say that she is not a robot but a living thing with lots and lots of prostheses.

Conclusions

Let us review our progress and try to say where this chapter has led us. If we were to build a pain-feeling robot, we would have to build one that was like us in respects that are important to having pain. So, we have looked at various facts about pain. That pains are awful in some degree and that you have a pain if you think you do are important, but useless in our task of building a pain-feeling robot. This is because we would already have to know that our robot feels pain, or feels something awful, in order to know that these facts hold of it. Pain behavior is important in our knowledge that other people have pains on particular occasions. But it is not very hard to see that we could get a robot to exhibit pain behavior by using components we do not believe to cause pains. Thus, satisfying the function of exhibiting pain behavior on the right occasions is not enough to give us a good reason to attribute pains to the thing that performs it. The next suggestion was that we look inside and attend to either the particular mechanisms that are involved in producing pain behavior or to the way the whole set is hooked together. Unfortunately, neither particular mechanisms nor the general plan of the whole set seem to be required for pain. This fact casts doubt on whether they have the right kind of importance for building a pain-feeling robot. We were unable to rid ourselves of these doubts, so, we were unable to say that we had any good reason to think that Robot Lul feels pains. We then looked at functions of a different kind, namely, those of interacting with particular drugs in characteristic ways. These functions have the advantage over the previous set in that they do seem intimately connected with pain. If morphine administered when there is a certain kind of activity in certain parts of a system suppresses pain, then it is reasonable to think that that kind of activity in those parts of the system is what causes pain. Unfortunately, to get this function en-acted, we will have to have a system made out of organic compounds, and this defeats our attempt to build a pain-feeler that is clearly a robot.

The kinds of functions we have just reviewed are all of those that appear relevant to building a robot that might feel pains. So, I con-clude that at least one of the following statements is the case. The robots we introduced up to and including Robot Ojh may have pains, but we have some reason to doubt that they do and no way of making it reasonable to positively assert that they do. Or, in building Prl we have built something that has pains but not something that is a robot. Whichever of these is true (or if both are), we can state this as a result: We have found no set of conditions under which it would be reasonable for us to claim that we had succeeded in building a robot that feels pain. This does *not* amount to a *proof* that there cannot be a pain-feeling robot. Proof would require us first to establish a com-plete theory of the causes of pains, and this we have not done. We have, however, made a persistent attempt to see how we might build a pain-feeling robot. Failing to find a way of doing it after such an attempt is sufficient to raise a reasonable doubt that it can be done.

This doubt is strong enough to combat the suggestion that is sometimes made that whether a thing feels pain depends on whether we humans would regard that thing with empathy. One may think here again of a robot like C3PO. We react to it on the screen as if it had sensations and feelings. One can certainly imagine that if C3PO were one day to walk the earth in real life, some would treat it like a brother or a sister. In a similar vein, some people are prone to making suppositions about believing by their pets. We can, however, often see these suppositions to be unjustified if we think carefully about the capabilities of animals. In the same way, the above argument should convince anyone who attributed sensations and feelings to a real-life C3PO that such attributions are not supported by reason.

Some readers may wonder whether our conclusion is not so strong as to put in doubt the reasonableness of attributing pains to people. After all, one may think, all I have to go on with your pains is your yelling, complaining, asking for pain killers, and avoiding dangerous situations. If that is good enough for my attributing pains to you, why is it not good enough for attributing them to a robot? The answer is that the list I just gave is emphatically not complete. The further information that I have to go on in your case is that you are constructed just like me. You were produced in the same way, you are made out of the same stuff, and all anatomical evidence points to your internal construction being very like mine. So I have good reason to think that whatever it is that causes pain is present in you as well as in me. A summary way of putting the argument of this chapter is to say that we do not have the same kind of reason to support attributing pains to robots. When we take a really careful look at what we are entitled to assume about robot construction, we do not find a reason to believe that robots can have events in them of the kind that cause pains.

If we put our conclusion together with the results of Chapter 3, we arrive at the following view. It is reasonable to doubt that robots have pains. The arguments involved can be extended to sensations and feelings. (For a quick example, a thing that can express genuine joy at the taste of chicken Kiev ought to be more than trivially different from a thing that would give the same behavior upon detecting the words "chicken Kiev".) So, it is reasonable to doubt that robots have sensations and feelings. If it is reasonable to have this doubt about robots, then it is reasonable to have it about computers. If robots and computers do not have sensations and feelings, then there is ultimately no point for them in the words that they manipulate; so it is reasonable to doubt that there is any such point for them. This lack, however, does not rule out the possibility of robots connecting inputs and actions with their words; and it does not rule out the possibility that computers may produce flexible verbal responses.

Chapter 5

A License for Artificial Intelligence?

The questions we have been discussing are, fortunately, interesting in their own right. But even if they had not been interesting, we would have had to consider them. This is because we could not have become confident that passing the Turing test shows intelligence until we were able to separate the question of intelligence from the question of understanding; and we could not be sure we had the right view of understanding until we were clear about its relations to word-world connections and to word-(sensations and feelings) connections.

From this point on, however, I am going to take it as accepted that passing the Turing test would show that a computer is intelligent. The question that now pushes itself to the forefront is whether a computer could ever be built that would pass the test. The main positive feature we used in arguing that the Turing test is significant is the flexibility of response that is required to pass it. So the main question we now need to investigate is whether it is reasonable to suppose that a computer could ever be built that would have enough flexibility to pass the Turing test.

To investigate this question we are going to have to know something about how computers work and something about what it is to compute. Perhaps it will relieve some and disappoint others to know that we will not be going into any detail about actual machines. It is only certain principles and general conclusions that we need to understand in order to investigate our main question. My aim is to include everything required for that investigation and nothing that is

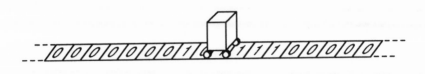

FIGURE 5.1

extraneous to it, however important it may be from a practical point of view, or from the point of view of the historical development of computers.

Turing Machines

As in Chapter 1, the place to begin is with the work of Alan Turing. Turing described a class of machines that now bear his name. For practical reasons that will soon be obvious, you will not find anything just like them in a computer store. Still, machines of this kind could be built, and they illustrate the basic principles that more practical machines embody.

A *Turing machine* (hereafter, TM) can be thought of as consisting of a reading and writing head and some tape. If you own a tape deck, you own a device of approximately this type. There are, however, several important differences. In your tape deck the head stays put and the tape moves past it. If you were going to actually build a machine of the kind in Figure 5.1, this is, of course, the arrangement you would choose; but it is more convenient in describing TMs to think of the head as moving along the tape. When you play or record on your tape deck, you usually go in one direction for quite a while; but in a TM you must expect to have to move back and forth. When you use your tape deck, you either play for a while or you record for a while; but in a TM the head will alternately read and either pass on or erase and write something else. Your music tape plays continuously; but in a TM the tape is divided into definite segments. Each of these segments has one character on it, one of a finite set of characters that the machine can respond to. (If the machine handles blank segments, "blank" is a character. Here, however, I have used "0" instead of blanks.) Finally, your music tape has a definite length. In the case of TMs, however, there is no telling how much tape you

$s_0$0NRs_0	$s_1$0NLs_2	$s_2$0xxx
$s_0$1NRs_1	$s_1$1NRs_1	$s_2$1Cstop

TABLE 5.1

might need. It is best to think of both directions as leading to a tape factory that stands ready to supply as much tape as may be needed.

Table 5.1 gives the design for our first example of a TM. Each of the six entries in this table describes one "move" that a TM may make as it goes step by step along its tape. Each entry has five parts. The following items explain what each part indicates.

- The first part of each entry is "s" with a numerical subscript. The "s" stands for "state" and the subscript gives the number of the state that the machine is in. You can think of a state as an arrangement of the parts of a thing. Managers who leave a store with the lights off, cash in the safe, alarm set, and doors locked leave it in a certain state. If they forget to put the cash in the safe, they leave it in a different state; if they remember the cash but forget to set the alarm, that is another state, and so on. You can also think of a state in terms of what the machine does if it is in that state. Table 5.1—a table of states, or *state table*—defines the states of a machine by what the machine does when it is in each state.
- The second part of each entry is one of the characters to which the machine can respond. It is essential that the characters be unambiguously distinguishable and that there be a finite number of them. Just to keep things simple, I am using the minimal set of two characters, "0" and "1". Larger alphabets would give you tables that would have to have more entries (one for each character that the machine might be reading), but the

number of steps involved in an operation of the machine could be much reduced.

The next "move" that a TM will make is entirely determined by what state it is in and what it is reading on the tape. To find out what the next step is, you look up the state table entry whose first part is the number of the state the TM is in, and whose second part is the character that is currently being read by the head. Then the next three parts of the entry tell you what the machine will do.

- When the machine reads a character on a given segment, either it will do nothing to the character or it will erase it and write a different one on that same segment. The third part of each entry corresponds to one of these options. Since I am using an alphabet of only two characters, I have indicated the writing element with "C", for "change (from 0 to 1 or from 1 to 0)" or "N", for "No change".
- The fourth part of each entry is either "R" or "L". This indicates that the head is to move one segment to the right or one segment to the left.
- The last part of each entry, like the first, is "s" with a numerical subscript. The subscript gives the number of the next state that the machine is to go into after it has completed the rewriting (if any). You can think of the change of state as happening while the head is moving, so that it is already in its new state when it arrives at the next segment and does its reading.
- There are two special cases. "Stop" means just what it says. When the machine encounters this after it has responded to the "C" or "N" instruction, it stops. "xxx" means that I can see that the machine should never be in the indicated state and reading the indicated character. So there is no point in bothering to say what it should do. If it ever gets into that

(a) . . . 0 0 1 1 1 0 0 . . .
        0

(b) . . . 0 0 1 1 1 0 0 . . .
         0

(c) . . . 0 0 1 1 1 0 0 . . .
          0

(d) . . . 0 0 1 1 1 0 0 . . .
          1

(e) . . . 0 0 1 1 1 0 0 . . .
           1

(f) . . . 0 0 1 1 1 0 0 . . .
            1

(g) . . . 0 0 1 1 1 0 0 . . .
            2

(h) . . . 0 0 1 1 0 0 0 . . .
          stop

FIGURE 5.2

state and is reading that character, either the head is broken or somebody has been messing around with the tape.

- In all the examples I am going to use, I will assume that when you turn the machine on, it is in the state, s_0. I will also assume that it is reading a 0 when it starts.

Figure 5.2 diagrams the operation of the TM whose state table is given in Table 5.1. The position of the number underneath the tape indicates which segment the head is reading, and the number itself gives the state. If the machine makes a change, the character in the changed segment appears as changed on the next line. The dots at the ends of the tape should be read as indicating that there are 0s forever. You can think of the tape as being produced with 0s already printed on each segment. Before we let the machine read a stretch of tape, we decide what string we want it to work on, and change some 0s to 1s accordingly. Now, this seems like a pretty simple-minded machine, and indeed it is. Even so, however, you should notice that it does more than reduce a string of three 1s to a string of two 1s. For

$s_0$0NRs_0	$s_1$0NRs_2	$s_2$0CRs_3	$s_3$0CLs_4
$s_0$1NRs_1	$s_1$1NRs_1	$s_2$1NRs_2	$s_3$1xxx
$s_4$0NLs_5	$s_5$0NRs_6	$s_6$0xxx	$s_7$0Nstop
$s_4$1NLs_4	$s_5$1NLs_5	$s_6$1CRs_7	$s_7$1NRs_1

TABLE 5.2

it will erase the last 1 of any string of 1s, no matter how long, once it has come to the end of the string. If we think of numbers as being represented by the number of 1s in a string, we can think of what this machine does in this way: it leaves us with a number represented on the tape that is one less than whatever number we gave it to start with. In short, this machine is a 1-subtractor.

Now that we have the hang of how to represent TMs let us look at one that is just a bit more interesting. If you have never worked with TMs before, it is important that you work through the state table in Table 5.2, in the way that we just worked through the one in Table 5.1. You can use the same initial string, that is, a string of three (or any number) of 1s flanked by 0s forever. Working through this example will take longer than working through the first example and there will be more changes. It might get a little tedious, but stick with it at least long enough to enable you to see what it does. That is, in the sense in which our first example is a 1-subtractor, what is this new machine of Table 5.2?

Although I will get around to answering this question (so you can check your answer against it) I want to go straight on now to introduce a third TM in Table 5.3. This table will be used to make an important point, so you should take the time to work through it. In this case, you should try two different incoming strings, as follows.

(i) ... 0 0 1 0 0 1 1 1 0 0 ...
(ii) ... 0 0 1 1 0 1 1 1 0 0 ...

The conventions are the same as above. In particular, it will be important that the tape segments extending to the right of what is shown are all 0. If you did not figure out what the machine of Table 5.2 does, you should go back and do that. For only then will you be

s_00NRs_0	s_10NRs_2	s_20NRs_2	s_30NLs_{10}	s_40NRs_4	s_50NRs_6
s_01NRs_1	s_11NRs_4	s_21NRs_3	s_31NRs_3	s_41NRs_5	s_51NRs_5
s_60CRs_7	s_70CLs_8	s_80NLs_9	s_90NRs_{10}	$s_{10}0xxx$	$s_{11}0Nstop$
s_61NRs_6	s_71xxx	s_81NLs_8	s_91NLs_9	$s_{10}1CRs_{11}$	$s_{11}1NRs_5$

TABLE 5.3

in a position to fully understand the point of the machine in Table 5.3. What this third machine does depends on what string you give it to begin with. Moreover, to see what it does in either case as having any interest, you must see the two strings above as divided into two parts, as indicated here.

$$(i) \ldots 0\ 0\ 1\ 0\ 0\ |\ 1\ 1\ 1\ 0\ 0 \ldots$$
$$(ii) \ldots 0\ 0\ 1\ 1\ 0\ |\ 1\ 1\ 1\ 0\ 0 \ldots$$

Once you divide the strings this way, you will probably see (if you did not before) that our third machine sometimes acts like our first machine, and sometimes it acts like our second one. More exactly, *for the part to the right of the break* in string (i), our third machine acts as a 1-subtractor; for the part to the right of the break in string (ii) it acts as a doubler, just like our second machine. That is, no matter how many 1s there are after the break in string (ii), our machine leaves us with a string of 1s that is twice as long.

Sometimes our third machine acts like our first one, and sometimes it acts like our second one. Which machine it acts like depends on what comes to the left of the break. The first 0 to the left of the break can be thought of as a way of separating the left side from the right side for the TM, which, of course, cannot read the vertical lines that I inserted to indicate to you where to make the break. It is the next two segments to the left that determine what the third machine will do. That is, whether, after any number of 0s, it gets a "1 0" or a "1 1" fixes whether it will treat the string of 1s to the right in the way that our first machine would treat such a string, or in the way that our second machine would treat it.

If we now introduce the most commonly used terms for what we have been describing, we will call the "1 0" or "1 1" on the left side of (i) and (ii) the *program*. The string of 1s to the right will then be distinguished as the *data*. The point of the last paragraph now comes out this way: How our third machine treats the data we give it depends on how we program it, that is, on what program we give it. If we give it one program, the result of its operations on the data will be just the same as if we had given the data string alone to our first machine. If we give it another program, the results of its operations on the data will be just the same as if we had given the data string alone to our second machine.

In this way, one machine can be two. That is, our third machine can also be our first machine (or, if we program it differently, our second machine). We can say that our third machine is *virtually* one of the others, meaning that it is "as good as" that other one, or that it "imitates" that other one. We can say that, when programmed to imitate our first machine, the *virtual machine* that is operating, when our third machine is operating, is our first machine. To keep this from getting confusing, all you have to do is to remember that whenever we speak of a machine as being more than one machine, we are implicitly making a division of groups of segments of its tape. Our third machine is our third machine, and *only* our third machine, with respect to the *whole* stretch of tape that it reads between starting and stopping. Our first and second machines work as we described them on the *whole* of the stretches of tape that they look at. Our third machine does on a *part* of the tape that it reads, what our first (or our second) machine does on the whole of the tape that it reads. We should be clear that there is nothing about the operation of our third machine in itself that makes a program-data distinction. It just marches away, step by step, according to its state table and whatever is on that tape segments that it reads. It is only we onlookers who realize that we can use our third machine to do what we could have done with our first or our second machine, by programming it in a certain way and then looking selectively at just a certain part of the tape for our answer.

We can extend this idea of one machine's doing what other machines do in two ways. Let us introduce the first one with a rough analogy. For a time, the actor Hal Holbrook went around "being" Mark Twain, that is, imitating Mark Twain's appearance, manner, and words. Of course, in another part of his life, after the show, for

example, Holbrook ate food that Twain never ate and talked about
things that Twain never heard of. Now, I want you to imagine somebody going around "being" Holbrook, that is, doing on Holbrook
what Holbrook did on Twain. Such an actor will also have his own
off-stage life. Part of his on-stage life will look like Holbrook's off-
stage life. In another part of his on-stage life, he will have to look a
lot like Twain, that is, like Holbrook looking like Twain.

Putting the matter without analogy, it comes out this way. Some
machine, say, M_x, operates on the whole of some stretch of tape,
which we can imagine to be flanked on both sides by 0s forever. We
onlookers can find a part of this stretch of tape, and a table for another machine, M_y, of which the following is true: The effect of M_x
on this part of the tape is just like the effect of M_y when this part is
the whole stretch that it (M_y) works on. But now, it may be that we
can *also* find a part of this part, and a table for yet another machine,
M_z, of which it is true that: The effect of M_y on this part (of a part) is
just like the effect of M_z when this part (of a part) is the whole
stretch that it (M_z) works on. In this case, of course, M_x will "be"
(virtually be, or be imitating) M_z as well as M_y. Which one we should
regard it as being (or, as imitating) depends on our point of view, or
on which part of the tape we decide to take as "data" and which as
"program".

There is, of course, no limit to this kind of development. We can
have actors who are imitating actors who are imitating actors . . .
who are imitating actors. And we can have machines that are (imitating) machines that are imitating machines . . . that are imitating
machines.

The second kind of development of the fact that one machine
can "be" another machine concerns the variety of programs that a
machine can receive. Our first machine really is not programmable at
all. It is a machine for subtracting one and that's it. Our second and
third machines are a little more interesting. We have seen that the
third machine can be programmed to be either of the first two machines. The second machine also can be programmed in such a way
that it will add two to whatever data string we give it or, again, so
that it will add six. These machines are still pretty limited, however.
If we had to settle for a single machine—for example, if we were
actually going to build a device that would pass from one state to

another in accordance with a given state table—we would want a machine that could "be" as many machines as possible. Then, if we wanted to use one of these other machines, we would not have to build it, we could just program the one that we already had built. It is natural to wonder how far we could go in this direction. It is natural to ask what is the smallest number of machines we would have to build in order to get to a point where we would never have to build any more (because we could accomplish the work done by any other TM just by giving the right program to one of the machines we already had). Turing himself investigated this question and proved an astonishing result: The answer is one Turing machine! That is, there are state tables that you can apply in just the way you apply the ones I have given in the examples and that have the following property. Suppose M is a machine that follows your state table. Let M_i be *any* TM you care to pick. Then there is some program that will cause M to imitate M_i. That is, M will derive the same output from the data portion of its input (that is, the part of its input that is not the program) that M_i would have produced if a tape just like what is data for M were the entire tape that M_i read. Any machine that has this property is called a *universal Turing machine* (hereafter, UTM).

Church's Thesis

UTMs can do a lot of something: They can do all that any TM can do. But how shall we describe *what* it is that TMs do? And *how much* of whatever it is they do can they do?

Our simple examples of TMs have subtracted and doubled. These are ordinarily called calculations and they are things that a pocket calculator can do. So it would be natural to say that TMs can calculate. You could also use the kinds of things you usually call "computers" to subtract and double. So it should also come naturally to say that TMs compute. But if we say that TMs calculate or compute, what exactly are we saying that they do?

If you think about this question, perhaps you will think of an example in which you calculate (without the aid of a pocket calculator). Most people balance their checkbooks by hand, so let us take that as an example. When you balance your checkbook, you have a procedure: You subtract earlier checks from your account first and add deposits at the correct times. In subtracting, you start at the right. If the lower digit is larger than the upper one, you remember to carry. You make an entry in each column and, when there are no more columns to the left, you are finished with that check. If you try to speak generally about what goes on in this case, you will probably say that you proceeded by using a *method*. In using your method, you follow some *rules*. You might also notice that the calculation does not depend on what you spent your money on, how much money you have, whether or not you are overdrawn, or how much money you anticipate receiving in the future. The calculation depends only on a few facts that are right there in front of you. You have to keep track of where you are in the course of the calculation—for example, you must not get distracted between your operation on one column and the next, or you may forget to carry. But so long as you pay attention to where you are and follow the rule that applies at each point in the procedure, you are calculating correctly and you will come out with the right answer. Since you have to follow the rules, in the right order, each time you calculate, you should be able to write down the rules. If you can do that, you can explain what you are doing (how you derived your result) and teach the method to other people.

   To put this succinctly, we can say that calculating or computing is proceeding according to a method in which you apply explicit rules step by step. This is good enough for many purposes. But suppose we get to wondering what kinds of things we can do by a method, or how much we can do by using methods? For example, can there be a method for doing science? Perhaps every reader of this book will have heard the phrase "scientific method". Yet many philosophers hold the view that there cannot be a method, either for doing science or even for telling whether a particular stretch of people's activity is "scientific" or not. If you are going to intelligently agree with these philosophers, or intelligently criticize them, you will have to be definite about what counts as a method. Well, you may say, using a method is proceeding step by step according to explicit rules. This, however, will only force us to ask what a rule is, and when exactly we are *applying* a rule. If you think this must be too easy a question, you might try thinking about this piece of advice: Accept the simplest view that accounts for the facts. Is this a rule? What counts as applying it? What is to count as the simplest view?

If we can ask whether there can be a method for doing science, we can ask the same question for mathematics. Certainly, we can imagine a science fiction story in which the people of Planet Gnirut have discovered a method for making mathematical discoveries. Once they found this method, they taught it to an army of clerks and set them to work. Naturally, they had no mathematics professors after that. The math clerks got paid the same as bank tellers and anyone who wanted a theorem got the clerks to use the method to produce it, or produce its negation, if it was a false claim. Now, must this story remain fiction forever? Or could it be like the submarines and moon explorations of older fictions that have become actual accomplishments? Clearly, to explore this question you will have to say exactly what counts as following a method or applying a rule. You will have to decide, for example, whether what we have now—universities with mathematics departments, journals, conferences, and so on—is or is not a *method* for producing mathematical discoveries.

This problem of articulating exactly what should count as following a method, applying rules, calculating, or computing was investigated by several mathematicians in the first thirty years of this century. Their aim was to produce a description of computing that would be precise enough to enable them to reason about questions like the possibility of Planet Gnirut in a clear and decisive way. They adopted a variety of strategies and they came up with several characterizations of what it is to compute. For example, computation was described by reference to a certain class of mathematical functions, and it was described by reference to a certain kind of very simple rule. One of the mathematicians who investigated this question was Turing. His description, naturally enough, referred to Turing machines: It said that to be computable is to be calculable by some Turing machine.

When a description of computability has been formulated, it is natural to ask what can be computed according to that description, and what cannot. Mathematicians also investigated this question. Once they had done so, another question seemed natural, namely, which description of computability is the widest or the narrowest? That is, which description allows for the most things to be computed,

or the least? Or, does it turn out that each way of describing computability allows some things to be computed that are excluded by some
of the others? Now, the remarkable fact is that all the different descriptions of computability turn out to lead to the same answers to
the question of what can be computed. Since the descriptions are
precise, this can be a *mathematical* result. That is, it is a theorem in
mathematics that whatever can be computed according to one of
these descriptions of computing also can be computed according to
any of the others. In this sense, despite their differences of strategy
and style, all the descriptions are mathematically equivalent.

One idea that is important for our purposes rests on the theorem
just described. It is not the same as that theorem, however; in fact it
is not a theorem in mathematics at all. This idea was developed by
the logician Alonzo Church and is known as Church's Thesis. There
are many ways of stating this idea, but for our purposes the following
seems the most useful. *There is a single property of being computable and
Turing and the other mathematicians who proposed equivalent views described it fully and correctly.* The support for this claim is that the
mathematicians who investigated computability did so independently. It is not obvious that their different descriptions lead to equivalent views of what is computable—that has to be shown by a proof.
If several intelligent people try to say clearly, carefully, and explicitly
what they mean by a certain term, and they give interestingly different accounts that turn out to be equivalent, that is a good reason to
think that they know what the term means and have all identified it
correctly. We can also look at Church's Thesis as a prediction that
no one will ever produce a description that is a convincing candidate
for what it is to compute but that differs from the other accounts on
what can be computed. The support for this prediction is that computability has been intensively studied by many mathematicians from
many angles. Surely, if there were an alternative conception that
seemed to be a view of *computability* someone would have thought of
it by now. This, of course, is not the kind of reason that certifies
something as a mathematical theorem. It is, however, an extremely
strong reason, which explains why Church's Thesis is very widely
accepted.[1]

Let us put together a few of the ideas we have mentioned. Anything that is computable at all can be computed by some TM. A

UTM can be programmed to do anything that any TM can do. So, anything that is computable at all can be computed by a UTM. We can now add that UTMs are not so hard to come by. Contemporary computers are equivalent to them. So, anything that is computable at all can be computed by contemporary computers. We must, of course, see to it that we have enough tape (or enough of whatever we are using to keep track of the rewrites of the read-write head). And we will have to keep in mind that it may not be so easy to discover what the right program is for a given computational task. Still, we have a reason for confidence in searching for a program for any computational task, for we know that if the task is computational at all, *there is* a program that will do it.

So far we have said nothing in this chapter about *intelligence*. We do not know whether that has anything to do with what can be computed. If we are to have a license for artificial intelligence, that is, a sort of permission to continue expensive and time-consuming efforts on its behalf, we must make a connection between intelligence and computability. It is, once again, to Daniel Dennett that we can look for an interesting way of doing this.[2]

Psychological Theories

In this section, we need to talk about some general features that any psychological theory ought to have. We will not actually produce any such theories and we will not assert even a single statement that is made by any psychological theory. Instead, we want to know what psychological theories are about and what form they might take.

It used to be that psychologists had a nearly automatic response to the question, "What does psychology study?" It was this: "Psychology is the science of behavior." Nowadays, that answer has associations that make some psychologists uncomfortable. Still, we can expect general agreement from psychologists if we describe their subject in this way: "Psychology is the science of behavior and its causes." This answer allows that at least part of the subject matter of psychology can be the functioning of the brain, in so far as that can be related in some fairly direct way to behavior.

The most important part of our description of psychology is that it is meant to be a science. I mentioned above that many today dispute the idea that there is a scientific method. Even these philosophers will agree, however, that sciences propose theories and that theories ought, so far as possible, to have certain characteristics. For one thing, they ought to be clear. There should not be any ambiguities or any need for guesswork about what the theory says about particular cases. Theories should also make predictions, and these predictions should be definite and as precise as possible. Vague pronouncements like "the weather will change" are not good science; if that is all a theory says, it makes no advance in meteorology and it is cheating to take the fact that the weather does change, in some way at some time, as supporting it. The better a theory about the weather is, the more its predictions must be made in definite degrees of temperature or inches of precipitation, with definite and relatively short time frames. The point is the same for any other science, including psychology. A good psychological theory must make predictions, and it must make them in terms sufficiently precise that we can definitely tell whether what is predicted happens.

When I say that "a theory makes predictions" I mean that people make predictions *by using the theory.* This, in turn, means that when different people apply the theory they generally come out with the same result. (To be more exact, they always come out with the same result, unless they make a mistake, just as all who balance a single checkbook must come out with the same result, unless they have made a mistake.) They come out with the same result because the theory guides them in their procedure. Now, all this is just a way of saying that a good theory must provide a method for *computing* what it predicts. Since psychology aims to be a science, it aims to provide theories that enable people to compute predictions of behavior and, perhaps, some aspects of the internal causes of behavior.

Predictions require some knowledge about the circumstances in which the prediction is made. The weather prediction for one locale is based on measurements of such things as temperature, humidity, and wind velocity in certain related places (the ones where the given locale's weather comes from). Election outcomes are predicted on the basis of information gathered in interviews and on past election histories. It is the same in psychology. If you advise your friend not to ask for a raise because (you predict) the boss will just get angry, you are basing your prediction on past observations about what obstacles in the work day have made the boss unreceptive to requests. In general, psychological theories must take account of surrounding circumstances, past histories, and perhaps the internal structure of participants in a situation; and it must relate these to predicted behavior.

Theories are preferred if their predictions are more precise than those of their rivals (while being equally well borne out). They are also preferred if they cover a wider range of events. A meteorological theory would be improved, for example, if it could be made to explain weather patterns at sea as well as those over land. A psychology that could explain people's errors as well as their correct performances would be better (other things being equal) than one that could explain only the correct performances. In an ideal limit, a psychological theory would enable us to explain every aspect of people's behavior.

Let us now imagine that we have an ideal psychological theory. It enables us to compute predictions for every aspect of behavior. We know that our computers are equivalent to UTMs. So we know that our computers can compute the predictions of the theory, provided they are given the same data that application of the theory would require. Let us imagine that we put such data into our computer's memory. Some of this data describes a set of things that someone believes and wants, along with character traits and abilities such as calculating, inventing analogies, and seeing spatial relationships. The data may describe an actual individual or an individual who does not actually exist but which our theory enables us to tell is a possible person. (The set of abilities is, for example, consistent.) Other parts of the data describe the current situation. Let us suppose that this part of the data describes a person in the Turing test situation. Running our computer on this information will give us a prediction of what the person will say. We can, of course, feed this prediction directly into whatever output device is used to communicate with the judge in the Turing test situation. The result will be that our computer ought to do well in the Turing test situation—as well as a person would be expected to do if we replaced the computer with a person. Passing the Turing test, we have argued, shows that intelligence is present. So, if we had an ideal psychological theory, all we would have to do is express it in program form and add appropriate data in order to have a computer that possesses intelligence.

This conclusion may very well lead you to question the assumption that an ideal psychological theory is possible. It can seem, however, that the denial of such a possibility amounts to mere mysticism. True, it is not actually a contradiction to suppose that there is no means by which people regularly respond in an appropriate way to new circumstances. But to suppose this really amounts to saying that people's behavior is continually miraculous. If that consequence seems extreme, then you must suppose instead that there is some way in which our brains work, some regular way in which they operate, that accounts for the flexibility of appropriate behavior that we exhibit. If there is a definite way that we work, there can be a good theory of it; if there can be a good theory of it, there can be a computer program that works out that theory's consequences; if there can be such a program, there can be artificial intelligence. We have as good a license to search for programs in artificial intelligence as we do to search for an ideal psychological theory; and since the alternative is mysticism, we have a very good license indeed for searching for both.

Questions and Conclusions

In one form or another, the ideas that we have reviewed in this chapter are very well known and very influential in supporting the confidence that there can be artificial intelligence. The argument we have just stated is, however, far from conclusive. Indeed, the question that argument tries to settle, our COULD THERE BE question, will occupy us for the remainder of this book. In this chapter, I will discuss only a few relatively straightforward points that do not require the further background that will be introduced in later chapters.

> Success in artificial intelligence may not be the same thing as making a computer that could pass the Turing test.

Passing the Turing test shows flexibility. This property, however, is not the property of giving the best response or the fastest response or the most reliable response. It is the property of giving a sensible (reasonable, appropriate, relevant) response over a wide variety of novel (not previously encountered) circumstances. Work in artificial intelligence is often not directed toward providing flexibility at all. Much of it is directed toward producing outstanding, reliable, and rapid response to a set of situations that allow complex variety in some ways but are quite limited in other ways. It cannot follow from an argument for artificial flexibility that we can produce artificial anything else.

We know that limiting flexibility often permits gains in speed and accuracy. A pocket calculator, for example, cannot do very many things but does what it does faster and more reliably than we do. What we do not know is how far we can retain speed and accuracy with greater flexibility. The argument in the preceding section will not show that a computer can be any faster or more reliable than people, if it is also required to be as flexible as they are.

Accuracy and reliability should be distinguished from excellence. In arithmetic, there is no difference: You cannot *improve* on 4 as an answer to $2 + 2 = ?$ But in many cases there is no way of specifying the right or best answer, even though we would recognize a good idea if one were presented. Think, for example, of policy questions, such as how best to respond to the actions of the government of China in the 1989 Beijing massacre. Now "intelligence" is sometimes used to mean "having better than usual ideas". It should be obvious, however, that an argument that computers might be made to exhibit the same flexibility as people cannot be an argument that they might have better-than-ordinary ideas. Whether we can get both flexibility and excellence in our machines remains to be seen, even if we become convinced that we can get flexibility.

The existence of a program does not guarantee the feasibility of running it.

In describing Turing machines, I mentioned that we had to provide for as much tape as we needed, and I imagined factories in both directions that stand ready to supply more tape. You can already see from our examples that some calculations require more tape than others. One reason for this is very obvious: If your data string is, say, twelve, doubling it is going to take more tape than if your data string is eleven. Since there is no upper limit on the size of the number that we might want to double, there is no upper limit on the amount of tape we might need. There is, however, another reason why you might need a lot of tape. There is no program for the machine in Table 5.1; but if you like, you can say that there is one that has a length of zero. The programs we examined for the machine in Table 5.3 were two segments long. You can easily see that there can only be two of these: Since nothing interesting happens until we come to a 1, the two-segment programs are either "1 0" or "1 1". The same principle holds for each number of segments: Assuming that the first must be a 1, there can only be 2^{n-1} programs of length n. If we want to write many programs, we will have to use longer and longer ones. If we have a UTM we can have programs for anything computable, but there is no upper limit on the number of segments we might have to use for the program.

We can, of course, increase the speed of computation and decrease the tape we use by enlarging our alphabet. We can increase the speed of our machines by making them of switches that can change "position" faster and by designing them so as to have less distance between their parts. But the point just made is a general one. So long as each operation of a machine takes a finite time, however small, there will be some calculations that take longer than any period of time you care to name. Therefore, the claim that artificial intelligence is possible cannot rest entirely on the *mathematical* fact that a UTM can calculate what any TM can calculate, or on this plus Church's Thesis that some TM can calculate anything that is calculable. It must be buttressed by some further argument to show that there is a feasible way of using a program that would provide intelligence, that is, one that could be run in the right sort of time frame and that would not require so many material resources as to be prohibitively expensive.

What the right time frame is, is not precise. People respond to questions and instructions at different rates. So, a computer that returned otherwise passable answers in a Turing test situation, but responded a little more slowly than the average person, would probably not do badly in the test. Let us now imagine a computer that is, say, half as fast as a slow person. That might be slow enough to make it do badly in the Turing test situation. I think, however, that if we agree that the first one has intelligence, we would probably also agree that this second one did. A third computer gives the same answers as the second; conversations with it are likely to be very strange, however, for it takes ten minutes to give responses that people give more or less right away. Here, I think that the tendency to agree that such a computer has intelligence will fall off sharply. There is a good reason why it should. Flexibility is responding in an appropriate way to a range of novel situations. If the response does not come until the situation is likely to have passed, it is not exactly a response *to the situation*.

I said that we needed an argument, over and above the one in the earlier sections of this chapter, for the feasibility of making artificial intelligence, even if not for the abstract possibility. This point stands despite the fact that feasibility has something to do with time of response and the limit on how much time a response could take and still be intelligent is not clear and sharp. It would be natural to respond to the request for a feasibility proof by giving the following argument: We are finite things and we do respond in a timely way, therefore the feasibility problem must have a solution and all that is left to do is to find it. This suggestion assumes, however, that *we* are Turing machines! Now, that is an idea that several philosophers have considered and it is one that we must talk about. We have to put off this question here, however, since further background is necessary if we are to be really clear about how to answer it.

> The argument for a license for artificial intelligence rests
> on a view of ideal psychology that is hopelessly
> misguided.

The famous psychologist B. F. Skinner sometimes argued that psychologists have no business speculating either on what goes on in the mind or on what goes on in the brain. What they ought to be doing is discovering correlations between what has happened to people and what they can be expected to do in various kinds of situations. Skinner's view, and the reasons behind it, have been debated many times from many angles. One obvious point, however, is this. Predictions, let us recall, are based on data. The data that are relevant for psychological prediction, on Skinner's (and many others') view, include what people have done in the past, and what has happened to them when they have acted. Any consequence of their past behavior might be relevant to what we should expect in a particular case. There is no one, however, whose history we know in any degree that approaches full detail. Thus, even if we had a perfect science that would enable us to start with people's histories plus descriptions of current situations and predict their actions, it would be utterly useless. We would never know enough about people's histories to apply it.

A similar point infects the argument for the license for artificial intelligence. It says that an ideal psychological theory would enable us to model a person and thus to make a machine that acted just like a person in the Turing test situation. But to actually carry through on this idea would require us to model a whole person. This is possible in principle, but it is not something we can do now, not something anyone really knows how to do now, and not something we are likely to spend money to learn how to do in the future. It is not the direction of actual research in artificial intelligence. Some work does have this direction in a limited form, namely, work on "expert systems". Some of these do attempt to model a diagnostician, a stockbroker, or a geologist, but they attempt to model only those aspects of experts' psychology that are relevant to medicine, investment, or prospecting. They do not aim to model the general psychology of a person so as to make predictions that could be used to exhibit the flexibility needed to pass the Turing test.

The points just made should lead you to think of a project that is different from the one I have been describing. This would be to find a program that provided a machine with a sort of *general* intelligence— an intelligence that is not tied to having particular psychological traits, to believing particular sets of claims, or to wanting particular kinds of things. If we could bestow such a general intelligence on a machine, then we would not have to worry about the myriad details of people's lives; we could get our machine to apply intelligence to any set of assumptions and goals we cared to give it. Now, of course, nothing that has been said rules out this possibility. But at the same time, we should be very clear that nothing we have said supports it.

The argument in the preceding section depends on the idea that if there is a way that people manage to be flexible it can be computed and therefore, by Church's Thesis, computed by a machine. You cannot legitimately argue from this that there is some completely different way of arriving at flexible response, some way that does not involve the particularities of actual people. Maybe there is, maybe there isn't. We shall have to keep our minds open until we find further arguments one way or another.

An analogy to the present case may help to clarify it. Picasso created a large, but finite, collection of works in his lifetime. So, there is a way of getting a person or a machine to be able to classify artworks into those done by Picasso and those not done by him. That is, we can list the characteristics of each work, the colors used, placement of objects in a painting, physical characteristics of sculptures, and so on—all in detail sufficient to distinguish them from every other artwork.[3] Give a computer such a list as data. Then, when works are described to it at a comparable level of detail, it can compare the list of characteristics with its list of Picassos and classify it as a Picasso or not. Call this the Exhaustive Method of classifying Picassos. Now, we can certainly imagine to ourselves another method, which I will call the Intensive Method. This would be to distill some relatively small number of stylistic traits that are characteristic of Picasso but are not found together in anyone else's works. Give the computer these traits as data. Then, when works are described to it in such a way that it can search for the presence of these traits, it can find them (or, enough of them together) and classify the work as a Picasso. Or, it can find them lacking and classify the work as not by Picasso. Now, the fact that people do develop a stylistic sense, and can often correctly decide who painted a work they have not seen before, may dispose us to believe that there must be some way of enabling a machine to use the Intensive Method. Perhaps there is. The point to notice, however, and the point that is analogous to the one I was making about general intelligence, is that the existence of a successful Intensive Method does not follow from the existence of the Exhaustive Method.

None of the three points I have made in this last section can cast doubt on the possibility of artificial intelligence in any of the ways that this phrase is likely to be understood. They do show, however, that the question of this possibility is not decisively and clearly settled merely by accepting Church's Thesis and recognizing the existence of UTMs. They show, moreover, that it is not so clear how we should proceed if we want to try to produce a computer that is intelligent. These questions, which are now so open, are among those that we will try to clarify in the chapters to come.

Chapter 6

Lucas and Self-Models

In 1961 J. R. Lucas published a now famous paper in which he used some mathematical results to argue against the possibility of what he called "mechanism".[1] In brief, his strategy was this: If mechanism were true, then some machine could be made that modelled a person, that is, that responded to inputs in just the way a person would. So, in particular, if mechanism were true, there could be a machine that modelled Lucas. But, Lucas held, a theorem proved by Kurt Gödel in 1931 could be used to show that no machine could model Lucas in one certain respect. Therefore, mechanism must be false.

When stated in detail, this argument turns out to be extremely interesting. It is, however, rather complicated and it rests on a considerable number of preliminaries. To help us keep track of where we are, I will list the main things we have to do.

1. Introduce *formal systems* and some of their properties.
2. Explain the relation between formal systems and mechanisms.
3. Explain what Gödel proved about certain formal systems.
4. Apply Gödel's result to mechanism. (This is the Lucas argument.)
5. Consider and evaluate some of the responses to Lucas's argument.

Formal Systems

To make a *system* in the sense we need in this chapter, you must set down one or more sentences, or sentence-like formulas, and then use them to derive further formulas. If you were taught geometry well, you have already worked with a system of this kind. You will recall that you were introduced to a small group of geometrical sentences labeled "axioms" or "postulates" and that you used these to prove some other sentences about geometry. Then, you could use some of these other sentences—called "theorems"—to prove further theorems, which you could use to prove still more theorems, and so on. The result was that instead of having a disordered bunch of sentences about geometrical figures, you had an ordered system in which accepting some of the sentences depended on accepting others.

When you studied geometry, you did your work in your own familiar language. There may have been a few special symbols, but for the most part your textbook was written in English. Moreover, when you were asked to give a proof of a new theorem, you used familiar methods of reasoning, and you succeeded if you could give any argument that was really convincing. The use of this familiar background is just fine for an ordinary system, but it is abandoned when we come to a *formal* system. Here, we have to specify what language we are going to use from the ground up, and we have to specify what counts as deriving one theorem from others or from axioms. These tasks are needed only in the context of a formal system and they are best explained by using an example. The example I shall use is a very, very simple one that is utterly useless for anything interesting. Nonetheless, it has the features that are characteristic of formal systems and it will enable us to understand the key concepts that we will need in order to follow Lucas's argument.

The first thing we have to do is to say what signs will constitute our formal system. Here, I will use A, B, I, and N. Other systems can have a longer list of signs. All that is essential is that there be only a finite number of signs and that they all be definitely distinguishable from one another.

The next thing we have to do is to say which strings of these signs are to be regarded as well-formed formulas (wffs). "Well-formed

The ABIN System

Signs: A,B,I,N

Well-formed Formulas: (i) The letter B followed by any non-negative number (0, 1, 2, 3, *n*) of Is is a wff.
(ii) If *x* is a wff, so is N*x*.
(iii) If *x* and *y* are wffs, so is A*xy*.

Axiom Scheme: Provided that *x* is a wff whose first letter is B, N*x* is an axiom.

Rule: Where *x* and *y* are any wffs, N*x* ⊢ NA*xy*

---

formula" is an analogue of "sentence". Strings of signs of our formal system that are not well formed will be analogous to incomplete sentences, like "The cat is on the" or to ungrammatical ones, like "John give a books to Mary last weeks." But these are only analogies, since sentences are composed of meaningful words and have a grammatical structure that has come about historically. Well-formed formulas are just strings of as-yet-meaningless signs. Their being well formed is stipulated by the person who is making the formal system. The stipulation for our example is part of the description of the ABIN system given in the accompanying table. You are to understand the entry for well-formed formulas to say that *only* the strings that (i), (ii), and (iii) imply to be well formed are well formed.

In specifying the wffs (and, later, in specifying the axiom scheme and the rule) the signs *x* and *y* occur. These signs are not part of the ABIN system. They are variables that indicate where strings of the signs that *are* parts of the ABIN system may be substituted. For example, ANBNBII is a substitution instance of A*xy*, with "NB" substituted for *x* and "NBII" substituted for *y*.

When Euclid made his system for geometry, he had a choice about what to use for axioms. He could have taken some of what in his actual system were theorems and made them axioms. Then, some of what are axioms in his actual system could have been derived as theorems. In a formal system, we can take this element of arbitrariness to extremes: The axioms are just whatever well-formed formulas we say they are. Eventually there is a price for arbitrariness, but it does not come in the form of incorrectness; instead, if you choose silly axioms, your formal system will merely be useless and uninteresting.

The ABIN system is pretty useless and uninteresting from most points of view. That is because I want it to be easily understood and therefore just barely as complicated as it has to be to illustrate all the concepts we are going to need. Thus, while we could have had many axiom schemes, our system here will have just one. An *axiom scheme* is different from an axiom; for unlike an axiom, an axiom scheme contains at least one variable, where expressions of some specified kind may be substituted. The result of the substitution is an axiom. The point of using an axiom scheme is to have a finite way of specifying an infinite set of axioms. Thus, our axiom scheme, Nx gives us the axioms

NB
NBI
NBII
NBIII
. . . .

This procedure is typical of the systems that are relevant to Lucas's argument.

Now that we have built a language and chosen an axiom scheme, we need to construct the analogue of giving a proof. The general idea here is to specify rules and count something as a proof if it arrives at a theorem from axioms *just* by applying the rules. The rules, of course, do not have anything to do with what the signs mean, since the signs do not have any meaning. They tell you, by reference to letters and their positions, what strings may be written down, given that you already have some other string or strings. Again, the choice of rules is arbitrary and the penalty for bad choice is not falsehood, or unreasonableness, but boredom. The rule for our sample system is given in the table. You are to read it as follows: "If you already have written down an expression of the form Nx (where x is any wff) then you may write a new expression of the form NAxy (where y also is any wff)."

Having rules permits the construction of proofs. A *proof* is a sequence of wffs that begins with an axiom and adds expressions to the
sequence only by applying the rules.[2] Here are a few examples of
proofs in the ABIN system.

1. NBI	2. NB	3. NBI
NABIB	NABNBII	NABIBI
NAABIBB	NAABNBIIABBII	NAABIBIBIII
NAAABIBBB	NAAABNBIIABBIINB	

A theorem of a system is any expression that is the last line of any
proof. Since the above proofs were written down one line at a time,
each line in them was at one time the last line of a proof. Thus, each
of the strings in the proofs is a theorem. Here are some more examples of theorems. You might want to write down their proofs.

NABNANBB
NAABIBIIBI
NAAABBIBNB
NAABIIBIABINABIBI

We are now completely finished with specifying the ABIN system. Of
course, it has an infinitude of theorems that we have not proved. We
know how to construct these proofs, however, and we do not need to
add anything further to enable us to produce as many of them as we
like.

Although we are finished with specifying the ABIN system, we
are not finished talking about that system. One thing about it that
follows easily and immediately from the way we have specified it is
that all the theorems in it are composed of just the capital letters A,
B, I, and N. Now, this statement, that all the theorems are composed of just those four capital letters, is not itself composed of those
letters. So, it is not a theorem *in* the ABIN system. It is, instead, a
theorem *about* the ABIN system. Theorems that are about formal
systems are called *metatheorems*. Since the statement about the elements of theorems in the ABIN system is the first theorem that we
have shown to be true of the system, we can call it "Metatheorem 1".

Let us have a few more examples. Metatheorem 2 states: Every theorem contains at least one B. This, again, is obviously not one of the theorems in the ABIN system. We do, however, have to look at that system in order to know that this metatheorem is true. That is, we have to notice that the single axiom scheme guarantees that every axiom contains a B and we have to notice that the rule never drops anything; it adds an A and some wff to whatever we had before. So, since we always start a proof with a wff that contains a B and we never remove anything, every line of a proof contains at least one B; so, therefore, does every last line of a proof, that is, every theorem. A similar argument, which you should make for yourself, proves Metatheorem 3: Every theorem begins with an N. It is also easy to show Metatheorem 4: No theorem begins with two Ns. For no axiom begins with two Ns, and the rule (which we must use to get anything besides an axiom) adds an A right after the first letter (which we know must be an N, by Metatheorem 3) of anything we already have.

These metatheorems are pretty trivial, but that is not true of all metatheorems. We can move to something that has a little more substance by asking whether we can show the ABIN system to be *consistent*. The first thing we must do is to say what such a claim means. I think we all understand the sense of the accusation that a politician has spoken inconsistently. This means promising one policy to one group and a conflicting policy, that is, one that can *not* be carried out if the first one is, to another group. Treating children inconsistently means treating them one way on one occasion and treating them in an incompatible way on another occasion. You know that you are not supposed to be inconsistent, that is, you are not supposed to contradict yourself: You are not supposed to say one thing and then imply that that is *not* true. If we take what is suggested by these cases and formulate it in a way that might apply to formal systems, we come out with this definition: A formal system is consistent if, and only if, it contains no pair of theorems such that one is the negation of the other.

Consistency is generally taken to be a virtue, and it seems that we would like the ABIN system to have it. Well, does it? Can we show that it does or does not? No; or, at least, not yet. This is because our definition of consistency mentions *negation* and we have said nothing about what counts as negation in the ABIN system. In fact, so long as we speak of the ABIN system only as a formal system, we cannot say anything about consistency.[3] This is because negation is a bit of meaningful content, and as long as we proceed purely formally, we proceed without assigning any meaningful content to the signs of our system.

Fortunately, we can depart from our purely formal outlook without losing the ability to reason carefully about what is true of the formal system. We do this by providing an *interpretation* of some or all of the signs in it. That is, we say what meaning we will attach to certain signs. We can then give reasons for believing certain things that depend on both the formal structure of the system and our decision about what meaning to give to signs in the system.

For example, we shall now decide that N is to be interpreted as negation. That is, an N followed by a certain wff is to be understood to be the negation of that wff. With just this one bit of interpretation in hand, we can argue for Metatheorem 5: The ABIN system is consistent. Every theorem begins with an N (Metatheorem 3). No theorem begins with two Ns (Metatheorem 4). So, no theorem has the structure of an N followed by a string that is a theorem. But N is negation. So, no theorem is the negation of a theorem; that is, the system is consistent.

The next question we need to consider is whether the ABIN system is *complete*. As before, we first need to know what the question means. There are two ways of explaining what completeness is, one very formal, the other less so. The formal explanation is this: A formal system is complete if and only if you cannot add any wffs to it without producing inconsistency. A camel is completely loaded if one more straw would break its back and a system is complete if adding one more wff would "break" it, that is, make it produce a contradiction. The less formal explanation of completeness will help us tie this concept to Lucas's argument. Let us go back to high-school geometry and try to think of what "complete" might mean as applied to it. Certainly, we would not fault a geometrical system for failing to include physics or chemistry. Nor would we fault it for not including false statements about geometrical figures. On the other hand, if there were some truth about squares or circles that we could state clearly, but that could not be derived from a set of axioms, we would probably find it intuitively correct to describe the system as "incomplete". That would be a good model for incompleteness as it is usually understood in other systems. In the case of the ABIN system, the analogous idea would be this: It is complete if every wff that is true is a theorem, but incomplete if there is some wff that is true, but not a theorem.

Can we now show that the ABIN system is complete, or that it is incomplete? According to the formal definition we can. Consider the string, NANBB. This is, first of all, a wff. Second, it is not derivable as a theorem of the ABIN system. This is shown as follows. Every axiom that has at least three letters begins with the letters NBI. One application of the rule to any axiom yields an expression that begins with NAB. A second application of the rule inserts another A right after the first N, so that the first three letters of the result of any second application of the rule must be NAA. The same reason shows that each further application of the rule yields an expression beginning with NAA. So, all theorems of three or more letters begin with either NBI or NAB or NAA. NANBB has more than three letters and does not begin with any of the possible combinations for theorems, so it is not a theorem.

Suppose we add NANBB to the set of theorems of the ABIN system; will we be able to produce an inconsistency? To answer this, let us note that the wffs that are related to NANBB by negation are ANBB and NNANBB. The first of these is not a theorem (by Metatheorem 3) and the second is not a theorem either (by Metatheorem 4). Moreover, the theorems that are derivable from NANBB by the rule all begin with the letters NA. Wffs related to these by negation would all have to begin either with an A or with two Ns; but the argument just given again shows that none of these is a theorem. So, adding NANBB to the ABIN system would add a wff to it without producing inconsistency. Therefore, Metatheorem 6: The ABIN system is incomplete.

Do we get the same result if we approach incompleteness less formally? To decide this, we must know whether adding NANBB is adding a *truth*. For this, in turn, we must know what it means. We cannot know this yet, for we have given no interpretation of A or of B, BI, BII. . . . These can, however, be given an interpretation and I now propose to do so. "A" is to be interpreted as "and"; that is, an A followed by two wffs says that both the first one and the second one are true. Further, I have decided to interpret the strings B, BI, BII,

. . . as false sentences. Any false sentences would do as examples, but let us choose "Mars is fertile" for B and "Jupiter is smaller than Venus" for BI. We can see that on this interpretation (including the interpretation of N as "not"), the axiom NB says that it is false that Mars is fertile; so, this axiom is true. The theorem NABBI says that it is false that both Mars is fertile and Jupiter is smaller than Venus. NAABNBIB, another theorem, says that it is false that both Mars is fertile and Jupiter is not smaller than Venus and Mars is fertile. A look at the rule should convince you that all the theorems are true. For, in effect, the rule permits you to move from the statement that a given sentence is false to the statement that the conjunction of that sentence with any other sentence is false.

Now that we have fully interpreted the ABIN system, it should be obvious that it is incomplete in the less formal sense, as well as according to the formal definition. NANBB is a wff. We have already seen that it cannot be derived in the ABIN system. But it is true. So, there is something that is true, that we can *express* in the ABIN language but that we cannot prove as a theorem in the system.

Formal Systems and Robots

Lucas's strategy involves trying to imagine a machine that is just like himself in what it says and does. If we could produce such a machine, we would surely call it a robot, and that is how I shall speak of it, even though Lucas does not use this word. Lucas means to show that there cannot be such a robot. The key premise of his argument, however, states a certain fact about formal systems. What we have to do in this section is to explain how or why knowing something about formal systems might be thought to tell us something about possible robots.

In brief, the required connection is a point-for-point correspondence between the operation of any robot and the structure of some formal system. In order to pursue Lucas's argument, we have to specify how such a correspondence is to be set up. Table 6.1 shows how to do this.

In Table 6.1 we have ignored several details that would be quite

Robots		Formal Systems
Inputs from sensors	→	Axioms
Operations of internal processing elements	→	Rules
Sequences of internal operations	→	Proofs
Motor or speaker outputs	→	Theorems

TABLE 6.1 Robot and Formal System Correspondences

important if you actually were going to try to build a robot. For example, sensors like TV eyes and microphone ears may have two kinds of inputs. Some may be words in, say, English, while others will be scenes that contain no writing, or noises made by the weather, passing traffic, or other nonhuman-voice sources. If we are going to imagine a robot that is just like Lucas, or just like you—a person, so to speak, realized in electronic-mechanical form—then we must suppose that both kinds of inputs are handled. We must suppose, moreover, that they get together, in this sense: The verbal instruction "Bring me an apple" ties up with the visual input of an apple in such a way that the visual input is recognized as relevant to carrying out the instruction. If we are to think of a corresponding formal system, we will have to think of a system of signs and rules for wffs that allows both strings of verbal input and strings of nonverbal input to be axioms— or be translatable into axioms—in the same formal language. Making either a robot or a formal system of this kind would be a formidable task. It is obvious, however, that we hear words by using our ears in the same way that we use them to hear other noises (and analogously for written words and the use of our eyes to see every kind of thing). Thus, at some level, there must be a common way of representing what is received by us. The operations that we perform on what we receive can then be thought of as operations on inputs that can all be represented in a common system.

The heart of the connection between robots and formal systems is the fact that the operation of a mechanical element can be represented by a rule that takes you from the input of that element to its output. If there were some uncertainty about what an element would do with an input, you could not write down a definite rule that would tell you what output to expect, given an input. But we are assuming that we have a *mechanistic* "person", that is, one made out of things like circuit chips, motors, gears, and pulleys. Ultimately, it is our acceptance of physics that leads us to believe that these things are not capricious, and that what they do depends strictly on what force is applied to them. Since our robot is mechanistic, its inputs are in the form of forces (electrical potentials, vibrating diaphragms, bending thermocouples, and the like) that have effects on its processing elements. Thus, for each of its elements, there is a rule that describes its operation.[4]

If each element operates in a way that can be described by a rule, then the operation of the whole set of elements can be derived by applying the rules in the same order as the operations of the elements.[5] Thus, we can think of the first processing (applying of a rule) on an input (axiom) as yielding a first result (theorem). Then the processing (applying a further rule) on that result (theorem) will yield a further change inside the robot (a further theorem). After enough steps of processing, the result that is yielded will be in the motors of the robot. These changes will determine the behavioral output of the robot and will correspond to the last theorems derived from the axioms corresponding to the input.

The importance of the robot and formal system correspondence for Lucas's argument can be put this way: If there is some feature that the processing done by a robot has, then that feature can be mirrored in an analogous property of the corresponding formal system. Lucas uses this point in a reverse sense. That is, he argues that there is some property that a formal system cannot have, and he derives the conclusion that there is an analogous property that a robot cannot have. If Lucas does have that property, then the robot cannot be just like him. The next thing we must do is to identify the property that is supposed to distinguish Lucas from every possible robot.

Gödel's Result

The linchpin of Lucas's argument is a result that was proved by Kurt Gödel in 1931.[6] One way to state the result is this: No formal system can be both consistent and complete for arithmetic. That is, no formal system can both be consistent and enable you to derive from its axioms every statement of arithmetic that is true. Lucas's statement of his argument, however, turns on the idea of a "Gödel sentence".

We will have to look just far enough into the detail of Gödel's argument to understand what this is. This will involve a little complication, but you should be clear about one thing. Nothing in this discussion comes anywhere near to *proving* anything. Gödel's argument is very long and very difficult. It has moved another logician, W. V. Quine, to say this: "That it [Gödel's theorem] is true is surprising, and that it could be proved is more surprising still."[7] Our efforts here are only directed toward getting a more detailed idea of what the Gödel result *says*, so that we can have some confidence about whether or not Lucas's application of it is legitimate.

Let us begin with some things that *can* be done. If you are going to have a formal system for at least some part of arithmetic, you will have to have a formal language. This will have to be a much richer language than the one in our trivial ABIN system example. It will have to allow for expressions that can be given interpretation as facts about addition or multiplication, facts about properties of numbers like being even or being prime, or being the fourth power of an integer, and so on. It will have to contain expressions corresponding to the fact that any number whose digits sum to a multiple of three is divisible by three, and other more complicated facts of this kind. Now, although you need more signs that the ABIN system's four in order to express as much as this, you do not really need so very many. Twenty will be more than enough. You can, in considerably less than a page, specify a set of signs and rules for well-formed formulas that will enable you to express the sense of any statement of arithmetic whatsoever.

Here is a second thing that can be done. Let us go back to considering our simple ABIN system for a moment, and let us assign numbers to its letters as follows.

N	A	B	I
1	2	3	4

Let us also write down the first few prime numbers in order: 2, 3, 5, 7, 11, 13, 17, 19. . . . Let us now generate a number for, say, NABIIABIB in the following way. For the *first* letter, take the *first* prime in the list and raise it to a power, according to the number that is assigned to the letter in that first place. For the second letter, take the second prime and raise it to a power, namely, the number that is associated with the second letter. Repeat this for all the letters and then multiply all the numbers together. In tabular form, we have:

Position:	1	2	3	4	5	6	7	8	9
Corresponding prime:	2	3	5	7	11	13	17	19	23
Letter:	N	A	B	I	I	A	B	I	B
Assigned number:	1	2	3	4	4	2	3	4	3
Result:	\multicolumn{9}{c}{$2^1 \times 3^2 \times 5^3 \times 7^4 \times 11^4 \times 13^2 \times 17^3 \times 19^4 \times 23^3$}

Now, what this enormous number actually is, is of no interest whatever. What does matter is, first, that we can generate this kind of number for every formula; second, that we get a different number for each different formula; third, that we can work back from a number to a formula; and, finally, that when we do work back, there is only one way of deriving a formula from a number, so that we always come out with a unique result. This last point happens because there is only one way to factor a number into primes. So, when we have factored down to primes we just count the number of times each one occurs and that gives us a number that we can look up to find the letter. Then, we know which position the letter has because of the position of the prime number in the series of primes.

Because there is just one number for each formula, and vice versa, we can think of the numbers that we derive by the above method as *codes* for the formulas. The importance of describing the coding process is that we can do the very same thing for the formulas of any formal system. In particular, we can do it for the richer language that has resources enough to express all the statements of arithmetic. The immediate result of these observations is this: A particular formula in any formal system for arithmetic will have an interpretation as a statement of arithmetic, and it will also have a single number associated with it.

The number codes for formulas of a system are called *Gödel numbers*. It might occur to you to ask what, for example, is the Gödel number of a formula like 2 + 2 = 4. The answer, however, is that there is no single number that is the code for this formula in all systems. There are many ways of setting up a formal system for arithmetic, and the Gödel number of a particular statement will depend on what system is used. It will also depend on the method of coding, of which there are many. You must think of Gödel's work on coding as having a very general conclusion, to the effect that *no matter what* system you set up, its formulas can be coded by numbers. This point should be taken as a model for what follows. That is, Gödel's further results are likewise general. They say that *no matter what* system you set up for deriving statements of arithmetic, you will be able to do certain things in it, and you will not be able to prove all the true statements unless the system is inconsistent.

Not every number is a Gödel number of a wff in a given system. For example, 24 is 8×3, or $2^3 \times 3^1$. If we look for the corresponding formula in the ABIN system (according to the same coding as above), we find that it is the non-wff BN. An analogous point will hold in any of the richer formal systems that are adequate for expressing statements of arithmetic: Not every number will be the number of a wff. Let us imagine that we have some formal system, which we will call PAT (Producer of Arithmetical Theorems). Some numbers will be numbers of wffs in PAT, some will not. Imagine that we collect all the numbers of wffs together; call the set of all these numbers "PATWFFNOS". We will now know what we mean if we say (where n is some particular number),

[1] n is a member of PATWFFNOS;

for, this is a way of saying that n is the number of a wff of PAT. Now, [1] is a sentence of ordinary English, not a sentence of the special formal language of PAT. However, although this is not something that is obvious, this statement, [1] can be expressed in the formal language of PAT. PAT has to have a language rich enough to express all ordinary arithmetical statements, and one of the things Gödel proved was that if a language can do that, it can also express things like [1]. Let us imagine that we have written [1] out fully in the language of PAT. Call the result "[1FE]" ("FE" for "Fully Expressed"). This is a formula of PAT, so it can be coded. Suppose h is its number. [1FE] is well formed; so it will be true that h is a member of PATWFFNOS.

This by itself is not so interesting, but we are now going to think of a similar numbering that has much more important results. Not only can you get numbers to code wffs, you can also code *proofs*. After all, a proof is just a series of lines and such a series can be thought of as one long line with a bit of punctuation marking the places where, as we ordinarily write proofs, we would move to a new line. Suppose, now, that we collect all the numbers that are numbers of proofs in PAT and call the set of all of them PATPROOFNOS. Then, a sentence like

[2] m is a member of PATPROOFNOS

is a way of saying that the sequence of lines (or, long line with punctuation breaks) that corresponds to the code number m is a proof. Analogously to the case for wffs, Gödel showed that if a system can express ordinary arithmetic, it will have wffs that express what [2] says. That is, there will be an expression, [2FE], that is a wff in the formal language of PAT and that has an interpretation on which it says what [2] says. This wff will, like all wffs of PAT, be able to be assigned a unique number.

If you understand what [2] says, then you should have no trouble understanding the next sentence,

[3] k is not a member of PATPROOFNOS.

This just says that the sequence for which k is the code is not a proof. As before, [3] will have a fully expressed form that is a wff of PAT, and it will have a corresponding number.

All the code numbers we have referred to are like our first example, in that we can uniquely determine the coded formula from the number. So, we can recover the actual proof from the code for one. By looking at the punctuation, we can tell what is the last line of a proof. The last lines of all the proofs in PAT are all the theorems of PAT. By now, it should be obvious both that not every number is a number of a theorem, and that every theorem has a number. Collect all the numbers of theorems of PAT and call the set PATTHEOREMNOS. Then

[4] j is a member of PATTHEOREMNOS

is a way of saying that j is the number of a theorem, and

[5] i is not a member of PATTHEOREMNOS

is a way of saying that i is the number of a formula that is *not* a theorem. As usual, these have full expressions as wffs in PAT and these fully expressed formulas have codes.

Let us imagine what would happen if things turned out as follows. We express [5] fully as [5FE] and calculate its code according to the same scheme we have been using to find the numbers in PAT-WFFS, PATPROOFNOS, and PATTHEOREMNOS. In imagining doing this task, we should remind ourselves that i in [5] is being taken to be some particular number (and not just an x or other variable for numbers). Now suppose what we find is that the Gödel number or code for [5FE] comes out to be this very same number i. Then, we would know that what [5FE] asserts is that the number of this very sentence is not in PATTHEOREMNOS, that is, that this very sentence is not a theorem. Moreover, we could conclude that if PAT is consistent, then what [5FE] asserts is true. This is because, if you *could* prove [5FE] in PAT, you could prove a contradiction. Because you could prove it, you would prove that i *is* a member of PAT-THEOREMNOS; but because you had proved it, you would have proved that the axioms of PAT imply what it says, and this is that i *is not* a member of PATTHEOREMNOS. So, finally, you would know that *if* PAT is consistent, then it has a wff that is *true* but that cannot be proved in it.[8]

Now, you might think that this is a cute trick, but one that could not be done. Or, you might think that if you set up a system just so, you will be able to find a formula that has the very number that the formula says is not a number of a theorem, but this will only happen in some systems that you will have to work pretty hard to find. But the amazing fact that Gödel proved is that there will *always* be sentences that work out like our [5FE], just so long as you have a system rich enough to produce most theorems of ordinary arithmetic.

Sentences that work like [5FE] are called "Gödel sentences". It should not surprise you to be told that a sentence is a Gödel sentence only relative to a system. A sentence that is not provable in one system may be a theorem in another system. The sense of Gödel's result is that no matter what formal system you propose for arithmetic, there will be true statements that are expressible in it but not provable in it. If the system is very simple, for example, if it lacks a way of expressing multiplication, then there will not be a Gödel sentence, but there will be much of arithmetic that is missing. If we have a system that does not have such obvious deficiencies, then there will be a Gödel sentence for it.[9]

Lucas's Argument

We now have all the materials necessary to follow the sense of Lucas's famous argument. If mechanism is true, Lucas holds, then some machine could be made that would, psychologically, be just like Lucas, or would be a model of you or a model of me. But, according to Lucas, there are facts about ourselves that resist being modeled in a machine. The key points are as follows. On the one hand, we are not inconsistent. We do not go around contradicting ourselves; if we stumble into doing so, we correct ourselves, and we do not simply accept all that other people say when they are disagreeing with each other. On the other hand, we can follow (given considerably more time than it took you to read this book so far!) Gödel's proof. So, for example, although [5FE] is not provable in PAT, although it is, so to speak, unknown to that system, *we* would be able to see that it is true. Therefore, whatever robot might correspond to PAT, *it* cannot do something that we can do, namely, see that a Gödel sentence for PAT is true. But there will be some Gödel sentence for any formal system that is up to containing most of arithmetic. So, if there is a robot that is alleged to be just like me, there will be some Gödel sentence that it cannot assert (the Gödel sentence of its corresponding formal system) but that I can assert (because I can understand Gödel and see that what the sentence says must be true). Put in summary form, the argument is this:

1. Properties of machines are paralleled by properties of formal systems.
2. All formal systems that are consistent are incomplete for arithmetic. Therefore,
3. All machines that behave consistently are incomplete for arithmetic.
4. I am not adequately modeled by any inconsistent machine.

5. I am not adequately modeled by anything that is incomplete for arithmetic. Therefore,

6. I am not adequately modeled by any machine.

Can a Machine Assert Its Own Gödel Sentence?

There have been many philosophers who have objected to Lucas's argument and it is time to look at some of their reasons. The main lines of objection correspond to two key premises, the fourth and fifth in the argument just stated. That is, it has been suggested that, after all, a person might be modeled by an inconsistent machine. It has also been held that a machine that modeled a person might be able to assert whatever sentences that person can assert, including the Gödel sentence of the formal system that corresponds to such a machine. Let us now look into these responses, beginning with the second.

One state table for a Turing machine corresponds to one formal system. If there is something that cannot be done in a formal system, then it cannot be done by scanning a tape and using what is read to determine how to move through the state table for the corresponding Turing machine. Matters get more complicated, however, when we turn away from "machines" in the abstract sense of something going through the states in a state table, and consider concrete, sensor-computer-motor devices. Such devices can always be regarded as being *many* abstract "machines". This suggests the possibility that some actual, hardware device could model me, if regarded in one way, but still assert the Gödel sentence of a formal system corresponding to me, if regarded in another way. If so, a concrete, material object machine might do what it is not supposed to be able to do, according to Lucas's argument—namely, assert its own Gödel sentence. We have to look into this order to see whether such a possibility is genuinely intelligible.

There are two ways in which a (hardware) machine can be more than one (abstract) machine.[10] The first of these applies to every material thing whatsoever. For example, my coffee cup can be regarded as a machine with a table of two states—empty (s_0) and nonempty (s_1). Let us use 0 to represent the operation of emptying the cup and

1 to represent pouring some liquid into it. Think of the "direction" R as corresponding to moving forward in time (which is where the next input will be found). Since adding liquid to a nonempty cup leaves it nonempty (even if overflowing) and emptying an empty cup leaves it still empty, we can represent the cup as instantiating this table:

$$s_0 O R s_0 \qquad s_1 O R s_0$$
$$s_0 1 R s_1 \qquad s_1 1 R s_1$$

This is a very simple table, but it will serve to illustrate how the physical states of a thing can be represented in (abstract) Turing machine style. Now, it should not be hard to see that we can also take the same thing—that is, the cup—and regard it as a hardware machine that corresponds to a different state table. This table will have three states, corresponding to the cup's sitting on its bottom, lying on its side, and standing inverted on its rim. (We can take lying on a side as one state, no matter which part of the side is touching the table.) The inputs can be taken to be the operations of turning the cup by 90 degrees clockwise or 90 degrees counterclockwise. R can be taken as before. You should be able to work out the table that corresponds to this way of regarding the cup.

Simple though these examples are, they should make it clear that what state table is realized by a material object depends on *how we regard* that object. It depends, that is, on which of the changeable properties of the object we choose to regard as relevant to defining its states, and which kinds of operations we choose to regard as inputs. Now, if we generalize this idea, it seems just possible that someone might suppose that things could turn out as follows. Take a certain fancy robot. Regard it one way, it is a model of me. Regard it in another way, however, and it will correspond to some other state table. Now, perhaps when we regard it as corresponding to some other state table, it asserts a sentence, say G_R. And maybe this very sentence is a Gödel sentence for me, or, to be more careful, the Gödel sentence of the formal system corresponding to the robot, when the robot is regarded in a way that makes it a model of me. In this way, the robot might both be a model of me *and* assert a Gödel sentence that it cannot assert when it is being regarded as a model of me. If this might happen, however, then it would seem to be no longer possible to distinguish the robot from me, for whatever sentence I could assert, the robot might also produce.

Admittedly, this is a complex and very special case. Our simple examples about the cup cannot really be taken to be a rigorous proof that such a case is possible. So, perhaps Lucas could argue that there is no real objection to him until we have a proof that there could be such a complex case. There is, however, a more interesting way of defending Lucas here. What we would need, in order to refute Lucas, is a robot that models *me*. Now, according to Lucas, I can assert a Gödel sentence for any system I am given. A robot that models me must therefore also be able to assert such sentences. But I do not assert what may be expressed by ways of regarding me that are different from the customary way in which you regard me and what I say. For example, for all I know, there is some way of dividing up discrete ranges of my body temperatures that could be put into correspondence with the dots and dashes of Morse code. So regarded, I may express all sorts of things. But I am totally unaware of all this; it has nothing to do with *me*, as far as any ordinary way I have of thinking of *myself* goes; and I do not *assert* anything that is expressed in this way. A robot that has something that fluctuates in response to my temperature likewise does not *assert* anything that it might be regarded as expressing by such fluctuations. So, a robot that expresses G_R only when we regard it in a way different from the way we customarily regard it would *not* be a robot that asserted G_R. Consequently, it would not qualify as a model of me, it if is true that I can assert that sentence.

When philosophers talk about who is who, that is, what is involved in a person's being the *same person* at different times, they usually emphasize certain psychological relations.[11] Thus, one moment of a person's mental life may be connected to some others through being *remembered*; other moments may be connected through being intentions to act on plans that have grown out of previous deliberation. We may add that people's beliefs change bit by bit, but not in a wholesale way, and that although a person can learn a new language and forget an old one over a long time, this cannot happen in a matter of days. When Lucas talks about a model of himself, he means a model that would preserve analogues of these psychological relations. Now, a requirement of such an analogue is that it be a model of the psychological relations under just one way of regarding it. If we did not demand this, we would have to allow, as our model of a person, something that expressed itself in many different ways, when in any ordinary sense, the person being modeled knows of only one. We would have to allow for something that expressed contradictory views in its different expressive modes. We would have to allow for something that did not preserve such psychological relations as memory between expressions in the different ways of regarding it. These allowances obviously depart far too much from what ought to be called a model of a person. Thus, we may say that for a robot to be a model of a person, in the sense that is relevant to Lucas's argument, it must be such a model *from a single way of regarding it.*

I said earlier that there were two ways in which a single (hardware) machine might be two (abstract) machines. The second of these ways might be thought of as meeting the condition we have just argued to be required for models of people. Let us, therefore, move on to consider it.

We need to remind ourselves of two facts that we have already explained. The first is that Gödel sentences are relative to a given system. Another way of putting this is to say that for each sentence that is a Gödel sentence of some system, there will be another system that will have large parts of arithmetic as theorems and also will have that sentence as a theorem. If we think of the situation in terms of robots, we will come out this way: If G_A is the Gödel sentence of (the formal system corresponding to) Robot A, Robot B may perfectly well be able to assert G_A. (I mean, here and in what follows, that Robot B asserts this, when we interpret what Robot B asserts in the customary way that we regard all its assertions, and not in the peculiar ways previously imagined.) The second fact is that there are universal Turing machines. Now, suppose that Robot A is alleged to be a model of me. Since I can imitate quite a few Turing machines (I can use quite a few algorithms, for example), Robot A can do so too. Perhaps it is a universal Turing machine. In fact, since Lucas has no right (and no wish) to exclude this possibility, let us suppose it to be so. It follows that it can imitate Robot B. That is, it can be given a description of the formal system that corresponds to Robot B and can work out from that what sentences Robot B will assert. But one of these is G_A! So, Robot A can, after all, produce what Lucas had said only I could produce. Thus it seems, once again, that Lucas cannot show that there must be a difference in ability (namely, to assert some sentence) between a person and each proposed robotic model of that person.

This proposal is an improvement on the previous case, for the following reason. A universal Turing machine is not simply disconnected from the machines that it imitates. There is an analogue of what we might call "psychological unity", in that it is *always* acting as a certain machine, no matter what other machine it is imitating, or that it virtually is. So, we cannot say, as we could before, that the production of G_A would be like interpreting my temperature fluctuations as code. Less precisely, but more intuitively, calculating is indeed something that we ourselves do. When we add a column of figures, we may make moves, both with pencil and in mental arithmetic, that correspond exactly to a process in a calculator, that could be represented by the state table of a certain Turing machine. But the results do not have the kind of psychological distance that my "expressions" as a temperature fluctuator would have. Thus, it seems, the difficulty that we encountered in our first attempt to get a (hardware) machine to be more than one (abstract) machine has been overcome.

This improvement, however, only appears to solve the problem. It is not really true that we assert everything we can calculate. We assert the results of our adding not because we went through a procedure, but only because we believe that the procedure is a good one. We can bring out the central point by noticing that we can have bad procedures. We can build machines that give right answers sometimes and wrong answers sometimes. We could understand how such a machine was designed and calculate what it would give for a new problem. That would be using a procedure, but we would not be asserting the result. We would, of course, assert *some* result, namely, one of this form: "Machine X will give 29 as the answer to $18 + 13$"; but we will not on that account assert an answer of this form: "$18 + 13 = 29$." Analogously, Robot A might calculate what Robot B will say and produce this sentence: "Robot B will assert that G_A." But this does not show that Robot A will *assert* G_A, because it does not show that Robot A will believe that Robot B knows that what it says is true. In fact, it might happen that Robot A never satisfies itself whether or not Robot B has proceeded correctly, and so never concludes one way or another about G_A. (It would be like knowing a person's views so well that you could anticipate exactly what that person is going to say, but being unable to decide whether this so consistently asserted view is true.) In this situation, Robot A would not be a model of a person, if that person could not merely *pronounce* G_A, or assert that Robot B would say it, but could actually *assert* that G_A. This, however, is what Lucas claims he could do. So the fact that, in a sense, one machine can be several, and produce, when regarded as one machine, what it cannot produce when regarded as another, does not show that a machine can do what Lucas said no machine could do.

Am I Consistent?

Let us turn to the line of objection to Lucas that attacks premise 4 in the summary statement of his argument. We may recall that the Gödel result shows that any system for arithmetic is incomplete *if* it is consistent. If Lucas can assert a Gödel sentence for any machine we care to compare him to, it may be that he cannot be modeled by a machine; but, then again, it may be that he *can* be modeled by a machine, just not by a consistent one. If Lucas wants definitely to assert the first of these possibilities, he must rule out the second. Lucas does explicitly attempt to do this and it will be convenient to begin by explaining what is behind his reasoning on this point.

The key argument turns on just a few facts about formal logic, which I will now introduce. Consider, first, this little bit of monologue that might occur at the end of a detective story.

> By this time, I had established that it would have been impossible for anyone but Jones or Smith to have committed the murder. For the longest time, I could not tell which it was. Then the letter from Green arrived. Despite considerable efforts at concealment, Jones could not hide the fact that the letter was of great importance. I began to suspect a romantic involvement. Sure enough, Jones was in

fact with Green on the night of the murder and
could not have committed it. This left you, Smith,
as the only remaining possibility.

If we abbreviate "Jones committed the murder" to S_1 and "Smith
committed the murder" to S_2, we can represent the reasoning in this
story as follows:

Either S_1 or S_2 is true.
S_1 is not true. Therefore,
S_2 is true.

The point of the little story is to show you that this is a type of
argument with which you are perfectly familiar. You have undoubt-
edly used it in your own reasoning and you are prepared to use it in
the future. Any robot that models you must thus have this bit of logic
in its repertoire, that is, it must be prepared to use this little pattern
of reasoning to draw conclusions from the sentences it asserts. The
point of introducing the abbreviations S_1 and S_2 is to help you see
that there is a general pattern of reasoning here that will apply no
matter what sentences we substitute for S_1 and S_2 (so long as we
substitute consistently throughout the argument).

There is another pattern of argument that we will need to use.
This one can be represented as:

S_3 is true. Therefore,
Either S_3 or S_4 is true.

This pattern may strike you as somewhat peculiar. One reason is that
the conclusion is so much weaker than the premise. In everyday life,
we usually want to use reasoning to enable us to conclude something
that is not obvious already, something that we did not clearly know
before. We do not generally want to say less than we know. We do
not generally introduce a new subject matter into the conclusion of
an argument, for the good reason that *usually* this would make an
argument invalid. Despite its departures from these common features
of reasoning, however, the argument whose pattern we just gave is
really quite all right. It is one we are all prepared to use. For example,

a college catalogue may contain a statement of this type: To graduate, you must take either Philosophy 103 or History 104. Students who have taken Philosophy 103 can be expected to reason this way: "I've taken Philosophy 103, so I have satisfied this requirement." Their satisfaction of the requirement follows, however, only if they are using the above pattern of reasoning, with "I've taken Philosophy 103" abbreviated to S_3 and "I've taken History 104" abbreviated to S_4.

I have dwelt on these two patterns of argument because they can be used to introduce a problem for any attempt to make an inconsistent robot that is supposed to model a person. One step that we need in order to understand this problem can be stated this way:

> *Unless we build in special precautions, an inconsistent*
> *formal system that contains rules corresponding to*
> *the two arguments we have just described will contain*
> *all of its wffs whatsoever as theorems.*

We shall shortly return to the questions of what this implies for robots and how it connects with Lucas's argument. For now, let us just try to see what is behind the italicized statement. First, recall that if a formal system is inconsistent, then there is at least one pair of theorems such that one is the negation of the other. Let us represent such an inconsistent pair as T and Not-T. To suppose that a formal system is inconsistent is to suppose that there is a proof in it that looks like this:

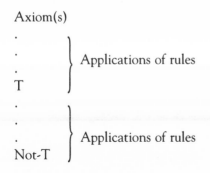

Axiom(s)

.
.
.   } Applications of rules
T

.
.
.   } Applications of rules
Not-T

That is, there is a proof of T and of Not-T. Now, if our formal system has rules corresponding to the above argument patterns, the proof can be continued so as to produce the line:

$$T \text{ or } S_x$$

where S_x is any well-formed formula. The reason is the second of the patterns we just introduced.[12] Now, Not-T is the negation of T, that is, it says that T is false. So, if the formal system has a rule corresponding to the first pattern (the one used by the detective), we can write a further line of the proof, like this:

$$S_x$$

But S_x was just *any* wff we cared to pick. So, if a formal system has rules corresponding to our two argument patterns and is inconsistent, then, barring special precautions, it has a proof of any of its wffs that we care to pick.[13]

Let us see how this might help with Lucas's argument. Recall that I said that our little argument patterns are ones that you are prepared to use. *Perhaps* you would not have been willing to use the second one before you saw how it worked out in a familiar example; but now, anyway, you are willing to use it. You have all along used the first one. So, any robot that is even a candidate for being a model of you now has to be prepared to reason according to rules corresponding to these arguments. Now, if such a machine were inconsistent—if it were willing to assert *even one* statement and its negation—then, barring special precautions, it could produce any well-formed sentence and do so while being regarded in just the one customary way that we regard it for all its productions. *You*, however, will *not* be willing to assert just any old sentence, even if there is *some* matter on which you contradict yourself. So, unless we could make a machine that had special barriers against asserting just any well-formed sentence, we could not make one that is both inconsistent and a model of you.

This way of putting the matter makes it clear that whether we can make a machine that models a person depends on whether we can introduce special precautions that will prevent it from asserting just any sentence if it even once stumbles into an inconsistency. Lucas, in fact, imagines some ways of doing exactly that. He imagines a machine that rejects the longer of any two proofs that lead to inconsistent conclusions. He imagines another machine that rejects certain of its rules if they are found to lead to contradictions. He dismisses these, however, as arbitrary and as failing to model the way people react to inconsistency. He goes on to consider some more complicated ways of avoiding the production of all assertions from an inconsistency, and again shows that they are inadequate models of our responses to perceived inconsistency.[14] From this discussion, he concludes that inconsistent machines can never behave the way that people do. They will either fail to accept logical rules that we accept (that is, the two I described above) or they will mindlessly assert every statement or they will block such mindless assertion by some arbitrary rule that is unlike any that people would find acceptable. In any case, they will fail to be models of *our* mental capacities. Thus, we cannot be modeled by any inconsistent machine.

This reasoning may sound plausible, but it cannot succeed. Lucas can indeed show that there are particular kinds of machines that do not model our responses to cases in which we are caught in a contradiction. This, however, is not enough. The series of ingenious failures to make a flying machine that took place in the late nineteenth century did not amount to a proof that an airplane was impossible. In the same way, a collection of plausible, but failed, attempts to model people's reactions to the discovery that they have asserted an inconsistency will not show that such a model is impossible. Moreover, it is not even enough to show that whole classes of simple strategies will not produce a machine that models people. The claim for which Lucas needs a proof is that *no machine can model our responses to perceived inconsistency.* The problem that Lucas has here is a consequence of the fact that the italicized claim is *very similar* to the main claim of the whole argument. That is, Lucas's main claim is that no machine can be a model of a person. The italicized claim is that no machine can model a certain portion of our behavior (that is, our responses to being caught in a contradiction). Anyone who doubts the main claim is surely going to doubt this subsidiary claim. No one who is not already persuaded that there is something so special about the human mind that it cannot be modeled by a machine will be willing to agree that this certain portion of human mental ability cannot be modeled by a machine. To avoid begging the question, by using something very like an assumption of the main claim in order to defend it against an objection, Lucas would have to offer an argument for the impossibility of machine modeling of some of our behavior (our reaction to finding that we have contradicted ourselves) that is completely independent of his main claim. But he offers no such general argument; he offers only the woefully inadequate citation of some attempts that obviously fail.

These remarks are, I believe, sufficient to show that Lucas has not provided a good reason why we should believe that no machine could model us. I doubt, however, that they will remove all the sense of puzzlement that thinking about Lucas's argument is likely to cause. So, I will add one observation that I hope will make the discussion more satisfying. In setting up Lucas's argument, we noted a correspondence between machines and formal systems. There is a certain kind of symmetry in this correspondence. That is, for each machine, there is a corresponding formal system, but equally, for each formal system, there is some machine that will operate in a way that that formal system describes. Nonetheless, there is also a kind of asymmetry between machines and formal systems. This is, that in a certain sense a formal system *always* contains *all* its theorems; but a machine has never derived all that it *can* derive. A formal system really corresponds to the *capacity* of a machine, not to its actual performance up to any given time. We can see the point of this by comparing your knowledge of arithmetic (your arithmetical capacity, so to speak) with your actually performed calculations. Since you learned arithmetic, there has *always* been something that you *could* have done, namely, obtain $277.89 by subtracting $34.57 from $312.46. But quite possibly these particular figures have never turned up, either in your checking account or in any other problem you have been called upon to do. (If you have in fact done this particular subtraction, there will always be some other that you have not done but that you could have done.) The formal system that represents you, if there is one, represents your capacity. The statement $312.46 - 34.57 = 277.89$ would be a theorem in the system, even if you have never done this calculation.

The relevance of this asymmetry is as follows. Contradictions in formal systems and their consequences—that is, all wffs—are all "there" all the time. But which sentences a machine "asserts" depends on which instantiations of axiom schemes it starts with and which rules, in which order, it applies. There will be many things, therefore, that a machine *can* assert that it *has not* asserted and that it *will in fact never* assert in its (presumably) finite lifetime. Lucas was right to argue that if a theorem is *not* in the formal system, then it cannot be asserted by a corresponding machine. But this does not license inferring in the other direction, that if a theorem *is* in the formal system, it *will* be asserted by a corresponding machine. So, the field is left open for this possibility: I am modeled by an inconsistent machine that would, *under some circumstances* assert a sentence and *under other circumstances* assert the denial of that sentence, and that in actual fact only one set of these circumstances arises in the machine's (or, correspondingly, my) life. And the field also is open for a possibility that is similar, except that some such pairs of circumstances have actually occurred, only not close enough together in time for us to have noticed the contradiction. Strange and humbling though it seems, I do not think we can fairly claim to *know* that this is not the situation we are in fact in.

Since I have been talking so long about the possibility that we are modeled by inconsistent machines, it might be thought that I am saying we can be modeled *only* by inconsistent machines, if we can be modeled by machines at all. This is, however, not a consequence of what I have been saying and my point was only that *we do not know* that we can *not* be modeled by inconsistent machines. So let us ask what it would be like if we could be modeled by consistent machines. In this case, we would each have a Gödel sentence that we would never assert. This does not mean, however, that we would deny such sentences. It means only that we would never be able to give ourselves a reason for asserting them. We must not suppose that it would ever seem to us that there is a sentence we are unable to assert. While we were thinking about such a sentence, we merely would not know whether we were never going to assert it, or whether we just had not yet come to a conclusion about it.

What I have just said may seem to beg the question against Lucas. He, I believe, would want to say that if any sentence G_F is the

Gödel sentence of the formal system F, then we *could* know that it is true. We could use Gödel's methods to show ourselves that G_F is unprovable in F, that it says it is unprovable in F, and that therefore it is true. To this point, however, I think we cannot do better than to quote the shortest and most elegant of the attempts to refute the kind of argument that Lucas advances. This argument is due to Hilary Putnam, and I believe it to be wholly successful. It is stated in terms of (Turing) machines, but at this point you should have no trouble in going back and forth between machine-talk and formal system-talk. Putnam's argument is as follows.

> Let T be a Turing machine which "represents" me in the sense that T enumerates proofs of just the mathematical statements I can prove. Then the argument is . . . that by using Gödel's technique I can discover a proposition that T cannot "prove", and moreover, *I* can prove this proposition. This refutes the assumption that T "represents" me, hence "I am not a machine" (Turing machine). The fallacy is a misrepresentation of Gödel's theorem, pure and simple. Given an arbitrary machine T, all I can do is find a proposition U such that *I* can prove
>
> (3) if T is consistent, U is true
>
> where U is undecidable by T if T is in fact consistent. However, T can perfectly well "prove" (write down a proof of) (3) too! And the statement U, which T *can't* "prove" (assuming consistency), I can't prove either! (Unless I can prove T is consistent, which is unlikely if T is quite complicated.)[15]

We can put this point in terms of our discussion, as follows. Regarding [5FE], we did not really come to know that it is true. We could say only that *if* PAT were consistent, what [5] said would be true.

In their response to Putnam, Nagel and Newman say that this begs the question, by assuming that any proof of U we could give would have to be one that a machine (T) could construct.[16] But Putnam is not arguing that we *can* be modeled by machines. He is taking only the agnostic position that our not being machine-modelable *does not follow* from the Gödel result. So, he can say that understanding

Gödel gives us a reason to believe (3), but not U. Maybe we could find some reason to believe U, but nothing in the argument so far shows that we could. So, as far as the argument from Gödel's result shows, we do not know that we could prove U; we do not know that there is a sentence we can prove but T cannot; and we do not know whether or not we can be modeled by a machine.

Chapter 7

Working on Sentences

In the last two chapters, we have considered two contrasting arguments. The first one attempted to show that artificial intelligence must be possible and the second one attempted to show that we cannot be machines. We have just seen that the second argument does not work, and so we do not have to worry that our "license" for AI will run afoul of something that Gödel showed. At the end of Chapter 5, however, I raised some doubts about the "license" that do not depend in any way on Lucas's argument. So, the position we are now in is that we do not know that we *cannot* be modeled by a machine, but we are not sure that we *can* be modeled by a machine either, or even whether there could be any machine that passes the Turing test. In this situation the only way to proceed with our COULD THERE BE question is to examine strategies we might use to try to make a machine that could do well at the imitation game. In this chapter, we shall begin this task by looking at just one such attempt, which we may call the *sentence-processing* strategy. Later we will encounter criticisms of this approach, and some alternative proposals on the COULD THERE BE question. In this chapter, however, we shall be entirely positive and emphasize the strengths and the plausibility of the approach under discussion.

Refining the Task of AI

We can begin to understand the sentence-processing strategy by describing the task that the Turing test situation presents. Let us notice that if someone utters just a single word or phrase, say, "trees" or "the northeast window" in your presence, you probably will not react for a while—you will wait for something more before you even think of replying. Of course, if nothing more is forthcoming, you may well ask if the speaker is all right, is intending to say more, or is, perhaps, testing your hearing. But there is nothing very specific that is called for by merely receiving a sentence fragment. Since there is no particular response to sentence fragments that shows off intelligence, it is not going to be very useful for interrogators in a Turing test to use many of them. Instead, we should expect the standard prompt in Turing tests to be a question or an instruction, that is to say, a whole *sentence*. Likewise, the answers one would expect in the Turing test are those given either in the form of sentences, or in words that express sentences when taken with their context, in the way that "Yes" in answer to "Is it raining?" expresses the sentence "It is raining."

We can sum this up by saying that the subjects in a Turing test essentially receive sentences and generate other sentences as replies. This pattern is illustrated in Turing's own examples. You should recall that it is also what happens in Searle's Chinese Room: What goes into the room are questions, and what comes out are answers. We can think of the approach to artificial intelligence that we will consider in this chapter as one that conceives intelligence as primarily the connecting of sentences to sentences. Making the right connections is the goal. In order to achieve this goal, certain tools are at our disposal, namely, computers.

Let us proceed by specifying the goal a little further. We have just said that passing the Turing test will require us to connect sentences to sentences. What will this take? Sometimes, it will take a *logically correct* connection. For example, an interrogator might ask what conclusion is to be drawn from the information that all bats are mammals and that all mammals are warm-blooded. Most people would answer that it follows that all bats are warm-blooded; and so, in aiming to build something that might pass the Turing test, we would aim to have something that would produce this answer. Sometimes the argumentative connection will not be deductive, as in this example about bats, but inductive instead. Thus an interrogator might ask what it would mean if Jones returned home and found her front door standing wide open. Several answers are possible: Jones might simply have left the door open when she went out, or a meter reader might have left it open. These are unlikely answers, however, and might make an interrogator wonder. This wonder could, perhaps, be put to rest by a sufficiently plausible follow-up story. Still, if we were trying to build something that would pass the Turing test, we would probably want to give it a structure that would lead it to say something about having been burgled, since that seems to be the most likely explanation of the open door, and the one that an intelligent person would suspect to be true. Finally, in some cases, we may have connections among sentences that are looser than those found in arguments. For example, an interrogator might say, "Make up a story about what might happen in a bar on a Saturday night." This is an open-ended invitation to produce some sentences. These might be quite various in different subjects but they would have to be connected in interesting ways if there is to be any chance of having their producer pass the Turing test.

We could add to these examples instructions to do arithmetic, invitations to play games, and requests to give specific information. The three kinds of cases we just described, however, are representative of a wide range of tasks, and attempts to handle them artificially would raise most of the characteristic problems in this area. So, I shall take these three kinds of cases as articulating and specifying the general goal of making a machine that would pass the Turing test. Let us now also try to specify the kind of tool that we are to imagine to be at our disposal in trying to produce these kinds of cases by artificial means.

One of the ideas we need here was introduced in the discussion of Searle in Chapter 2. You may recall that although the man inside the Chinese Room worked on questions that were written in Chinese, he did not understand the characters of that language. He therefore could appreciate them only by their *shapes* and not by their meaning. The shape of a word or character is a physical property that has only an arbitrary connection to its meaning. This is true even in onomatopoeia. The *spoken* word in onomatopoeia does have some (but still rather remote) connection to meaning: *boom*, for example, sounds a little bit more like an explosion than some other words, say, for example, *look*. But there is nothing about an explosion or its noise that makes it natural for it to be represented by a word composed of a roundish part with a line sticking up on the left side, two circles, and an upside down fork. Yet, the man inside the Chinese Room could work on Chinese characters only in the way that you could work on *boom* just by noting the shapes of its letters.

We need to have a term that will enable us to refer easily to this somewhat unfamiliar way of regarding words. An appropriate one for this purpose is "formal". Using this term, we can say that the man in the Chinese Room can work with Chinese characters only in a formal way, or only on the basis of their form, meaning that he can work only by looking at properties of the characters that, like shape, have nothing to do with meaning. The contrasting term, which is used to indicate that a connection with meaning is involved, is "semantic". Ordinarily, you do not pay much attention to the form of familiar words; you treat them semantically, that is, you look right through their shapes and think only of what they mean. Occasionally, you may treat words formally. For example, you may notice that, despite their meanings, *short* is a longer word than *long*; or, you may note that *eerie* is quite unusual in being a short word yet having three letters the same.

The importance of understanding these terms is this. To the extent that we think of computers as dealing with words, we must think of them as proceeding formally. One way of thinking about this is to remind yourself of how the man in the Chinese Room works. Searle described him in the way he did because the formal mode of the man's operation illustrates the formal mode of a computer's operation. We can add to our understanding here by recalling the Turing machines that we described in Chapter 5. The marks on the tape— the 0s and 1s—have no meaning for the machine; they are just so many shapes. The only thing that is essential for the machine's operation is that the different shapes must be distinguishable by the reading head, and that repetitions of each kind of shape on different squares of the tape can be recognized by the machine as being the same shape.

It is convenient to introduce the idea of form with reference to shapes of words. Once we have understood the term, however, it should be easy to see that shapes are not required. Independence of meaning, distinguishability, and repeatability can be achieved by sounds, as is done by all except some onomatopoetic words. These properties also can be exhibited by either spatial patterns or temporal patterns of punched holes, light flashes, magnetized particles, or electrical charges.

I just now described the man in Searle's Chinese Room as "proceeding formally". I have explained "formally", but what do I mean here by "proceeding"? Again, let us look at both the Chinese Room and Turing machines. In the Chinese Room, the man inside works by looking up *rules*. Let us recall what kind of rules these are. They are rules that refer to shapes of the Chinese characters that the man receives and that tell him to write down such and such further shapes provided that such and such other shapes have been found on certain slips of paper in the room. The man's "procedure" consists in doing what the rules say. Since the rules treat the characters only in so far as they have certain shapes, and say nothing about their meaning, the rules are formal rules. Saying that the man proceeds formally is thus saying that he follows formal rules, that is, rules that refer only to the formal properties of signs. We can easily see that the same holds of the operation of Turing machines. We can think of the entries in the state table as rules. They are rules for which way to move, whether to rewrite what is on the tape, and what state to go into next. They connect these things with the current state, and with what the reading head is reading. The reading head, however, only detects the shapes of the 0s and 1s that occur on the tape. So, the Turing machine proceeds by following rules that are formal ones, that is, rules that refer only to the formal properties of the signs on the tape.

We can now summarize the key problem of artificial intelligence, as this is conceived by the approach we are considering in this chapter. On the one hand, the goal to be achieved is a semantic one. That is, the sentences that a computer receives as inputs are to be connected to sentences it gives as output in such a way that the *meaning* of the output sentences shall be appropriate to the *meaning* of the input sentences. For example, in our first case, the output sentence was to be one that logically followed from the input sentences; and what logically follows from sentences depends on what they mean. In our second and third cases, the output sentences were to be probable on the basis of input sentences, or they were to be relevant to the subject matter of input sentences. Again, relations of probable support and relevance depend on meaning. On the other hand, the means that are to be used to achieve the goal work only formally. The problem, then, is to get formal procedures to accomplish semantic goals.

The Core of the Solution

When we describe the task in this way, it may seem impossible to carry out. Yet, we have already had an example that contains the germ of a possible solution to the difficulty. This is the ABIN system of Chapter 6. Let us remind ourselves of the relevant points about that system. First, we can work in the ABIN system in an entirely formal way. Everything up to (but not including) Metatheorem 5 was done with no semantics at all. All we have to be able to do is to recognize the difference between the letters A, B, I, and N, and understand the rules that refer to occurrences of these letters. And yet, the manipulations that the rules allow accomplish a semantic goal. That is, for any two sentences, S_1 and S_2, "Not both S_1 and S_2 are true" follows logically from "S_1 is not true." This deductive argument is built into the rule of the ABIN system. As a result, all its theorems are true, provided that the axioms from which they are derived are true. On the intended interpretation that we gave in Chapter 6, the axioms can be read as saying of some sentence that it is false. So, whenever we give a false sentence as an interpretation of "BII . . ." in an axiom, the axiom is true, and all the theorems derivable from that axiom in the ABIN system are truths that logically follow from it.

It is true that the ABIN system is extremely simpleminded. It was made that way so that it could introduce basic principles with a minimum of complexity. This simplicity may lead you think that the connection it makes between formal means and semantic goals is just a trick, or something that will work only for a very small class of simpleminded cases. It is very important, therefore, to be clear that the *kind* of connection between formal and semantics I have just illustrated can be made across a very wide spectrum of deductive inference. It is the business of an important part of logic—the part called "symbolic logic"—to find rules that can be stated purely formally and that correspond to deductive arguments. This branch of logic is highly developed and has found very powerful sets of rules. These rules need not be numerous—twenty-five is more than enough—but when applied successively they can generate all the arguments that one would need to use in mathematics. That is, their application is entirely formal, in exactly the sense that the ABIN system illustrates, but the interpretation might be a proof in geometry, arithmetic, or set theory.

We have, then, a clear way of seeing how a purely formal tool might achieve a semantic goal. The problem that might have sounded impossible is already solved, in a way that at least in principle is easily understood. There are, however, several questions that arise when we try to think about extending this core solution to more interesting cases.

Extending the Core

The solution as I have described it applies to sentences that are connected by deductive argument, that is, where one sentence is a conclusion deduced from other sentences. But we have seen that in order to pass a Turing test a machine would have to make at least two other kinds of connections among sentences. The question naturally arises, therefore, as to how we might extend the solution we have described to these other kinds of cases.

Let us recall that the second case we discussed was that of sentences related by inductive argument. The distinctive feature of this kind of argument is that the conclusion we draw does not absolutely have to be true, given our evidence; the conclusion only has to be well supported by our evidence. Now, even though the connection between premises and conclusion is not the tight one that it is in deductive arguments, we can still propose rules for drawing inductive conclusions. For example, suppose we have never opened a can of vegetables that did not contain what the label said it contained. I can, in fact, not recall ever having done so. So, I always expect a can to contain what the label says. This is, however, an induction: My evidence (never having opened a mislabeled can) certainly does not show that such a thing is impossible. There *could* be some mislabeled cans; I even suppose, on the strength of a version of Murphy's law (if something can go wrong, it sometimes will) that such a thing has happened. Thus, there is not a perfectly tight connection between my evidence and the conclusion that the can I am about to open contains what its label says it contains. It is nonetheless *always* all right for me to draw that conclusion. That is, it is thoroughly reasonable for me to expect the can to contain what the label says; a real doubt in an ordinary case would be evidence of mental imbalance. (I am assuming that there is no evidence to the contrary, that, for example, I did not buy this can cheap from a reduced-price rack that said, "Cans whose labeling is uncertain".)

If we now imagine trying to build a machine that would pass the Turing test, it would seem reasonable to give it an *inductive rule* that parallels the one I use. The case of the cans is, of course, a special case of a general rule, one that would go something like this: Whenever a large number of cases has exhibited a regularity (or, co-occurrence of several properties), and there have been no exceptions that you know of (no cases in which all but one of the properties did occur and the remaining one did not), draw the conclusion that the next case will exhibit the same regularity. To get a machine to apply this rule, it would have to recognize cases of regularities, and it would have to do so by formal means. This is no easy task, but we can sketch how, at least in principle, it might be done. We have been imagining all along in this chapter that a machine receives sentences as inputs and produces sentences as outputs. It is therefore natural to suppose that its background information has been given to it in the form of sentences. These will be composed of words, which can be recognized to be the same or different by formal means. Furthermore, it will have been indicated which sentences are about events occurring at roughly the same time and place and which sentences are about different situations. Implementing these ideas is not a trivial task (in fact, none of the tasks we are assuming here is trivial in practice) but it is not hard to see the general nature of what must be done. Think of someone describing the people at a gathering you had to miss. You may be told what so and so was wearing, that so and so got drunk, what so and so said, how so and so reacted. You have to know when the same person is still being described and when the reporter has moved on to someone different. To get you to know this, the reporter gives you cues, for example, repetitions of a person's name or pronouns. So, you can imagine that when a machine is given sentences that describe various people or events, there must be indicators of when the same person or event is being further described, and when something different is being described. Once we have this much, we can have our machine examine the *words* used in describing different cases and answer the question whether a certain word or phrase, say, "Label says 'peas'", is often found with another, say, "Can has peas", and whether or not there is ever a situation where the first is found together with "Can does not have peas". Once we see that a machine could answer questions like this on a purely formal basis, we also can see that it could apply the inductive rule given above to get from "Here is another case of a can labeled 'peas'" to "This can probably has peas in it."

Like the ABIN system, this inductive case is extremely simple. It does the job, however, of showing how there is no impossibility in the idea of a machine *following formal rules* in order to arrive at *a semantically correct* result. Let us take care to emphasize the point that the *correctness* that the rules guarantee here is not the correctness of the result but the correctness of the inductive reasoning. This is just as it is with us: Inductive reasoning can never guarantee its result, but nonetheless there is correct and incorrect inductive reasoning.

Let us turn to our third case. Here we imagined an interrogator asking for a story about what might have happened in a bar on a Saturday night. This case is unlike our previous examples, because there is no single response that is particularly likely to be given; many different stories might be told. A story might center on two people meeting and becoming romantically interested, or it might center on a fight or on the reactions to a televised sporting event. The variations could be enormous, and the limits depend only on the imaginations of the people involved.

It may seem that no rules could be relevant to a case with such a wide range of possibilities. There is something right about this appearance, and we shall return to it in the next section of this chapter. What we should notice here, however, is that there are still rules that must be observed in telling a story. To begin with something very simple, the names of the characters must stay the same. What they do must be possible and even probable in the situations they are in. Applying this rule depends on other rules. For example, suppose that every remembered case of people going to a bar (whether the memory be that of a machine or of a person) involves their ordering something to drink. Then a storyteller (whether machine or human) would be expected to include no sentence in the story that conflicts with a sentence that describes a person in a bar as having ordered a drink. When would there be such a conflict? Whenever a deductive or an inductive argument leads from the given sentence to "Person P has been in a bar for a while but has not ordered a drink." If a machine can recognize deductive and inductive arguments by purely formal means, then it can recognize conflicts by purely formal means; and if it can do that, it can follow, by purely formal means, a rule not to produce sentences that lead to conflicts. A positive rule can be phrased in terms of what is usual: Any sentence is allowed in a story if it attributes what usually happens, provided it does not conflict with anything previously said. The usual might be known either by being directly informed that such and such an association of features of a situation is usual or by reviewing remembered cases and finding that one feature goes with another in more than half of the cases. Either way, the usualness of an association can be recognized formally. So, a machine that proceeds formally can follow a rule that depends on recognizing usualness.

What I have been describing is not a recipe for producing deathless literature. But then, that is not something most people, including, I fear, myself, are able to produce. A machine that can proceed as I have described will produce a story that relates typical events and avoids logical errors and unexplained improbabilities. It would have to have a lot of information about what goes together; but then, so would any person who could respond to the request for a Saturday night bar story. The organization of this information, as we shall see later on, presents formidable difficulties. I am certainly not claiming to actually have a program that will succeed in writing a story that you cannot distinguish from a human production. Nonetheless, we can make out the general outline of a view that holds some promise of solving the key conceptual problem before us, that is, maintaining the kind of semantic relevance and plausibility that we find in stories, by using only formal means.

Open and Closed Tasks

In the last few paragraphs I have been trying to focus on the principle of the solution to creating AI that the sentence-processing approach offers. This has become more and more difficult as I have progressed, because the details of application that would be needed have been getting more and more complicated. It may even seem to some readers that the account I have been developing is getting less and less believable. Now there is a key addition that this account needs. Earlier, I was able to put it aside without difficulty, but now it has become pressing and the time has come to explicitly attend to it.

The point we must get clear about can be suggested by an experience that will be familiar to many from high school math courses. Once you learned a little, you were able to check a proof in the book to verify that it really did prove what it said it proved. Finding your own proof, on the other hand, was generally a much different and much more difficult task. Let us articulate part of what is involved in this difference by thinking about a very simple example. Can you turn a bear into a colt in four steps? That is, can you turn the word "bear" into the word "colt" by changing each letter just once and in such a way that you have an English word at each step? This is what I shall call an *open* task, because it is not "bound", that is, not hemmed in by rules that you can use to find the steps. You have to think of some words that differ from "bear" in only one letter (this itself is an open task; no rule leads you to any particular candidate word) and see if you can think of one after that that shares two letters with "colt". There is no rule for what word to start looking at, and there is no rule for which place in the word it would be useful to try a variation. By way of contrast, it is a much simpler task to determine that the sequence bear, beat, boat, bolt, colt is a solution. This task I shall call a *closed* task, because there is a rule for doing it: Match each entry with the entry of an English dictionary to check that they are all

English words, then list letters of adjacent ones, cross off letters that occur in both lists, and check that there is only one letter left in each list.

Open tasks are found everywhere. For example, suppose I ask you whether all bats are warm-blooded. You have to think of something that will convince you one way or another, but there are no rules you can go by to bring the relevant facts to mind. Perhaps, even so, it will occur to you that bats are mammals and that one of the distinguishing features of mammals is that they are warm-blooded. Once this has already occurred to you, you will be able to check to see that these facts support the conclusion that bats are warm-blooded. There is a general rule that covers the case, namely, "If all As are Bs and all Bs are Cs, then all As are Cs." But nothing like this covers your finding the relevant premises in the first place.

This example concerns a deductive connection, but the same point holds for inductions. For example, perhaps you want to buy a stereo. You do not want to feel you have paid too much, but you want one that will satisfy you for a long time. Now, within your experience there may be cases with relevant properties: cases where you were too conservative and were not satisfied later, and cases where you were extravagant and came to regret your choice. If you can think of the right experiences, perhaps you can form a strong inductive argument of this form. "Every time in the past that I chose an item with properties X, Y, and Z, I was unhappy later; every time that I chose an item with properties U, V, and W, I was satisfied. The Super-Vanadyne components have properties X, Y, and Z while the Vibra-True/Accu-Sone combination has properties U, V, and W. Therefore, I will be satisfied with the Vibra-True/Accu-Sone combination." This argument conforms to a proper inductive rule. But there is no rule by which you are going to find the right cases from your past that will make the premises of this argument true. You may, of course, find that they occur to you if you think hard about what has pleased you or made you feel you spent too much, but if they do it will not be because you followed a rule.

The telling of a Saturday night bar story involves many difficult open tasks. Toward the end of the previous section, I mentioned, for example, that a story should not contain any sentences that conflict with each other. I explained that conflicts could be recognized by purely formal means. While this is correct, it glosses over an important problem: Not only must the conflicts be checked and recognized, the conflicting claims must be found in the first place. Likewise, the evidence of the conflict can be checked by rules, once it is presented. But it is an open task to find the evidence.

We can sum up the discussion of this section so far by saying that we must find a formal means of performing open tasks, if we are ever to have a sentence-processing machine that passes the Turing test. Let us now try to think about how we might get this job done.

Here is an idea for one possible solution, which we may call "the exhaustive method". Since checking can be done by rules, we can just check everything. Suppose, for example, that an interrogator asks whether bats are warm-blooded. The open task is to find premises that will lead to either a yes or a no answer. The exhaustive method is to examine all the cases contained in memory and list all the properties that are recorded about bats and all the properties that are recorded about warm-blooded things. Then other instances of these properties can be looked up, and all their properties recorded. This process can be repeated indefinitely. Then there can be a comparison of the properties for each case to see whether there are properties that always go together. Whenever such an association of properties is found, the sentence can be formed that says that all things of one kind have a certain further property. Then that sentence can be tried out with other sentences to see if they yield a good argument for the statement "All bats are warm-blooded." If such a combination of sentences is found, the machine can produce a yes and stop; otherwise, it goes on until all combinations have been tried. If no success occurs, it produces a no and stops.

If there are several cases of mammals that have been recorded as being warm-blooded (and no cases that are mistakenly recorded otherwise) and if there are several cases of bats that have been recorded as being mammals, then the exhaustive method will eventually produce the desired yes answer. But this way of responding to our problem is not only exhaustive but exhausting. It is a method so inelegant that one could only laugh at it, or cry, if it were to be taken seriously. It is a practical impossibility for any kind of approximation to artificial intelligence, because it results in an enormous amount of wasted activity. (Just think of all the facts about possession of ribs, geographical distribution, eating habits, number of fingers, eye structure, and so on that would be duly reviewed but are irrelevant to the desired conclusion.) It is a theoretical mistake for at least two simple, connected reasons. First, at the time we started to record cases, we would already have to have decided what the properties are that we think will ever be relevant to any question that will ever come up. But this is not a list that we know how to limit. So, we could never be satisfied to stop listing properties for even the first case we wanted to record. Second, the more cases and the more properties we have in our list, the more comparisons are required by the exhaustive method. This method, in fact, leads to *exponential explosion.* The problem that this phrase refers to can be illustrated easily by thinking about the following task. Suppose there are four quarters, and the question is whether any two of them are exactly the same (that is, in date and mint mark). To find out, you have to compare coin 1 with each of coins 2, 3, and 4 (three comparisons), then coin 2 with coins 3 and 4 (two more), and finally coin 3 with coin 4, for a total of six comparisons. Now suppose the same question, but with eight coins. Here you need seven comparisons on the first round, then six, then five, four, three, two, and one, for a total of twenty-eight comparisons. The lesson to be learned from this example is that the number of comparisons increases much faster than the number of items to be compared; for, we doubled the number of items in the task, but the number of comparisons went from six to twenty-eight. When we consider applying the exhaustive method to any interesting case of artificial intelligence, we can see that the number of comparisons is going to be astronomical.

These are some of the reasons why it is generally agreed that the exhaustive method is worthless. Fortunately for the sentence processing approach, there is another method, *heuristic search.* The idea of this method is to cut down on the number of items that need to be reviewed, by giving a *rule* for proceeding that will usually find relevant properties fairly quickly. We can illustrate the idea by reference to a simple example from algebra. Since equals added to or subtracted from equals give equals, we can add or subtract *anything* to or from each side of an algebraic equation. We will often get a solution to a problem fairly quickly, however, if we add or subtract a term that is already present. Thus, although if we are given

$$x^2 + x - 2 = 4,$$

we can perfectly legally move to

$$x^2 + x - 2 + x^3 = 4 + x^3,$$

we will do much better to move to

$$x^2 + x - 6 = 0,$$

which we will do within four tries if we go by the suggested rule.

Another kind of heuristic search is possible if we classify properties. Thus, suppose we think to put in a rule to the effect that whenever the term "warm-blooded" occurs in a question, the first thing that should be examined is the circulatory system of whatever else the question is about. Suppose further that when we recorded information about bats, we divided it into facts about flight, facts about eating, facts about the circulatory system (one of which is that bats are warm-blooded), facts about mating behavior, and so on. Then we would be able to cut down the search to just seeing whether "warm-blooded" occurs in the list of properties of the circulatory system of the bat. Of course, if the warm-blooded character of bats is connected to something else, for example, "temperature information", then we will either save nothing or terminate the search with a wrong answer. But if we have been clever and careful about how we have classified our facts, we can expect a large reward in eliminating wasted comparisons.

The art of what I am calling heuristic search is highly developed. There are different strategies (we have seen two), and there is nothing easy about actually making it work in particular applications. To go into it any further, however, would be to begin to do artificial intelligence work proper. Here, what we need to do is emphasize a certain theoretical point and remind ourselves how it fits in. The point is that heuristic search allows for a machine to proceed *by rules* that are *purely formal.* So, whatever the practical interest or the practical problems may be, we have a theoretically satisfying solution to the problem for AI, as the sentence-processing approach understands it. Sentences are inputs; there are formal rules for processing them; where there are open tasks, there can be heuristic formal rules for bringing possible solutions to the fore and nonheuristic formal rules for checking the results. If we have the right deductive and inductive logical rules, we will avoid violations of good reasoning. If we have enough information and good heuristic rules, we will be able to find what is typical and what will work. When a sentence has been generated by heuristic rules and has been certified by logical rules, it can be printed out. These remarks explain how a machine that proceeds purely formally can achieve semantic goals. The remainder of the problem of making a machine that passes the Turing test is one of finding the right rules.

Why Sentence Processing?

In solving the problem of making formal machines achieve semantic goals, we have removed the main theoretical obstacle to developing AI through the sentence-processing approach. Removing one obstacle, however, does not provide a guarantee of success. One possibility is that the practical difficulties may be so many as to render the project unfeasible, even though theoretically possible. Another possibility is that there are other theoretical difficulties. These might be less obvious than the one we have just solved, but they might nonetheless prove fatal to the sentence-processing approach. In the next chapter, we shall in fact be looking at some arguments that are designed to demonstrate such difficulties. It is necessary, therefore, to ask what reasons we have for positively expecting the sentence-processing approach to work. In this section we will look at one such reason.

Before looking at the positive case, we should note that the sentence-processing approach is *not* supported by the "license for AI" that we described in Chapter 5. The argument of that chapter leads to the conclusion that our computers can calculate any calculable function and therefore, if we have a definite psychological theory, our computers can calculate its results. But that argument says nothing about what form a good psychological theory will take. It is, in fact, compatible with the "license for AI" that the only good theory of our behavior would be a theory of how our individual neurons and muscle cells act and react. So long as such a cell-by-cell theory gave a definite recipe for calculating its results, a computer could run a calculation and produce an output corresponding to the theory's prediction for each specified input. A cell-by-cell theory, however, is quite different from one that rests on a sentence-processing strategy. So, the view that the sentence-processing strategy will work does not follow from the argument for the "license". We must therefore look for a different sort of argument, if we are to find support.

There are many arguments that have been given in support of the sentence-processing strategy.[1] My aim here is not to improve on these, nor is it to offer a proof that this strategy must work. I will be satisfied with the more modest result of showing why it has at least *seemed* to many that it must work, and why proposals to abandon trying to make it work seem to have to give up something important.

An obvious point that is relevant here is reflected in the arrangements for the Turing test: Subjects in the test must use language. This means that subjects must in *some* way "process" sentences. That is, since they receive sentences as inputs, they must be able to *do* something with them that starts a series of changes leading to relevant outputs. Moreover, it is easy to see that the subject in a Turing test will not succeed if it responds only to features of sentences such as their length, or the time between their presentations. This is because these factors could be the same even though the interrogator is asking completely different questions. What I hope this makes clear is that subjects in a Turing test must, if they are to have any chance of success at all, respond to the input sentences *as sentences*, that is, they must respond to the components as different words (and to the fact that the same word is repeated). They must respond to differences of word order. For example, they must treat the piece of information that John loves Mary differently from the piece of information that Mary loves John. But if they are able to do this, then they *are* "processing" sentences at least at the beginning of whatever goes on in them.

This fact is connected with some others. One of these is that at least some of our intelligence seems to involve reasoning in language. So, for example, I may reason like this.

> If abstaining is regarded as a kind of voting, then a majority of voters is anything more than half of the number you get by adding the pros, plus cons, plus abstainers. In this case, since the abstainers add

> nothing to the pros, while still counting in the number of which more than half is needed for passage, an abstention has the same effect as a negative vote. But people may abstain because they think they do not understand the issue and that the best outcome will occur if the vote is left to a majority of those who do. So, an abstention ought not to count the same as a negative vote.
> Therefore, abstaining should not be regarded as a kind of voting, but rather as a case of not voting.

This is, of course, a final statement of a case for reducing the number of which greater than half is needed for passage of a motion. It seems, however, that it must parallel the process by which belief in the conclusion was arrived at. That is, it is hard to imagine how someone could have come to have this reason for this conclusion without having realized that (1) if abstainers are counted as voters, they have the same effect as negatives, and (2) abstentions ought not to have the same effect as negatives. Then, these realizations must have been connected in some way. If this much is accepted, then there is a strong suggestion that between the time when the question of what to do about abstentions arose and the time when this conclusion was reached, some sentences that express the meaning of (1) and (2) were internally produced and connected. Further, if this is granted, it seems natural to suppose that other sentences were reached and that the whole process is one of having rules that apply to linguistic structures produce further linguistic structures to which further rules are applied in turn.

The points I have just been making suggest the sentence-processing view, but they do not prove it, because they are compatible with an alternative, conflicting view. I do not want to give a careful outline of this view here, because it is complicated and because I will explain a more sober version of it later on. But it is important to be able to at least conceive of what an alternative to the sentence-processing view *could* be. So, I am going to be very crude and very metaphorical about it. I am not going to take the view in this form very seriously and I hope you will not either. All that the next paragraph is supposed to do is to show that there is some conceptual "space" for

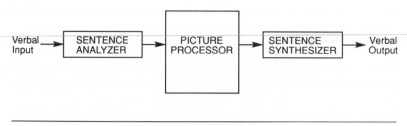

FIGURE 7.1

a view that is compatible with the facts mentioned so far, yet differs from the sentence-processing view.

I will call this alternative view the "picture-processing myth". According to this myth, there is a front-end sentence processor whose output is pictures. (See Figure 7.1.) This processor does indeed respond to grammar. It associates some words with pictorial elements that it gets from memories of having perceived things that the words refer to, and then it arranges those elements. Part of the arrangement goes according to the directions provided by other words. Thus, "John was standing in his house" might produce a picture of John in a standing posture in a typical room, while "John was standing outside his house" might produce a picture of John in a standing posture with his feet on grass and the exterior of a house looming in the background. Other parts of the arrangement depend on word order; thus "John loves Mary" might produce a picture of John looking tenderly at Mary, while "Mary loves John" might produce a picture with the tender look going in the other direction. "Mary and John love each other" might then produce a picture of Mary and John looking tenderly at each other.

The picture-processing myth continues by supposing that once sentences have been transformed into pictures, the processing obeys rules that are defined entirely by reference to pictures. This is not easy to imagine, but the following example will help. We have a lot of experience in walking around objects while looking at them. For example, if you walk from the front yard of a house around to the back yard, you may be vaguely aware of how the house looks from various points on the journey. Now, suppose you have a picture of a house and the question is how the situation in the picture will look to someone standing at a different place. We can imagine that you find the answer by having your brain start with the picture and change in the way it usually changes when walking around objects that look like those in the picture. This would be a case of operating directly on the picture, and not on sentences that might describe the things depicted.

The third part of the picture-processing myth requires another processor, this time going from pictures to sentences. When the last picture that is needed has been produced, this output-end processor converts it into sentences, by procedures that are the reverse of those described for the front-end processor.

As I indicated, we will eventually discuss a more serious alternative to the sentence-processing view. The business of this chapter, however, is to clarify the strengths of the sentence-processing view. We can further this project by considering some objections that a proponent of sentence processing might naturally raise against the picture-processing myth. Perhaps the weakest objection of this kind is that we do not yet have a very clear idea of what the rules or methods of picture processing might be. A more significant point is that the picture-processing idea has no obvious application once we come to abstract concepts. For example, what is a picture of an abstention supposed to look like? Or a picture of the fact that abstentions ought not to have the same effect as negative votes? Further, the myth has to allow for a good deal of sentence processing anyway, that is, at the beginning and the end. It seems terribly inelegant to admit that there is that much sentence processing and then propose that, in addition, there comes a kind of processing of whose workings we have little idea anyway. The more elegant alternative is to say that we start with sentence processing and we continue with it right up to the sentences we give as output.

These are significant objections, but it is not too hard to see something a little stronger. To introduce this further point, let us allow our imaginations a really free rein in an attempt to imagine how the picture-processing myth might be worked out. Let us imagine that "All bats are mammals" gets processed into a large picture with other mammals—elephants, lions, cats, dogs, antelopes, and so on—that has a disproportionately large bat right in the center. Let us further imagine that "All mammals are warm-blooded" gets pictorialized in this way: All pictures of mammals that are produced or maintained during the next five minutes have lines on them where their main arteries and veins might be, and these lines are glowing (representing radiating heat). Now, if these methods of depicting are in place, it is automatic that the large bat in the center will have glowing blood vessels. That pictorial result will be what corresponds to the conclusion that bats are warm-blooded. All we need is an output processor that will use the inverse of the input processor's methods and take this pictorial result into the words "All bats are warm-blooded."

This example may add some content to the picture-processing myth, but the proponent of sentence processing will not be impressed. To see why, let us begin with a point that Wittgenstein made about pictures and images.[2] Taken by itself, the image of a bat with glowing lines could be a picture of anything. It could be all that is needed to represent "All mammals are warm-blooded." But it could just as well be a representation of a condition in which you will never, ever find a bat; and that condition could be warm-blooded, or in the process of electrocution, or surrounded by a glowing net, or surrounded by the hand of Satan or—quite literally—anything you can imagine. If we are to take it as representing "All bats are warm-blooded", that is only because we suppose that the image of the bat represents bats and the image of the glowing net represents vessels with warm blood in them. But *now these elements of the picture are being taken to be functioning as words.* All the input processor has done is to *translate* "bat" into a picture of a bat and "warm-blooded" into a picture of a glowing network. But the rules for operating with these pictures must be exactly parallel to those for operating with the words "bat" and "warm-blooded", if the pictures are to represent what we are supposing they represent. Apart from being cumbersome, the switch to pictures is no more significant than the switch from thinking in English to thinking in French. Finally, if there are rules for operating with the words "bat" and "warm-blooded", then we can express these in a computer program and get the computer to operate on them in the same way we do.

Let us sum up by stating in literal terms the lessons we have learned from our myth and our earlier discussion. If the sentence-processing approach is misguided, then either artificial intelligence is not possible at all, or it is possible only by simulating our operation on a cell-by-cell basis,[3] or it is possible only by some genuinely alternative kind of processing. Such an alternative must

> Take sentences as inputs;
> Derive a nonsentential result from input sentences;
> Work on this nonsentential result in a way that
> does not reduce to the sentence-processing
> approach in however subtle a way; and
> Yield sentences as outputs.

As long as it is not clear that there is an alternative view that meets these requirements, there will be reason to pursue the sentence-processing approach.

Chapter 8

Doubts About Sentential AI

In this chapter, we are going to look at some problems for the sentence-processing approach to AI just described. These problems are not intended as objections to AI in every form; that is, they are not intended to show that there could never be a device made of electronic hardware that could pass the Turing test. Instead, they support the view that even if there could be *some* kind of artificially intelligent device, it could not work only, or mainly, by processing sentences. Since we need to keep this point clearly in mind, it will be convenient to have a short phrase that will abbreviate "the sentence-processing approach to AI". I shall use the term "sentential AI" for this purpose.

The problems we shall review are of three kinds. The first is that sentential AI has failed to live up to expectations, and that the nature of the failure does not point to optimism for future development. The second can for the moment be simply introduced by its name, "the knowledge access problem". We shall see how this problem arises directly out of the strategy for sentential AI given in Chapter 7. Finally, we shall look at some physiological facts. These show that there are differences between the operation of our brains and the operation of computers whose design seems most natural for sentential AI.

Dreyfusian Doubts

In this section I will be presenting an argument that occurs in several works by Hubert L. Dreyfus and, more recently, by him and his brother, Stuart E. Dreyfus.[1] The Dreyfuses have put forward several interesting arguments about AI, but I am not going to try to survey them all. Instead, I shall concentrate here on just one of them. I shall, moreover, not review the many cases that they describe in order to support their conclusion. The interested reader can find these cases in the books listed in note 1. What I do want to do here is only to make clear what *kind* of evidence it is that the Dreyfuses provide, and to state exactly what this evidence shows.

Let us begin with a fact that is sometimes clearly recognized within the sentential AI research community.[2] This is that terms and names of programs in AI have often had a wildly optimistic character. Perhaps the most famous example is the "General Problem Solver". This sounds like a program that you could turn loose on more or less any old problem with hope of success, but in fact it is no such thing. Similarly, the "Teachable Language Comprehender", does not comprehend language. Such terms as "natural language interface", "story-understanding module", and "ego loop" all have suggestions that go far beyond actual performance.

The optimism of AI researchers can be shown not only by looking at the names they give to programs but also by comparing their predictions with observed accomplishments. Turing made a prediction in 1950, to the effect that by the year 2000 there would be a machine that would fool interrogators 30 percent of the time. Since we are getting close to the turn of the century, but not close to any such performance, one does not hear this particular expectation repeated any more. The tradition that Turing started, however, that is, of making predictions that later had to be abandoned, has proved to be a long and vigorous one.

Taken by themselves, these remarks show very little. It is, after all, healthy for researchers in a field to be optimistic. They are not likely to succeed in discovering very much if they are not hopeful. If the predictions of sentential AI researchers have proved much too optimistic, that may show only that the work is harder than was thought. We certainly are not entitled to draw the conclusion that the work *cannot* succeed.

The Dreyfuses, however, find a characteristic and disturbing pattern in the failed predictions, and this pattern provides a more serious argument. The optimistic predictions for sentential AI are not usually drawn out of thin air; they are made on the basis of some actual achievements. These achievements, however, usually lie in the early stages of the development of a new idea. The disturbing pattern is that even though new ideas and new techniques for producing results in AI have genuine interest and surprising successes, their promise does not pan out as time goes on. Instead, attempts to develop and extend a new idea lead to difficulties, which prove to be ever more complicated. Researchers come to doubt the promise of the new technique and eventually abandon it in favor of some newer idea.

The Dreyfuses do not merely observe that this pattern of development exists; they have an explanation for it. They hold that the early successes of new strategies in AI are explained by the fact that when an idea is tried out for the first time, a lot of simplifying assumptions are made. Researchers consider particularly simple cases, in the hope that they can find out whether the new idea will work at all. They assume that if the idea works in the simple cases, they will be able to gradually add to it so as to handle the more complex cases. The problem, however, is that the simplifying assumptions turn out to be essential to the working of the new idea. The result is that, when they are removed, we find that the new idea does not prove helpful after all.

The idea of beginning with simple cases is, in general, an attractive one. People have said, for example, that if Galileo had tried to begin by explaining the complicated case of the motion of falling leaves, instead of balls rolling down an inclined plane, he would never have discovered anything. But let us look at one of the cases the Dreyfuses cite, to see how beginning with simple cases might not be such a good idea in AI research. This is the work of Schank and Abelson on story-understanding programs. We have encountered this work before, in Chapter 2. You may recall that John Searle used it as the basis for the arrangement of his Chinese Room. In Chapter 2 we naturally followed Searle in assuming that Schank's work was a complete success, for his argument was supposed to show that *even so*, there would be no understanding of the story. Now, however, we want to pay attention to the actual limitations of the efforts to make programs give good responses to questions about stories.

Let us recall that Schank's method was to give the computer a script that contains a description of typical relations among things that are often found together. For example, in a newspaper story about an accident, we will often find mention of cars, victims, weather conditions, ambulances, hospitals, when people were released from the hospital, injuries, allegations of blameworthiness, and speeds. But not all of the facts about each of these things will be mentioned in every accident report. Since an accident-report script contains typical relations among such things, it has information that can fill in what a particular report does not provide. That is why it can have some success in answering questions about items in a story that are not explicitly answered in the story itself. It is this ability that Schank regards as indicating that the computer understands the story.

What the Dreyfuses point out is that the success that we can achieve by this method depends on restricting the stories we use to very typical ones about very stereotypical situations. The moment we introduce something unusual, the program will fail miserably. Let us have an illustration of the kind of difficulty that arises. If you read in the newspaper that no date had been given by which some accident victims were expected to be released from the hospital, you would probably conclude that their injuries had been serious. But you would not draw this conclusion if the story also contained the remark, "The hospital press agent said that there had been difficulty with the computer in the records department." You would think that, although the accident victims *may* have been seriously injured, it is also possible that they have already been released, but that this fact has not been properly recorded. Now, a program that has information only about the typical relations among items in an accident scenario will completely miss the relevance of the computer difficulty in the records department. So, when faced with a story that is just a little more complicated than the ones it succeeds on, it will fail.

There is a very natural reply to make here. It is that we can easily restore the competence of the program to answer questions correctly. All we have to do is to add another script, say, a record-keeping script that will contain information about who gives information to whom, how it is recorded, and so on. Then, when this script is connected to the accident script, the resulting program will enable the machine to appreciate the relevance of computer breakdown in the records department and to conclude that the lack of an expected release date is, in this case, not an indication of serious injury.

The Dreyfuses are not impressed by responses of this kind. The problem they point out is that there are many, many special circumstances that might be relevant to the scene covered by a script. The point of a story about an accident—and therefore the right answers to questions about it—might be affected by whether the victims are acquainted, by the make of the car ("Uninsured Ferrari Totalled: Owner Under Observation"), by the particular day or place, by the fame of a victim, or by anything else you can imagine. For this reason, a general solution to the problem of dealing with unusual circumstances cannot be covered by adding one script: There will have to be special additional scripts for each of the many kinds of complication. Furthermore, there may be interactions among sets of special circumstances, and these will have to be provided for by carefully organizing the results of two or more additional scripts being called upon at the same time.

If we were to try to add to the original script idea to get a wider class of stories understood, we would have to increase the complexity of the original script by adding more scripts. But it is not merely additional complexity that is the main problem we need to see here. It is also true that the new scripts, like the original one, would have to be written by people. These people would have to use their intelligence to think up what special circumstances might be relevant, and how they should be handled. This begins to sound like the hopelessly impractical procedure of the Block machine in Chapter 1. But, once again, this is not the central problem on which we must focus. The central problem is the one that illustrates the pattern that the Dreyfuses find repeated again and again. This is that the script idea will work for simple cases, but it contains absolutely nothing that helps to generalize it to more complex cases, no kernel of an idea that shows how special cases can be handled without writing a new script for them. *It is the fact that we restrict the stories to simple, very stereotypical cases that permits the appearance that we are succeeding at something.* The success essentially depends on the restriction. So, the success does not show us how to begin to make intelligence; it does not show us a method that we can improve and refine by adding complications.

It shows us only a method whose conditions for (limited) success are directly undercut by the very fact that we loosen the restrictions and try to handle a wider class of stories.

The scripts of Schank and Abelson were only an illustration of a pattern. The Dreyfuses intend the results of their discussion here to be taken generally. That is, they are explaining the success of early work with new ideas in AI by the fact that simplifying restrictions are made, and they are explaining the later disappointments by claiming that the early successes *essentially depend* on those restrictions. If this is right, then we cannot regard early successes as encouraging first steps toward artificial *intelligence*. For we must remember (from Chapter 1) that a key property of intelligence is flexibility, that is, the ability to cope with new situations in general and not merely with those that satisfy some simplifying restrictions.

We should stop here for a moment and take a little time to think about the character of the argument so far. First, let us notice that it is an *inductive* argument. This means that it is not intended to be conclusive in the way that mathematical proofs are. It is somewhat more like an argument for practicing music. There is no mathematical proof that you will not be a great musician if you do not practice, but that does not mean that there are not good reasons to practice. If we are going to think of the Dreyfuses' argument as an inductive one, however, we have to be sure that we understand *which* inductive argument it is. It is *not* merely that sentential AI has not succeeded up to now and so probably will never do so. This is not a good argument; after all, no team has won the Superbowl three times, but that is not much of a reason for thinking such a thing will never happen. A hundred years ago, no one had been able to make a heavier-than-air flying machine; but that would not have been a good reason for thinking that there could never be one. The Dreyfuses' argument must instead be taken this way: Attempts to produce sentential AI have all depended essentially on simplifying restrictions; but intelligence requires flexibility, which means that it cannot depend on restrictions; and therefore, the attempts that have so far been made to produce sentential AI have represented no progress at all toward their goal. Then the general inductive point is that we have reason not to expect success from an enterprise that is making no progress toward its goal.

Historical Note: It is interesting to observe that Descartes, who gave essentially the same test as Turing, recognized something rather like part of the Dreyfuses' point. The relevant passage is this one, which occurs shortly after the passage quoted in Chapter 1.

> Although machines can perform certain things as well as or perhaps better than any of us can do, they infallibly fall short in others, by which means we may discover that they did not act from knowledge, but only from the disposition of their organs. For while reason is a universal instrument which can serve for all contingencies, these organs have need of some special adaptation for every particular action. From this it follows that it is morally impossible that there should be sufficient diversity in any machine to allow it to act in all the events of life in the same way as our reason causes us to act.

That is, a bunch of devices (compare scripts, programs) that depend on special circumstances do not explain flexibility, however clever or interesting or useful in their own way they may be. Trying to obtain flexibility by combining special-purpose devices would require there to be an unfeasably large number of them.

In drawing this conclusion it is very important to realize that we are *not* saying that research in sentential AI is uninteresting or that no use can be made of it or that there is not progress in *some* direction. (Such a conclusion would certainly be ungrateful, to say the least, in light of the fact that this book was written on a word-processing computer!) AI researchers have learned from mistakes, introduced new ideas, and made practical innovations. The level of chess playing has improved. The conclusion to which the argument we have been reviewing leads is only that advances in the field of sentential AI research do not amount to progress *toward* the *specific* goal of producing artificial intelligence. They do not give us reason to think that progress is being made toward making a machine that will do well on the Turing test.

A frequent reaction to presentations of this argument of the Dreyfuses' is that AI is a young science and we must just wait longer for it to succeed. If this is all that is said, the proper response is that the Dreyfuses are certainly not drawing any conclusions from the mere fact of AI failures; their argument is instead based on a recurring pattern that those failures exhibit. Sometimes, however, it is added that the Dreyfuses' argument is not a *mathematical* refutation of the possibility of sentential AI. This is true, but it is often not appreciated how extremely weak this response is. The lack of a mathematical refutation is precisely no reason for thinking that sentential AI is possible: The proper conclusion would be that we have no mathematical proof one way or the other and some inductive reason against the possibility of sentential AI. To the absence of a mathematical refutation it is often added that the Wright brothers also were doubted in their day, but they succeeded in the end. This addition, however, trades on a very biased choice of analogy. There were many who noticed that birds flap their wings and who tried, quite unsuccessfully, to build flying machines that worked by flapping. The Dreyfuses are not arguing that it is impossible to produce artificial intelligence by any means whatsoever; they are arguing that the sentence-processing approach to AI will not work. We are not entitled to assume that the sentence-processing approach is the airfoil of AI when the Dreyfuses are arguing that it may be the flapper of AI instead.

We should take care to notice that the Dreyfuses' argument is not directly based on the properties of computing machines. The facts that they are made of silicon chips or that they run on electricity or that they move from one definite, discrete state to another are not made use of in the argument. The assumption the Dreyfuses are attacking is that AI can be achieved by a sentence-processing strategy. Such strategies depend on rules that retrieve stored information that can syntactically interact with other retrieved information to produce a useful output. The Dreyfuses' point is that you can get such a strategy to work pretty well in a limited area but that the success depends essentially on the limitations. So, when you try to widen the area, instead of building comfortably out from a secure foundation, you instead undermine the conditions that were necessary for the original success.

This last observation brings us very close to a somewhat different problem for sentential AI, which we will now explore. I should repeat here, however, that the Dreyfuses have other arguments to offer. We shall return to one of these below; the remainder can be found in the works cited.

The Knowledge Access Problem

In Chapter 7, I showed how sentential AI leads directly to the need to deal with open tasks by syntactical means, and I introduced some ideas about how to do this. I accentuated the positive and focused on explaining how the solution was supposed to work. The argument we must now consider aims to show that, after all, no solution will actually succeed.

Let us briefly recall one of our examples from the last chapter. We supposed that a question had been asked about whether all bats are warm-blooded. We further supposed that a machine had information in its memory that was relevant to answering this question, namely, the sentences that all bats are mammals and that all mammals are warm-blooded. If these sentences occur together in an argument whose conclusion is "All bats are warm-blooded", it will be an easy task for the machine to formally evaluate the combination as valid, and to answer the question by printing a yes. The hard part, however, is to get these two pieces of relevant information retrieved from memory, and retrieved at the same time.

The guaranteed solution was to bring every pair, then every triplet, then every quadruplet, then every greater n-tuplet of stored sentences together with each of the answers to the question and evaluate the result for validity. This, however, leads to exponential explosion, just as in the problem of finding coins of the same date. The result of adopting it would lead to billions of unproductive operations. It was for this reason that it was necessary to introduce heuristic rules and clever ways of classifying or organizing information.

The criticism that we now want to review holds that heuristic rules and clever classifications cannot succeed in solving the problem to which they are a response. The problem is that there are two aims that are in fundamental conflict. On the one hand, the point of having more knowledge is to increase the ability to respond relevantly, and correctly, to new situations. For this purpose it is not enough merely to possess some knowledge. It must be possible to bring that knowledge to bear on a new situation. It must be brought out of storage and put into use. This need points in the direction of letting a new situation call up as much knowledge as possible; but this is what leads to the exponential explosion problem. So, the fundamental point of the methods we introduced in Chapter 7 is to cut down on the amount of knowledge that is retrieved in any one case. This, however, leads to the opposite problem, namely, a tendency toward failure to make use of relevant information even though it is stored in a machine's memory.

A natural response to this situation is to try to effect a compromise. There are reasons, however, why this is difficult. Any arbitrary rule for searching, or any arbitrary way of organizing information, will work wonderfully in some situations but dismally and stupidly in other situations. Perhaps the simplest such strategy, and the easiest to think about, is randomizing. That is, suppose we have a rule that tells a machine to retrieve the first one hundred sentences it comes to on a purely random search of memory. Now, if the relevant information is in these sentences, we will have solved whatever problem we had in a very short search. It is obvious, however, that this is not a good strategy to use, since most of the time, we would miss relevant information entirely.

Random selection can be regarded as absence of a genuine search strategy. Surely, we can use our intelligence to pick out rules for searching that will improve on random search. This idea is indeed correct, but it leads to the following problem. The solutions that should be counted as clever solutions, or good solutions, to a problem depend on what the problem is. Therefore, when we improve on randomness, we can improve only *in relation to some class of problems*. For problems outside this class, our "clever solution" may be even worse than randomness, for it might even guarantee that a certain piece of information will *never* be retrieved. It is, however, built into the Turing test that *any* sort of question may be asked. We do not know in advance what interrogators will think of. So, we do not know which class of problems we should pick as the ones for which we should build in clever solutions. If we happen to guess wrong, the

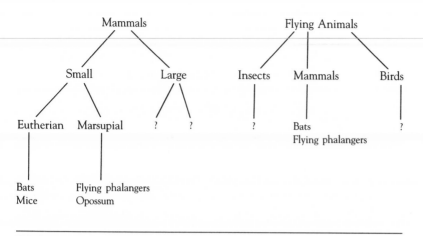

FIGURE 8.1

clever solution we build in for one class of problems may result in very inadequate answers to the questions that actually get asked.

One possible response to this is to say that computers are getting larger and faster and that we just have to wait until we have enough capacity to build in clever solutions to all kinds of conceivable questions. Then we will have a machine that passes the Turing test. This, however, is almost equivalent to the desperate expedient of the Block machine that we discussed in Chapter 1. It improves on it a little, because it allows solutions for classes of questions, not just individual ones. But there are still too many classes of questions for us to expend the effort to work out clever solutions to them all. The reason is that there is no one way of carving up questions into classes. To see why, consider the organizational trees in Figure 8.1. The first of these trees might be helpful if we were asked to name some small eutherian mammals. The second would be less helpful for that, but more helpful if we were asked for some mammals that fly. If we knew which question we would get, we would know which scheme to use; but if we did not, committing ourselves to one scheme might put us at a disadvantage. Both questions, however, could be regarded as questions about small mammals and both could be regarded as questions about flying mammals. There is no intelligent way to decide what class we should put the questions in, unless we already know which classification scheme we are using in our storage of information, and therefore, which kind of organization of the questions will be a better match to our apparatus for generating answers. But if we do not know what the questions are going to be, we will not have any good way of deciding on the best scheme for trying to generate answers.

The moral of this simple illustration is that mere increase of size or speed is not an intelligent approach to the knowledge access problem, that is, the problem of finding *relevant* information without spending most of the time reviewing irrelevancies. Once this point is appreciated, an alternative response may be sought. One such response might be to make a virtue of necessity and settle for clever solutions to specific problems. If we can just make sure that only one sort of question is asked, we may be quite successful at organizing information storage to produce ready answers. Now, this may be exactly the right strategy to adopt from a commercial point of view. Let us be sure to notice, however, that from the point of view of our guiding problem, it amounts to giving up. That problem was to make a machine that could pass the Turing test. That means a machine that is flexible. To restrict our problem area is exactly the same as abandoning the aim of producing flexibility, and is, therefore, to give up trying to produce a machine that might pass the Turing test.

These remarks ought to remind you of the Dreyfuses' argument in the previous section, and this is a good place to return to their work and deepen our understanding of their case. We saw, let us recall, that AI research has exhibited a pattern of interesting ideas that turn out to depend essentially on simplifying restrictions. We now have in hand an explanation of *why* this pattern is found. Restricting the scope of possible questions does allow for clever solutions to the knowledge access problem. Relaxing the restrictions requires adding more clever solutions to a wider range of problems. This is feasible for a while. But when we try to lift the initial restrictions so that we can approach the flexibility of human performance, the problem becomes hopelessly complex. We have not got the resources to work out clever solutions to everything, and relying on getting a *very* clever solution to one thing exposes us to stupidity on something else.

There is another fact to which the Dreyfuses call attention and that will enable us to put the point here in a slightly different way. Under some condition or other, anything we know may be relevant to anything else we know. This perhaps can be most easily seen in the case of jokes, which often depend for their interpretation on bringing together knowledge that is not typically related. (Remember, the interrogators in Turing tests could perfectly well tell a joke. They could not wait for laughter since laughter requires a body and cannot be conveyed on a printer—typing "Ha, ha, ha" is not laughing. But they could [1] expect some printed reaction indicating that the joke had been understood, for example, "Very funny" or "You are such a wit", and [2] they could ask for an explanation of why the joke is supposed to be funny.) In the terms of our recent discussion, this means that a solution to the knowledge access problem within sentential AI must allow for bringing any combination of sentences that we know together under some conditions or other—that is, under conditions in which they would all be relevant. But the only ways we have of dealing with knowledge access depend on clever solutions that find special combinations relevant to particular kinds of problems. This discrepancy between the demands of the knowledge access problem and the means we have for dealing with it amount to an explanation of why the history of AI that the Dreyfuses detail has exhibited the pattern they find.

One response that may seem attractive here is to argue that there *must* be a solution to the problem, even though it is not obvious, because WE are intelligent and so WE must have solved the problem. If this does seem attractive, however, it is only because it is being assumed that WE are sentential processors. We did indeed see some reason to suppose this at the end of the last chapter. In the following section, however, we will find some facts about ourselves that point in the opposite direction.

Some Brain Facts

Some of the arguments that occur in the remainder of this book depend on a certain amount of background information about the brain. In this section, I want to go just far enough into the construction and operation of the brain to provide this required background. This is not too difficult a task, but we must clearly understand the following warning. What we need to take from the brain sciences in order to continue our discussion of the possibility of artificial intelligence is relatively simple. But the sciences themselves, like their object of study, are extremely complex. If we were to be just a little more detailed than I intend to be here, we would find all kinds of exceptions, doubts, disagreements, and complications—not to mention the complexity that grows out of the large number of elements in the system. Moreover, the fact that some phenomenon does not seem to be important now does not mean that it will not be realized to be important in the future. Fortunately for us, however, there is a level at which there is an agreed upon general picture of how most of the brain's elements that are relevant to our behavior work most of the time. It is a picture that those who currently debate the possibility of various kinds of AI agree in presupposing. This common ground is what I shall be describing.

The parts of the brain with which we must become familiar are *neurons* and *synapses*. Neurons are individual cells and they have nuclei, metabolic functions, and boundaries just like other cells. Estimates of the number of these cells in the brain run from a hundred billion (10^{11}) to a hundred trillion (10^{14}).[3] With possibly a few exceptions, neurons have a direction: They receive input at one end and deliver output at the other end. Both input and output ends generally have many branches—a tree with a many-fingered root system connected by the trunk to its many-fingered crown is an appropriate image (except, of course, for size). The familiar fact that trees take in water and nutrients through their roots and give out oxygen through the leaves on their branches can remind us of the directionality of neurons, and we can thus speak of their input ends as "roots" and their output ends as "branches". (See Figure 8.2.)

Where do the roots of neurons get their input, and where do the branches send their output? Some neurons get their input from special sensory cells, for example, those in the retina of the eye, or those in the inner ear or nasal passages. And some neurons give their output to muscle cells, making them contract and causing parts of the body to move. But the vast majority of inputs to neurons come from other neurons, and the vast majority of outputs likewise go to affect other neurons. In thinking about the way neurons are organized, we should not think of them laid end to end in a single line. Neither, however, should we think of them as a disorganized mass like the tangle of trees that you can see pressed up against a bridge pylon after

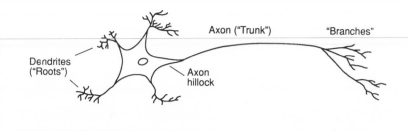

FIGURE 8.2 Generic drawing of a neuron

a spring flood. A useful image would be a pile of forests layered one on top of another. This image will be especially useful if we remember that not all trees are the same size or shape; there are, for example, relatively compact ones, like Christmas trees, and others that spread widely, like an oak. Some are short, some are taller (and so would reach all the way through one layer to the next one). We can also increase the realism of the image significantly if we allow some trees to be upside down. This image of layers of forests allows us to picture the fact that many cells influence many other cells. In such a pile of forests, the branches of each tree can lie near the root systems of several other trees, and the root system of each tree can lie near the branches of many others, but there can still be a certain orderliness to the arrangement, and limits to the region of influence of any single element.

The branches of neurons lie close to the roots of the neurons they affect but generally do not actually touch them. Between a small area of a branch and small area of a root (or the cell body) lies a little gap called a synapse (Figure 8.3). Charged particles emitted from a small area of a branch can cross this gap and have an effect on another neuron when they arrive at the corresponding area on the surface of its root system. The number of synapses through which a neuron receives stimulation from the branches of other neurons varies with different types of neurons, but the range for the number of synapses possessed by the root system of a single neuron is in the thousands to tens of thousands.

If the root system of a neuron receives enough stimulation from the branches of nearby neurons, it will send an electrochemical signal down its *axon* to its own branches. This signal is an all-or-none affair, so it is quite *unlike* the continuous process by which water moves from

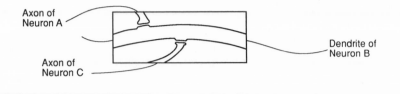

FIGURE 8.3 Close-up drawing of some synapses

the roots to the branches of a tree. Instead, it is discontinuous, like a bullet, or better, a series of bullets, moving from gun to target. For this reason, the signaling along the axon of a neural cell is generally called *firing*. The *amount* of signal—the size of the bullet, so to speak—is the same in each firing. The *rate* of firing, however, is variable, with the range being from zero to about a thousand times a second. The speed of the signal along the axon is in the range of ½ to 120 meters a second.

I said that a neuron will fire if it gets "enough" stimulation from the branches of nearby neurons. Let us look into this and see in a bit more detail just what determines whether a neuron will fire. There are several points to keep in mind.

- A high rate of firing in a neuron will produce more effect in the neurons it synapses onto than will a low rate.
- Some synapses are excitatory and some are inhibitory. Suppose the synapse between Neuron A and Neuron B in Figure 8.3 is excitatory, and that the one between Neuron C and Neuron B is inhibitory. This means that an increase in activity in Neuron A will make it more likely that Neuron B will fire, and that an increase in activity in Neuron C will make it less likely that Neuron B will fire. In the remaining points, I shall refer only to excitatory synapses, but analogous points having, so to speak, the opposite sense, hold for inhibitory synapses.
- Synapses vary in their efficiency, in comparison both with each other and with themselves at

different times. That is, their efficiency can
change in the course of time. By "efficiency" I
mean the amount of effect that activity in a
branch on one side of a synapse has on the
neuron on the other side of the synapse. A low
rate of firing in a neuron with a highly efficient
synapse onto, say, Neuron B might produce the
same effect as a high rate of firing in a neuron
whose synapse onto Neuron B was of low
efficiency.

• Whether a neuron will fire depends on conditions
at the place where the axon is joined to the cell
body. This is called the *axon hillock*. Different
synapses lie at different distances from this area,
and it takes some time for a disturbance at a
synapse on a root to travel through the cell and
reach the axon hillock. How much time depends
on how far away the synapse lies. The speed of
this process is slower than the transmission of
signals down an axon when a neuron fires.

Significance of These Facts

These remarks about the brain lead to some very significant conclusions, which we should now make explicit. The fact that firings of a
given neuron are the same size and are discontinuous suggests a "digital" or discrete-state operation. This fits in with the requirement of
Turing machines (see Chapter 5) that they be definitely in one state
or another at each time. Everything else about the operation of the
brain, however, suggests exactly the opposite. Rates of firing can vary
continuously, as does the distance between synapses and the axon
hillock. A neuron may receive input from hundreds of other neurons,
at thousands of synapses. The effect produced at the axon hillock of,
say, Neuron B of Figure 8.3 by a single firing of Neuron A is, therefore, no more than the effect produced on you by a single voice in a
large crowd. Moreover, because the effects of inputs arrive at the
axon hillock at different times, we must not compare the situation to

an organized crowd led by a conductor but instead to a disorganized crowd in which people speak at times unrelated to the speaking of others. What the axon hillock is responding to, therefore, is not discrete signals, but the average excess of recent excitatory activity over inhibitory activity. If this average excess is high for a time, the neuron will fire rapidly; if it is not, the neuron will fire less rapidly, or not at all. Both the average excess and the firing rate are continuously variable quantities. Thus, the effective operations of neurons are continuous and therefore quite unlike the discrete state operations of the switches of digital computers.

There is a further point that is closely related to what we have just seen. It is not only the individual units in a digital computer that are effectively in one position at each time. The state of the whole machine is determined by the states of all its units, and the whole machine must be in one definite state at a time. In order for this requirement to be met, the units must be synchronized. That is, as far as their effective operation goes, any changes of state that they undergo must happen at the same time. They must, so to speak, march along together, taking their steps at the same time, like the members of a drill team. In contrast, the firings of neurons in the brain are like a bunch of strollers whose footsteps are taken at any time they please. There is no synchronization, that is, there are no time divisions with sharp boundaries that make all the brain units to be effectively in just one state during each division.

There is another point of difference between brains and computers that we should know about. I mentioned that the speed of transmission along an axon was in the range of ½ to 120 meters a second. This may seem rapid, but it is tortoise-slow in comparison to the speed of electrical transmission in a wire. The transmission of disturbance from a synapse on a root to an axon hillock is slower still. There is also a delay of about 1/1000th of a second for charged particles emitted by a branch to cross a synapse. Finally, a neuron cannot fire indefinitely fast; the upper limit, we said, is about a thousand times a second. Relative to, say, the speed at which we can type or talk, these processes in neurons are very rapid. In comparison to the speed at which elements in a contemporary digital computer work, however, they are very slow—on the order of a million times slower.

These remarks about times lead to a further conclusion. We can begin to see what it is by elaborating on our analogies of the drill team and the strollers. All the units in a digital computer that are going to change in order to change the computer's whole state change effectively at the same time. Since this is analogous to members of a drill team taking one step together, let us just call the time between changes "one step". This is a fixed time in computers, so there will be a definite number of steps that it takes to solve a problem. This number will be equal to the time it takes to reach a solution divided by the time required for each step. Now, things are a lot messier when we come to the unsynchronized neurons in the brain, and because of the lack of synchronization we cannot give a neat definition of "one step". Let us recall our analogies, however. We could listen to the resounding clomp of a drill team's collective footstep and count off the number of steps it takes the team to get from one place to another. With a bunch of strollers generally moving in the same direction, we could not listen to or watch their feet and count off a definite number of steps for the whole group, because some may stroll faster than others, making their feet land at different times, and the length of stride will vary. Nonetheless, we need not be at a total loss for comparison with the number of steps taken by a drill team. For example, we could count the number of steps taken by each stroller between two points, and then take the average number as the number of steps that it takes the group to pass from one point to another. Or, we could find the average time that it takes a stroller to take one step, and then divide the time it takes for the whole group to pass between two points by that average-step time. If we identify the result as the number of steps taken by the group of strollers, we will have something roughly analogous to the number of steps for the drill team. If we apply the same idea to brain operations, we will identify the number of steps in a task as the time it takes to complete the task, divided by the average time it would take for a disturbance at a synapse in a root to have an effect at a synapse in a root of a following neuron (that is, the average time it would take for a signal to travel in the neuron from root to axon hillock, from axon hillock to branch tip, and then across the synapse from branch tip to root of the following neuron).

If we put together these definitions of "step", and the facts about relative transmission speeds from the last paragraph, we arrive at the following result. The rate at which steps are taken in a brain is much slower than the rate at which they are taken in a digital computer. Again, the comparison of rates is about a million to one. There is, however, something more important. Consider a task that takes one second. There are many of these that clearly exhibit intelligence. We can see this by thinking of decisions about whether sentences are true. Some of these, like "Your name is John Jones", will be made so fast they would be hard to measure, and others, like "The sum of 33,472,935 and 5,385,649 is 38,858,584", will take a lot longer. But there will be many, like "If giraffes have hooves, they are like horses in some respect", that take about one second for deciding yet clearly require intelligence. (After all, we have to understand English to understand the question.) Now, the rates are such that one second allows for only about a hundred steps of brain operation.[4] The interest of this fact is that all the attempts to get similar tasks done by sentential AI on digital computers require hundreds of times more steps.

Let us now recall the argument that led us to consider the brain facts we have been reviewing. We had given a description of how sentential AI reasearch has run into difficulty. We had also shown how the knowledge access problem explains why these difficulties must arise. But then the thought occurred that we are intelligent, and so there absolutely must be a solution to the problems that research in sentential AI has encountered.

Now we see, however, that we are not entitled to use any such argument. Computers have discrete states and are synchronized; we have unsynchronized elements that operate in a continuous way.[5] So, we cannot argue that our being able to do a thing shows that a digital computer can do it. Further, there are no brain facts that we know of from which we can give an independent argument that all our intelligent productions are due to sentence processing. (The fact that we understand English or some other natural language shows that we do process sentences; but it does not show that this is the *only* kind of processing that lies behind our intelligent activities. It does not even show that the *process that enables us to make use of sentences that we hear* is itself a case of sentence processing, except in the sense that that is its *result*.) So, we are in no position to argue in this way:

> We are instances of beings who produce
> intelligence entirely by sentence processing.
> Sentence processing can be programmed on a
> digital computer.
> Therefore,
> There must be a solution to the knowledge access
> problem (namely, programming our sentence-
> processing methods on computer).

Of course, we cannot use the general fact of our difference from computers to argue that computers *cannot* exhibit intelligence either. But,
our discussion of the brain does give a good inductive argument
against supposing that our intelligence is a result of sentence processing. This argument goes as follows.

> All plausible strategies for arriving at intelligent
> results by sentence processing require upwards of
> thousands of steps for intelligent tasks of the sort
> we can do in one second.
> We can do these tasks in about 100 steps.
> Therefore,
> We are doing these tasks by some means other than
> processing sentences.

A Complication

Ever since we introduced Turing machines in Chapter 5, we have
had a clear model for *discrete states*. This is because a Turing machine
is defined by its states and because part of the definition of a state
involves the next state that the machine as a whole goes into. It
follows that a Turing machine has to be in exactly one state at a
time, and that different states are clearly distinguishable from each
other. From this it follows that any piece of computing machinery
that is used to embody a Turing machine state table must have discrete, clearly distinguishable states, of which it is in just one at each
time. Let us call such a piece of machinery a *discrete state machine*.

Now, if we speak a little loosely, we can say that discrete state machines are also *digital*. This is because "digital" often is used with the meaning of "in one clearly distinguishable state at a time". Moreover, a common illustration of a digital device is also an illustration of a discrete state machine: I am thinking of an ordinary light switch, which, for all practical purposes, is either definitely on or definitely off at any given time.

What we must now make clear, however, is that a discrete state machine *need not be made out of digital elements*. There is, of course, a certain naturalness about making discrete state machines out of digital elements. So long as you synchronize the timing of changes in the states of digital elements, building a device out of them will automatically give you a discrete state machine. But there is nothing necessary about this approach. "Discrete state" describes the operation of the whole machine and does not directly describe what it is made of, or how the discreteness is achieved. Discrete state operation can be brought about by nondigital elements. For example, by adding sugar to my coffee in very small amounts, you can produce a continuum of states among which I cannot reliably distinguish. But the only ones that matter to me are (1) not sweet enough, (2) drinkable, and (3) so sweet it is too cloying to drink. That is, from a certain point of view, I function as a device with three discrete states. Here is another example. An organism that contracts a disease may suffer for various lengths of time, may be in various degrees of health and nutrition to begin with, and may have disabilities of various kinds if it recovers. Still, there will be a discrete state result in one respect: the organism will either live for two weeks after it contracts its disease, or it will have died by that time.

If we apply the moral of these examples to brains or their parts, we can see that it is possible that at some level they function as discrete state machines. The simplest application of this idea occurs at the level of the firing rate of single neurons. We have seen that this rate is a continuously variable quantity; but it is conceivable that all that really matters is rapid firing as opposed to slow firing, that is, firing above a certain threshold rate as opposed to firing below that rate. We need not, however, limit ourselves to thinking of single elements. For there could be clusters of neurons that are effectively either "on" or "off", and that contribute to the relevant operations of our brains only in this way.

Now, where does all this leave us with regard to the arguments of this chapter? The answer can be given in three claims.

1. We do not have a *proof* that the brain does not operate as a discrete state device (even though many brain facts suggest that it does not operate in that way).

2. We have *no reason* to think that it does operate as a discrete state device.

3. Even if there were a level at which the brain operated as a discrete state device, the slowness of brain hardware limits the number of computational steps that could be involved in producing our intelligent behavior.

Claim 1 prevents us from using the following very simple argument: We know that we are not discrete state devices, and therefore we know that we cannot operate like a Turing machine. Claim 2, however, certainly entitles us to reject the idea that there "must" be a solution to the knowledge access problem within sentential AI, on the alleged ground we are examples of such solutions. That is, as far as we know, we may not be discrete state devices, so as far as we know, our intelligence may work on principles quite other than those that could apply to contemporary computing machines, and quite other than those that are involved in sentential processing.

Finally, the limitation on the number of computational steps stated in Claim 3 still supports the argument that was given at the end of the last section. Briefly, our hardware is too slow to do what it does exclusively by sentential processing. This point does not depend on what we think about whether or not we are discrete state devices, because the higher the level at which one may suppose we are discretely organized, the more neurons must be involved; so the slower must be the processing, and the fewer can be the number of computational steps.

We have now arrived at just the kind of uncomfortable spot that philosophers seem to like to get us into. On the one hand, we have an argument, from Chapter 7, that seems to show that we *must* be working on sentences when we exhibit intelligence. In the present chapter, on the other hand, we have encountered another group of arguments that suggest that we *cannot* be getting our intelligence that way. In the next chapter, we will look at a suggestion for an alternative approach, that is, a suggestion about how we might get AI that is *not* sentential.

Chapter 9

Parallel Distributed Processing

In Chapter 5, we needed to have an understanding of certain ideas that are basic to the operation of contemporary computers. To provide this, we did not look at the latest, most sophisticated examples of computer technology; instead, we introduced the very simplest kind of computer, the Turing machine. The hope was that by discussing a simple case, the basic principles would stand out all the more clearly. We have now come to a place where we need to understand the basic principles of a new breed of machines, called *parallel distributed processors*. Research on the design of such machines is being conducted at a furious pace and there are now many variations on the basic idea, some of them quite complex.[1] We shall, however, proceed as before. That is, we will look at some very simple models, with the aim of bringing out in a clear way what the basic principles of their operation are. By doing this, we will be able to understand the key points in which this new work differs from sentential AI, and why it is believed by many investigators to hold great promise of succeeding where sentential AI has run into problems. Our simple models will also provide a sufficient basis to understand some doubts that have been raised about these new machines.

Being Connected

Let us begin with the diagram of Network I in part (a) of Figure 9.1. In this little "machine", inputs arrive from the left on the lines of the

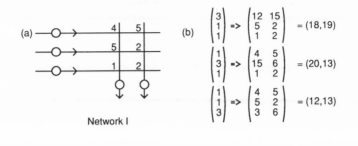

Network I

FIGURE 9.1

three horizontal *units*. You can think of these lines as wires. The inputs arrive simultaneously, or, to put it differently, one whole input consists of three parts, namely, the impulses in each of the three units. The output consists of impulses in the lines that emerge from the two vertical, or output units. The impulse in an output line depends on three things. First, it depends on the properties of the unit itself. For example, one kind of unit (the kind used in Network I) simply passes on what it receives. Another kind of unit has a threshold that prevents any output from occurring unless the total input exceeds a certain value. Other units may have more complicated relations between their inputs and their output. Second, the output of a unit depends on the strength of the impulses in the input lines that are connected to it. Third, it depends on the strength of the *connections* that the input lines make with it. The numbers at the intersections in Figure 9.1 (a) represent these *connection strengths*, or, as they are also called, *weights*. A weight of 5 is a comparatively "efficient" or strong connection—an impulse in an input line connected in this way has a relatively large effect on the output line. A weight of 1 is an inefficient or weak connection—an impulse in a line connected in this way will have relatively little effect on the output line. The total output of an output unit in Network I is the sum of what it receives through its connections to input lines. So, to find the impulse in a single output line, you must multiply the impulse in each input line by the strength of the connection that it has with that line, and then add up the results for all of the input lines. Three examples of this calculation are given in part (b) of Figure 9.1. Reading the left, single column from top to bottom gives the impulses in each input line,

FIGURE 9.2

from top to bottom. The double columns in the middle give the input times the connection strength for each input onto each output unit. The pairs of numbers at the right are the sums of the columns in the middle. Reading them from left to right gives you the total output on the left and right output lines.

Simple though it is, Network I has several properties that are worth noticing. To begin with, let us look back to the last chapter and compare our new machine with brain tissue. There is an analogy that will be clear from examining Figure 9.2. In this analogy, input units correspond to neurons whose axonal branches affect the roots of other neurons, namely those to which the output units correspond. The intersections of lines in the diagram correspond to synapses, and the different numbers correspond to different strengths of synaptic connection. (In Figure 9.2, connection strength has been represented by size of the branch ending: the larger the bulb, the stronger the connection. This is a representational device that is not to be taken literally.) The numbers given for inputs on each line and the numbers calculated for each output line correspond to firing rates in analogous neurons.

This comparison is only an analogy and, like all analogies, it is limited. There is, for example, nothing in Network I that corresponds to the fact that different inputs to a neuron take different times to reach the axon hillock. Nor are there any inhibitory connections in Network I. But although the analogy is limited, it is very important. One reason is that it has general application; we shall soon see that its appropriateness is preserved or increased by many of the complications that can be added to Network I. The analogy is important also because of what it suggests about the possible rewards of improving on the basic idea of Network I. If our brains enable us to be intelligent, and we can make a machine that works in a way that is analogous to a brain, it seems plausible that we could make a machine that would make a robot intelligent. If it could do that, there ought to be a way of hooking its output up to a printer so as to produce good answers in a Turing test situation. No arguments of this kind are taken by anyone to be conclusive, but they play an important role in encouraging investigation.

Let us now turn from the construction of Network I to its operation. What does it actually do? And how does it do it? One way to describe what it does is to say that it calculates, or computes. This may sound odd, because it doesn't *do* anything. It doesn't set and reset switches, nor does it go through a procedure in which we can identify steps. For example, there is nothing at all that corresponds to carrying a one over into the tens column, even though the second and third examples in part (b) of Figure 9.1 require such an operation in our standard way of doing arithmetic. It does not apply a rule in order to derive outputs from inputs. Nonetheless, for each three-part input, Network I produces an output pair. It does so in a regular way; that is, it does not produce just some pair or other each time you give it an input, it produces the same result for the same input.

The interest of this kind of computation may be understood better if we describe what Network I does in another way. It *associates* each three-part input with an output pair. The reason this is interesting is that association is one of our own important abilities. For example, we associate the faces of our friends with their names: We receive the sight of their faces as input when we pass them on the street, and we are able to say "Hi Sue" or "Hi Jim", or whatever the appropriate name is, as output. We associate capital cities with countries, different wines with different foods, different expectations of weather with different appearances of sky, and so on. So, a machine that can associate ought to capture our attention. Once we look at Network I in this way, however, a further point should strike us:

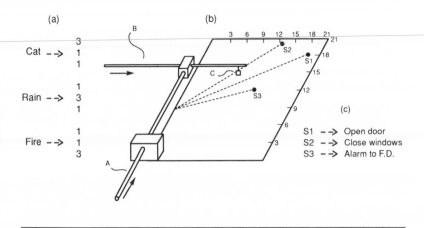

(a)

Cat — ⟶
3
1
1

Rain — ⟶
1
3
1

Fire — ⟶
1
1
3

(b)

3   6   9   12   15   18   21

S2
S1 ⟋18
⟋15
S3
⟋12
⟋9
⟋6   (c)
⟋3
B
C
A

S1 — ⟶ Open door
S2 — ⟶ Close windows
S3 — ⟶ Alarm to F.D.

FIGURE 9.3

There are several associations (three in Figure 9.1) but only one net-work. This property of storing several associations in the same set of connection strengths, that is, in a single network, is an important and general property of the systems we will discuss in this chapter.

We will be able to see a further important point most clearly if we give Network I a little job to do. For this purpose, let us imagine that Network I's input units are hooked up to something roughly like sense organs, and that its output lines are hooked up to some motors that operate an arm. The whole device, let us suppose, operates as a primitive household robot that lets the cat in, closes the windows when it rains, and sends an alarm signal to the fire department in case of fire. Figure 9.3 diagrams how part of it works. We are going to assume that the sensors—photoelectric cells and smoke detectors, for example—are arranged and connected to the input units in the man-ner indicated in part (a) of Figure 9.3. That is, a cat approaching the house causes voltages of 3, 1, and 1 in the first, second, and third input lines to Network I; and the onset of rain or a fire causes the other patterns of voltages indicated. Network I then yields voltages in the output lines corresponding to the values in part (b) of Figure 9.1. The first (or, left) of these is hooked up to a motor that slides Bar A (in part (b) of Figure 9.3) in the direction indicated by the arrow. The second (or, right) output line runs a motor in a box mounted on Bar A. This box slides Bar B to the right. The contact C is suspended from Bar B. When it hits a switch, motors are activated that perform the operations given in part (c) of Figure 9.3. The contact of C with a switch also cuts off the current for a while, and springs return both bars to the resting position at 9, 0. The dotted lines indicate the path that C would take from the resting position to each of the switches, if given the appropriate input.

The device in Fig. 9.3 (b) is not to be thought of as a precision instrument. There is some play in the rod mechanism, and the switches are not points but discs that the contact will trigger if it touches any point on the edge. This is analogous to the fact that we do not always throw switches with exactly the same grip or force: There is a range of movements that will get the job done. Because of this imprecision, no significance is attached to differences of one or two points in the output values. The outputs of Network I, as far as their use in this machine goes, fall into just two classes, high (18, 19, and 20) and low (12 and 13).

Robot Qrh, as we shall call this machine, is no doubt far too inefficient to take seriously as engineering. It is, nonetheless, useful for thinking about the importance of devices like Network I, which we might think of as Robot Qrh's "brain". Speaking metaphorically, we might say that Robot Qrh knows that it should open the door to let the cat in. It knows that it should close the windows when it rains, and that it should call the fire department when there is a fire. Moreover, being a robot and not just a disembodied brain, it acts on its knowledge so as to bring about useful results.

We must, of course, not get carried away with our metaphors. Robot Qrh is so simple that it should be obvious that attributing *knowledge* of anything whatever to it is gross anthropomorphism. But let us play along with the metaphor for a moment, because it suggests a useful question. Robot Qrh does not find out what to do about the cat just at the moment when the cat shows up. It must know it all along, since it is prepared to let the cat in *whenever* it may arrive. That knowledge must, therefore, somehow be *stored* in it. How is this done? We have already seen how: The knowledge is stored in the connection strengths between the input units and the output units in Network I. (And so, remarkably enough, is the knowledge that the windows should be closed when it rains and that the fire department should be summoned in case of fire.) But now we must further notice that if this knowledge is ever to be used, Robot Qrh must be "told" that a cat is now present. How is this done? It is done by the arrival of the *input pattern*—that is, it is the fact that the three lines each have the values that they do, that corresponds to the fact that a cat is approaching. In a similar way, the action to be taken is determined by the *output pattern*. It is not, for example, the fact that there is a high value on the first output line that corresponds to closing the window, since that is shared with the pattern that results in opening the door. Nor is it the fact that there is a low value on the second output line, since that is shared with the pattern that results in sending an alarm to the fire department. It is only the combination of values, or the pattern of the several values, that corresponds to the presence of a certain situation, or the direction to carry out a certain action.

The commonly used term for what we have just described is "distributed representation". "Distributed" refers to the fact that the meaning 'cat' or 'open door' can be found only in the pattern of activity of several units. "Representation" is used in the following way. Since, for example, a cat (and, of the items in our example, only a cat) causes the 3,1,1, pattern, you can tell that there is a cat present if you know that Network I is receiving that input pattern. This makes it natural to say that the pattern represents the presence of a cat, or that the pattern is Network I's representation of the presence of a cat. Likewise, you could tell what action is forthcoming if you knew how Robot Qrh is constructed and what output pattern Network I is producing. So, it is natural to think of the output pattern as representing the action.

We can now explain the sense of the title of this chapter. "Parallel processing" refers to the fact that several things happen at the same time. This contrasts with "sequential processing", in which one result is calculated, and then fed into another calculation, which must therefore take place *after* the first calculation is completed. In a machine like Network I, there is no such sequential calculation. The activations on the different input lines have their effects all at the same time. The term "distributed processing" has a double role. First, as we have just explained, the representations of useful elements of a situation and representations of actions are distributed over several units. Second, the "knowledge" that Network I has is distributed over all the connection strengths in the network. Since both the parallelism

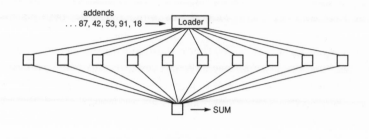

FIGURE 9.4

of operation and the distributed character of representations and of knowledge are important and distinctive, "parallel distributed processing" (often abbreviated PDP) has become a standard descriptive term for the processing illustrated by Network I and other networks to be described in this chapter. Another frequently used term for the same kind of processing is "connectionism".

Before developing our understanding of PDP, I want to make a brief remark about a kind of processing that is *parallel* but *not distributed*. Many current articles in the popular press about "parallel machines" refer to machines of this nondistributed kind, but from our point of view they are not very interesting. The example of the simple parallel adder diagrammed in Figure 9.4 will help to explain why. Let us imagine that we have many occasions on which we want to add 100 numbers. We have a machine that can do this, but we find it disappointingly slow. Suppose that loading in the numbers is a relatively fast operation, that it is the adding itself that takes the time, and that the time it takes to add is proportional to the number of items to be added. Then, the following strategy can improve our speed. Take, say, ten of our adders. Instead of loading 100 numbers into one adder, we will load ten numbers into each of our ten adders. These ten adders will do their adding at the same time; this, recall, is what makes a machine *parallel*. Then, we will let their ten outputs feed into an eleventh adder, whose output is the final result.

Looking at this in one way, we can see that it is inefficient: it requires the addition of 110 numbers, whereas if we used just one adder, we would have to add only 100. But since blocks of ten of these additions can go on at the same time, this machine is about five times as fast as our single adder. (That is, it takes one tenth the time for the ten adders to add, and then another tenth for the eleventh adder to sum the outputs of the first ten. The loading time, we assume, can be about the same.) So, if speed is our primary aim, this kind of parallel machine will serve us well. It should be clear, however, how different this parallel adder is from parallel *distributed* devices like Network I. It should also be clear that the advantage of the parallel adder is purchased only at the price of increasing the care with which the problem must be set up. The overall structure of the problem is still sequential, and the need for synchronized operation is still present. If we build a piece of hardware that looks like Figure 9.4, it will be strictly limited to its task of adding and will not be flexible at all. If we have hardware that we can program to work like our parallel adder, the program will have to contain instructions that get the outputs of the ten adders sent to the eleventh one. This illustrates the point that this kind of parallelism will work only if the problem, and the method for solving it, is completely understood before work begins. Moreover, this kind of solution is tailored to the specific problem at hand and therefore does not contribute anything new toward providing the flexibility that we know to be required in a machine that would pass the Turing test. This is why I said that this kind of parallelism is not interesting for our purposes, however commercially exciting it may be. We will find that this point becomes stronger and stronger the more we understand about the features of PDP. Let us, therefore, return to its development.

Getting Connected

Some readers may have wondered where I got the numbers for the weights in Figure 9.1 (a). Now, the truth is that I just played around with pencil and paper until I got a network that had the properties that I wanted to use for illustration. This is all right for my limited purpose, but as a general procedure for finding weights, it has at least three terrible defects. One is that I first cooked up some numbers for Network I, and then imagined a job that it might do. That is, I built Robot Qrh around it. But in most cases, there will be a task that is already given, and what we need is a way to find a network with weights that will do that task. My procedure gives not a clue as to how to do this. Second, there is the problem of complexity. Six weights are not so many to keep track of, but if we want a ten by ten network (which is not large by comparison to currently investigated networks) that will be one hundred weights. Trying to find useful weights for a network of this size by trial and error is completely out of the question. If we ever want to build a machine with either theoretical or commercial interest, we will have to have some strategy for finding useful sets of weights. Finally, let us recall that one of the attractions of PDP is its analogy with certain facts about brain operations. But we cannot suppose that the strengths of the connections between our neurons are preset in such a way as to make our brains useful networks. So, we cannot preserve the attractive analogy unless we can explain how a network can come to develop appropriate weights. In short, however interesting connected networks may be, the whole idea will be useless unless we can find a strategy for *getting* connected with useful weights in the first place.

Fortunately, PDP researchers have developed several methods for doing this, and we will now explain one of the most important of them. A good way to begin to do this is to return to the analogy between PDP systems and brains. We talked about the fact that branches of one neuron do not in general touch the roots of another neuron. They lie close to them but are separated by a synapse. A firing that arrives at the tip of a branch causes particles to cross the synapse, and this causes an electrical disturbance in the root of the adjacent neuron. Now we must add the fact that *the efficiency of a synapse is variable*. That is, the *amount* of disturbance in a root that is caused by the arrival of a firing at the tip of the branch on the other side of a synapse can be different at different times. Analogously, in typical PDP systems, *the efficiency of a connection (that is, the connection strength, or weight) is variable*.

We must now ask *how* the changes in connection strength might take place. Here again, we should look to the brain. One thing we should notice is that, for the most part, synapses are isolated.[2] That is, they simply lie between small areas of two neurons, and there is nothing else that they are connected to. If there is a general rule by which the synaptic efficiency changes, it must be a *local* one, that is, it must depend only on conditions at the location of the synapse. What might these conditions be? The generally accepted view is that

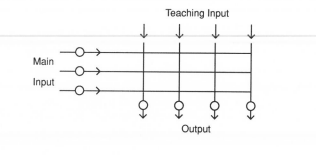

FIGURE 9.5

change in synaptic efficiency depends on relations among changes of firing rates in the neurons on either side of the synapse.[3] Now, analogues of these facts are typically embodied in connectionist systems. So far as possible, changes in weights are made according to local conditions, that is, conditions that affect only the two units to be connected. And the relevant point about these conditions is their activation, the analogue in units of rates of firing in neurons.

To understand more clearly how such systems work, we should describe the operation of a *pattern associator*. Figure 9.5 is quite similar to Figure 9.1, but it shows the output units as capable of receiving input from two sources.[4] One of these is represented, as before, as a set of lines coming from the left in the diagram. Let us call this the "main input". The other is represented as a set of inputs coming from the top. The pattern imposed from the top is sometimes called the "teaching input", because it represents the pattern that we want to be associated with the main input. It will help us to understand the potential usefulness of pattern associators if we imagine a context in which we might want an association. Thus, suppose I am trying to learn some Chinese. My instruction book tells me that the Chinese word for "not" is pronounced "bu". Let us imagine that I have a little network in my brain that has the same structure as Figure 9.5. Let us also imagine that when I read "bu" out loud, a certain pattern of activation is produced in the teaching input lines, and that this is what causes a certain pattern in the output lines. Further, let us imagine that these output lines are connected to muscles in such a way that it is that pattern on these lines that causes the sound that my mouth makes to be "bu". The result of what we have imagined so far is that there is a connection between reading "bu" on the page and intending to pronounce it, and actually pronouncing it. But now what I want to happen is to have this word come out when I want to say "not" in Chinese. So let us imagine that there is also a pattern on the main input lines that occurs when and only when I want to do this. Then my problem will be solved if the weights at the connections between these main input lines and the output units can be adjusted in such a way that when the main input lines have the pattern corresponding to "not"-in-Chinese, the output lines will have the pattern corresponding to "bu".

The method for doing this weight-setting that I will describe here is called the *delta rule* ("delta" for "d", and "d" for "difference"). The delta rule governs the change at each connection, and it gives the change in local terms. Consider a particular connection, say, between a main input line, i, and an output unit, o. The strength of the connection, $W_{i,o}$, may be positive, negative, or zero. Suppose that trying to express "not" in Chinese causes an input on line i, which we can represent by I_i. This input will be one among several that contribute to the total activation of o, which we can represent by A_o. The contribution to A_o of line i will be I_i times $W_{i,o}$, and A_o will be the sum of analogous quantities for all the input lines. Now suppose that after we try to express "not" in Chinese, we look at our instruction book and pronounce "bu". This will produce a second activation on o. Let us call this one T_o, for "teaching (or, target) activation of o". The central idea of the delta rule is that we should change the weights to make the effect of input to o match the target for o. For example, if the actual activation in o that occurred when we tried to express "not" in Chinese is less than it should have been in order to produce the correct result, we should increase the weight; if the actual activation was more than it should have been, we should reduce the weight. Equivalently, we should subtract the actual activation from the target activation in o and change the weight proportionately to this difference, that is, proportionately to $T_o - A_o$. This will be positive, denoting increase, if the actual activation is too little (A_o is less than T_o) and negative, denoting decrease, if the actual activation is too much. There is a further consideration. If the input, I_i was very small, it cannot contribute much to the output result, and there is no point in changing the connection weight to o very much; if, how-

Historical Note: Frank Rosenblatt (1928–1971) was a pioneer in the development of the kinds of machines we are describing in this chapter. He called his machines *perceptrons* and described them in a 1962 book whose revealing title is *Problems of Neurodynamics: Perceptrons and the Theory of Brain Mechanisms* (Washington, D.C.: Spartan Books). He applied what he called an "error correction procedure" (a version of what is now called the delta rule) and he proved what he called a "convergence theorem", which showed that the procedure would lead to solutions, if they were possible. Below is a diagram of a typical elementary perceptron, derived from p. 99 of Rosenblatt's book.

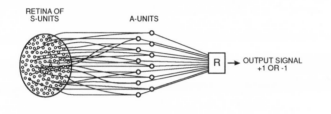

ever, it is large, a relatively larger change in $W_{i,o}$ will bring us nearer the target sooner. Putting these two points together, we have,

Change in $W_{i,o}$ is proportional to I_i times ($T_o - A_o$).

Notice that as we get close to where we want to be, $T_o - A_o$ becomes smaller, and so the changes become less. We should also remind ourselves that this way of changing the weights is applied for the corresponding values at all of the intersections between each input line and each output unit.

To apply the delta rule to our problem, let us imagine that we are trying to build a machine that can express "not" in Chinese. Perhaps, in an early trial, it brings out a wrong word. This means that at least some of the input line activations did not produce the right output activations. Now we tell the machine the right answer, that is, we do something analogous to looking into our language instruction book and reading "bu" there. We can do this by putting in the pattern that will produce "bu" as output. Now, taking these two events together, each connection between an input line and an output unit has "experienced" three quantities: the main input (I_i), the resulting activation in the output line (A_o), and the target activation (T_o). It thus has the information that is needed to change the weight of that connection by the delta rule.

What will be the result of changing the weights in a pattern associator according to the delta rule? The answer is that if there is a set of weights that will associate the input pattern with the desired output pattern, successive application of the delta rule will find it. This is a very important point, for without it, it would be hard to know whether the delta rule was really an improvement over trial and error. It is also important that this point can be generalized to several patterns. For example, Robot Qrh's brain stored associations between three input patterns and three output patterns. If we want a good way to discover the weights for such a brain, we will have to have a method that will find weights that will store all the desired associations in the same network. To apply the delta rule to this problem, we present an input pattern, followed by the target output pattern, followed by weight change according to the delta rule. Then we do the same for the next input-output pair, and so on for each pair of patterns that we want the network to associate. When we have finished the set of patterns, we must start through them again (not necessarily in the same order), applying the delta rule after each one. We must expect to have to cycle through the pattern set many times before we arrive at the right set of weights.

There are some limits to what we can do here. If the input patterns are very similar, networks will tend to confuse them, and it will take a large number of cycles to associate them to different output patterns. Moreover, if we try to associate too many patterns on the same network, some of them will be so similar to others that we will introduce confusion. So, there will be some upper limit to how many associations we can store in a network of given size. If we respect these limits, however, a set of weights that will produce the desired multiple associations will often be possible, and when such a set is possible, the delta rule will find it.

Let us now look at a somewhat different kind of network, called an *autoassociator*. A brief look at the diagram in Figure 9.6 will show that what is new here is the feedback connections.[5] In an autoassociator, there is no distinct teaching input, but the patterns presented as

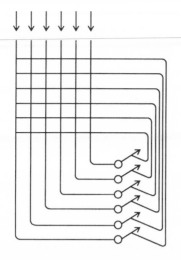

FIGURE 9.6

main inputs (i.e., at the top of the diagram) function as both main input and teaching input. A pattern is presented, and connection weights between the feedback lines and the units of the network are changed according to the activation levels in each of the intersecting lines. Then a second pattern is presented, and the weights are again changed. The process is repeated several times for each pattern to be learned. If an appropriate set of weights can exist, this process of adjusting the weights upon repeated exposure to the input patterns eventually will find it.

What do we mean here by an "appropriate" set of weights? Auto-associators learn the presented patterns in such a way that the patterns can be reconstructed as a whole from a partial presentation. For example, Kohonen, Lethio, and Oja autoassociated patterns of inputs corresponding to digitalized, computer-graphic faces. When incomplete or blurred graphics of the same faces were presented after learning, the autoassociator produced graphics of the faces that were restored or clarified, and were very close to the originals.[6] The general point illustrated by this example is that the "appropriate" weights in an autoassociator are those that permit the reconstruction of each of the patterns that have been learned when partial or degraded versions are presented. It should be obvious that, as in the pattern-associator case, too great a similarity of patterns, and consequently, too many of them, will cause confusion. Within limits, however, autoassociators can learn to recognize whole patterns from parts, through repeated presentation of sets of patterns.

The distinction between autoassociation and pattern association is not sharp. You may, for example, think of an autoassociator as a pattern associator that associates a part of a pattern with the whole pattern. Let us think about this in terms of some examples, which also will make it evident why autoassociation should be of interest to anyone who is thinking about the possibility of artificial intelligence. Take the example of a car parked halfway into a garage. If you stand to the side of the garage, you will see only the rear half, but you will not take yourself to be seeing a strange sort of two-wheeled vehicle. You will complete the scene and expect to see the front half if you walk around the front of the garage. That is, the part of a typical pattern—the shape of a car—that you do see causes you to think of the whole pattern. (Even if, for some reason, you suspect that someone sawed a car in half and lined up the cut with the garage opening, you will still think of what you are seeing as half a car.) Here, it is natural to think of a whole pattern and one of its parts; however, many cases that strike us as involving association between distinct patterns can be thought of as involving parts and wholes. For example, we associate our friends' faces with their names. We can think of this as learning a face pattern and a name pattern and associating them. But we can also think of the face and the name together as one complex pattern. Then the presentation of part of it, for example, the face, causes completion of the pattern whose other part corresponds to the name. In this example, completion in the opposite direction can work too, that is, the presentation of the part of the pattern corresponding to the name may cause the pattern to be completed, so that we think of what the face looks like.

Hidden Units

The two kinds of networks just described are fundamental for understanding how PDP works, but they are somewhat limited. One limitation has been indicated in such phrases as "*if* an appropriate set of

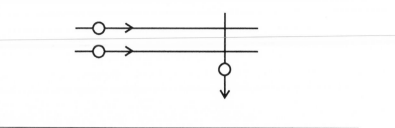

FIGURE 9.7

weights can exist". For it can happen that there is no set of weights that will enable a pattern associator to give the desired results. We will illustrate the problem here, and the kind of solution that can be given to it, by describing a standard and very simple case. This is known as the "exclusive or" or the "XOR" problem. Imagine that we want a rather primitive quality control robot in a shoe factory. If there is nothing at a certain point on a conveyor, that is all right, and if there is a pair of shoes, that also is all right. But if there is a right shoe and no left one, or a left shoe but no right one, we want the robot to sound its buzzer. That is, we want the buzzer to sound if there is *either* a right shoe *or* a left shoe, *but not both*. If we imagine that the shoes occupy distinctive positions—say, being on the right half and being on the left half of the conveyor—then we can represent this problem as involving four input patterns: $(0,0)$ is no shoes, $(0,1)$ is a right shoe without a left one, $(1,0)$ is a left shoe without a right one, and $(1,1)$ is a pair of shoes. One the output side, there are two relevant "patterns"—let us say (0), for the buzzer's being off, and (1) for its being on. The problem, then, is to associate the patterns $(0,1)$ and $(1,0)$ with (1), and the other two input patterns with (0). Now, if we use a network like the one in Figure 9.7, we cannot succeed. No matter what weights we have, if positive input in either single line is enough to turn the output unit on—corresponding to the pattern, (1)—then the combination of both will also be enough, thus associating $(1,1)$ to (1) and not to (0), as desired.

There are several ways in which we might complicate things in order to solve this problem. One simple solution is diagrammed in Figure 9.8. In this diagram, the numbers inside the circles are thresholds. The sum of the weighted inputs must equal or exceed the threshold in order for a unit to give output. Outputs of all units are

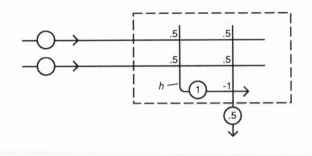

FIGURE 9.8

assumed to have a value of one; that is, each unit's output line is either on or off. Notice that the unit we added to Figure 9.7—the one labeled *h*—has a negative weight onto the output unit. This means that when it is activated (when its threshold is reached), the output unit is inhibited. The effect is to subtract 1 from what the total input to the output unit otherwise would be. Inspection of the diagram will show that the output line is on in just those cases where one of the input lines, but not both, is on.

In giving this solution to the XOR problem, we have introduced a unit that is called a *hidden unit*. This term just means that the unit is neither an input unit nor an output unit of the *whole* network. Unit *h* does, of course, receive inputs and give outputs; but this receiving and giving is from and to other units composing the network, not from or to something outside it. It is "hidden" inside the dotted line box in the diagram, that is, it cannot be "seen" from outside the box.

The moral of the XOR problem is that hidden units can be used to solve a problem that cannot be solved in a simpler network. This point is of general application; that is, the use of hidden units permits the solution of many, many association problems that cannot be done by PDP networks without them. In remembering this result, however, we should recognize that many different arrangements of connections are possible. For example, in Figure 9.9(a), unlike Figure 9.8, output units of the network receive their inputs *only* from hidden units. Networks may have several layers of hidden units. There may be feedback from any layer to any earlier layer. Finally, there may be "feedsideways", that is, *lateral* connections among units, as diagrammed in Figure 9.9(b).

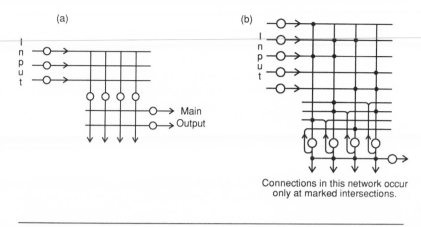

FIGURE 9.9

In thinking about the variety of possible PDP networks, we should keep in mind that any of the connections may be either excitatory or inhibitory. There are also, as we have noted, several alternative schemes for changing weights. The program of PDP research thus covers the investigation of a class of machines that have many differences from each other, but that are related by many similarities. The most important of these similarities is the fact that the connections between units are variable.

We should also be aware of the fact that there is more than one way of diagramming the connections among units. For example, Figure 9.10 is a diagram of a nonelementary perceptron reproduced from Frank Rosenblatt's book.[7] Figure 9.9(b) was derived from it, and you should verify that the two representations are equivalent. Many PDP researchers use the style of Figure 9.10 for representing their networks.

Attractive Properties of PDP Networks

There are a number of properties that make PDP machines attractive and in this section, I want explicitly to identify some of them. Not every PDP machine has every property, or every property in the same degree. Nonetheless, I will just talk about the attractive properties and not be very specific about which machines do what. Partly, this is because the subject is still being investigated, and there is not now

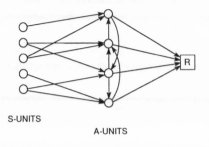

S-UNITS

A-UNITS

FIGURE 9.10

any agreed upon classification that makes it easy to say which kinds of networks will do what jobs best. Partly also, many of the networks are inspired by the net-like character of the brain. Because there are so many neurons and because synaptic connection efficiencies are variable, many kinds of networks might occur in various parts of the brain. For example, some collections of neurons might be connected with lateral connections, or with feedback, but other collections might not. This makes it plausible to assume that desirable properties of PDP networks can be realized in one part of the brain or another.

One word of caution before we begin. My aim in the present section is to describe what it is that excites people about PDP as an approach to AI. This may at times give the impression that everything about PDP is positive and that there are no problems. Later on, we shall see that things are not so simple. We must, however, understand what the attraction of PDP is, in order to understand the point of some of the objections to it. The present section, therefore, is just about the attractions of PDP.

Graceful Degradation

Sequential or serial processing, that is, nonparallel processing of the kind done by familiar computers, is highly sensitive to defects. A small amount of damage to a circuit chip, for example, can result in totally crazy performance. You can get a clear image of the reason for this if you recall the Turing machines we described in Chapter 5. Damage to a computer is analogous to rewriting the next-state numbers in the state table. A little reflection should convince you that rewriting even one of these is likely to give a table that is completely useless, as far as the original task is concerned. Similarly, as many a victim of user-unfriendly programs will testify, a small defect in the entry of data may throw the entire operation off track.

Typical PDP networks behave quite differently. Instead of being "brittle", that is, suddenly collapsing into uselessness, their performance degrades "gracefully". This means that they *gradually* perform worse and worse as more and more damage or defective input is encountered. We have already seen an important example of this in the autoassociator. Here, when only part of a pattern was given, the network restored it. Such restorations are not always perfect, but they are recognizable. The effect of incomplete information is not total failure, but only imperfection in the result. The same situation holds for hardware damage. In the small networks we have used for illustration, the failure of one unit would, of course, make a very significant difference. In larger networks, however, where there may be fifty or more units, the failure of a few units to work does not wipe out usefulness; the results are still recognizable approximations to the original performance.

This property is interesting from a purely commercial angle, since it is good to have machines that can still be used when they are partly broken. But the real importance of graceful degradation is that it suggests a similarity to human performance. We do not do as well without a piece of relevant information as we do with it; but neither do we come out with crazy or utterly pointless results. We arrive at something correct, although vague, or incorrect, but somewhere close to right. There are also many kinds of injury to the brain that leave noticeable changes in people, but do not result in a general loss of intelligent behavior. Graceful degradation in PDP networks provides a model that may turn out to explain how these facts about human performance are possible.

Content Addressable Memory

One of the problems that we described regarding sentential AI was the problem of getting items of information retrieved on occasions when they are relevant. Sentential AI does this by various search strategies, which we saw were difficult to make both feasible and flexible. We might be able to solve this retrieval problem if we could have a *content addressable memory*, that is, a memory in which items are caused to be retrieved by the content of what the sense organs (or, input units) are receiving. An attractive feature of PDP is that it shows how content addressable memory is possible. For example, when you see your friends, you often need to retrieve their names. If names and faces have been associated in the same network, there is no need for any kind of search; instead, the presentation of the face pattern automatically activates the pattern for the name. In this way, a feature of PDP systems seems to answer very directly a problem that was one of the most serious that sentential AI encountered.

Content addressable memory works when the presented pattern and the one that represents the item to be recalled are stored in the same network. We might describe what happens as an interaction between such patterns. The next property is another result of such interaction.

Generalization

We have seen that imperfect input can cause a PDP network to re-construct a pattern. "Imperfect" input, however, is just input that is *similar* to an expected input, but not quite the same. So, we could put the point by saying that a range of similar inputs can give rise to the same, or similar, output pattern. Now, suppose we take one pattern, call it P_1, and train a network to associate it with another pattern, P_2. Then a range of inputs that are similar to P_1 can all give rise to the associated pattern, P_2. We can then say that the network "gener-alizes" the association of P_2 to items similar to P_1.

To see the interest of this situation, imagine that we represent various animals in a network by patterns that correspond to their features, such as number of legs, hairiness, relative positions of nose and teeth, type of extremity endings (claws, hooves, fingers), size, and so on. And suppose that we take one pattern, say, the one that has all the right features for a chimpanzee, and associate it with an-other pattern, say the one for liking bananas. Then, when we put in the pattern of features corresponding to a gorilla, which will be quite similar to that for a chimp, we will get out the pattern that represents liking bananas. The network, we can say, has learned that chimps like bananas, but has generalized the connection to chimp-like animals.

Notice that the interest of this kind of generalization does not depend on its being always correct. For all I know, gorillas may not like bananas, but this would not diminish the importance of the generalization just illustrated. The reason is that, as we saw in Chapter 1, it is not correctness that defines the flexibility that the Turing test tests for. It is not optimality of response, either. Intelligent people are neither infallible nor are they good at coming up with optimal solutions to problems on the spot. What they are good at is coming up with likely, or believable, or reasonable conclusions or suggestions that are relevant to the current context. Even if gorillas turn out to hate bananas, concluding that they probably enjoy them on the strength of the information that chimps like them, and gorillas are a lot like chimps, is something characteristic of intelligent performance.

We should notice that the kind of generalization I have just described does not depend on our specifying in advance *which* features of animals will turn out to be relevant to making associations. In order for the association with bananas to generalize to gorillas but not to, say, cows or fish, there must *be* some features in the representation patterns that are common to chimps and gorillas and distinct from those in the patterns that represent cows and fish. But we do not need to tell the network which ones these are. The network finds them, so to speak, by itself, as a consequence of the weight-adjustment process.

Prototype Formation

We can all think of what a typical dog looks like, or a typical bird, or a typical tree. We can call representations of such things *prototypes.* Prototypes contain the most frequently repeated features of a group of things that are not exactly alike but have many overlapping characteristics. We do not have to be told to try to pick out a prototype. Instead, exposure to a bunch of different kinds of animals, for example, results in our grouping them around various prototypes. Now, in certain PDP networks, combinations of features that often come together tend to be connected by relatively high weights. If these networks are trained on groups of things that have considerable overlap in their features, and much less overlap with things in other groups, they will tend to connect the more overlapping items together. They will do this automatically, that is, without having to have the members of a group already identified as being in the same group. For example, if features of different kinds of dogs, different kinds of fish, and different kinds of birds are presented to these networks, prototypes of dog, fish, and bird will be formed, corresponding to the most common features of each kind. If you then present the features of a new kind of dog, the dog prototype will be activated. Similarly, new kinds of birds or fish will activate the relevant prototypes.

The interest of this property of some PDP networks is that we, too, discover groupings among things without having to be first told which things go into which groups. Noticing such groupings in a new case would, in fact, be an important test of flexibility. We can well imagine an interrogator in the Turing test situation rattling off a list of this kind: cups, books, pipes, bricks, silos, TV sets, thimbles, recreational vehicles, and so on, and asking how to group them. I suppose that an answer that puts alternate items of the list together would be taken as evidence of intelligence. Now, a PDP network that represented things by their shapes, among other things, might also group alternate items in the list together. This is because the odd-numbered items would all activate a hollow-cylinder representation, while the even-numbered items would activate a representation for rectangular outlines.

Rule Generation

The properties described so far show how PDP networks can associate a range of similar patterns to some further pattern. Suppose now that we have a network of which the following specifications are true.

1. The network has been trained on several different input patterns, which fall into three kinds, A, B, and C. That is, As are all

somewhat different from each other, but they are more like each other than they are like Bs or Cs; and the same holds for the Bs and the Cs.

2. Some of the As have been associated with an output pattern of, say, X, which is quite distinct from patterns Y and Z. Y and Z also are distinct from each other. Some of the Bs have been associated with the Y output pattern, and some of the Cs with the Z output pattern.

3. The output patterns are connected to motors that carry out three different actions, let us say P (for the X output pattern), Q (for the Y output pattern), and R (for the Z output pattern). These actions might be thought of as instances of speaking; for example, they might be cases of reporting the presence of things or issuing orders. But they may also be thought of as actions such as opening a door, or turning on the lights.

In a network of this kind, generalization will connect the other As—the ones that were not used in training—with the X pattern and the action, P. The case will be similar for the other Bs and the other Cs. The result will be that the network will behave exactly as if it were following the rule to do P if A is present, Q if B is present, and R if C is present. Yet, nowhere is there any representation of a statement of such a rule. The rule is *found* by the network from the repeated associations (or *regularities*) in the material that is taught to it; the rule is not *given to* the network by being told to it. If we combine this with the fact that PDP networks can discover groupings of similar things on their own (that is, without being told), we can see that they can discover both groupings of things among which rules can hold and what the rules are. The interest of such an ability will, I think be clear. For, although we can be told rules, rules that we are told must at one time have been discovered. So, intelligent beings must at least sometimes be able to discover rules on their own, that is, from their experience, without having to have that experience structured by rule-statements from outside themselves.

The properties I have just been describing do not exhaust the attractions of PDP networks. They do, however, demonstrate the kind of advantage that researchers expect PDP to provide in the development of artificial intelligence, and in the understanding of our own intelligent abilities. In the next chapter we will keep our promise to consider some flies in the PDP ointment. First, however, we shall end the present chapter by introducing, and resolving, a little puzzle.

Conundrum: Does PDP Exist?

The results and properties I have explained in this chapter are real enough, but the machines I have described are not. The people who did the research I have summarized did not put patterns into machines whose elements had variable connections. What they did do was to first, design a parallel, variable-connection machine. Then they described, in mathematical terms, how the elements of such a machine *would* work *if* they were to build one, which they did not do. Instead, they wrote a program for a conventional, sequential-processing computer that would figure out how each element in their hypothetical machine would react after each presentation of an input, and how each weight would change if it changed according to, for example, the delta rule. Then they had a computer of the familiar type run the program and figure out what the parallel machine would have done if they had really built it.

The wisdom of this procedure should be clear. It would be very expensive to actually build a new type of machine and in any case, we cannot know right away exactly which kind of machine we ought to build. So, it is much better to use conventional computation to figure out what different machines will do and to put off actually building one until we are sure we have found a useful design. But the situation does invite puzzlement: After all, are we discovering what PDP machines can do, or what conventionally designed computers can do? The answer must be both, but some further explanation seems required.

We know that we can use computers to help us model such things as the behavior of hurricanes and the development of economies. This is done by studying what we want to model, analyzing it to find significant elements, and discovering relations among these elements. The identification of elements and relations constitutes our theory of what we are going to model. Once we have the theory, we can express it mathematically, and write a program for calculating the mathematical results. When the program is run, the output represents what the theory says will happen, if the situation is as our input described it. Now, if we can do this with hurricanes and economies, there is no reason we cannot do it with machines for which we have a fully explicit design. Our knowledge of the design, its elements, and their connections corresponds to our "theory" of what we want to model, and the relation between the theory and the programming on a sequential machine is the same as it is in any case of computer modeling.

The second thing we need to say here takes us back to Chapter 5. I explained there how one machine can be, or be like, or imitate another machine. At the time, I had in mind the imitating of one Turing machine by another Turing machine. However, there is a point that still holds when we consider the present case of a Turing machine[8] imitating a machine that is conceived along quite different lines. Recall that when one Turing machine is another, there is a difference in what counts as their data, or input. One machine, with no program, operating on some input, "is" another machine. But this second machine's input is not the whole of what counts as input for the first one. Now, analogously, when we run a PDP research program, we have to give our sequential computer a lot of input. *Some* of this input corresponds to what will be input for the PDP machine, but there must be much more. That is, some of the input for our sequential machine will, in effect, have to tell it which units are connected to which others, what the initial connection strengths are, and what is the rule for changing them. So, as in other cases, when a sequential machine "is", or is imitating a PDP machine, *its* input is different from (in fact, larger than) the input to the PDP machine. So, *it* is calculating one relation between its (total) input and an output, which *we* can use to discover what relation holds between a *different* input (the part that would be input for the PDP machine) and output.

I think these remarks will remove any sense of contradiction that may have appeared to hover about the idea that (to put it loosely) you can do *parallel* distributed processing on a *sequential* machine. But perhaps we are not quite sure what we should say if the following situation were to arise. Let us suppose that someone actually builds a PDP machine—let us call it FRANKIE—and that it is wonderfully successful. I mean, of course, that when we put FRANKIE in the Turing test situation, it fools the interrogator close to 50 percent of the time. If you have gone along with what I said in the early chapters of this book, you will conclude that FRANKIE is intelligent. Even if you did not buy what I said, I ask you to go along with it for this and the next paragraph, just for argument's sake. For I now want to imagine that someone examines FRANKIE's PDP construction in detail and writes a program that is to be run on a sequential machine that predicts exactly what FRANKIE will do. Let us call this sequential machine that is running the FRANKIE program JOHNNIE. There might, of course, be a time problem about JOHNNIE: element-by-element calculations require large computational resources and therefore long running times. But let us suppose for a moment that we can overcome this problem. In that case, we can substitute JOHNNIE for FRANKIE in the Turing test situation, and once again have a machine that does very well on the Turing test. The question is: Shall we also say that JOHNNIE is intelligent?

Here, we have come upon some real content to the idea that there might be interestingly different *ways* of producing intelligent performance. Some may be inclined to say that FRANKIE succeeds at the Turing test in something like the *way* that we do, and that the way in which JOHNNIE succeeds is different enough from the way FRANKIE succeeds that we should not allow that JOHNNIE is intelligent. My own view, however, is that we should say that JOHNNIE is intelligent. JOHNNIE will, after all, exhibit flexibility, and that will not be due to looking up results that some other intelligence has already worked out. It will be flexibility that results from a construction that is entirely within JOHNNIE, so that JOHNNIE is a producer of its flexibility and not merely a conduit for it. This point is compatible with some further points that I believe properly locate the sense of strangeness that I think we feel about JOHNNIE. First, it is unimaginable that JOHNNIE's construction corresponds to the way that we humans produce our flexibility. JOHNNIE's construction is one that could not have *evolved*, but must have been *bestowed*. (Nonetheless, *what* is bestowed is, I have argued, intelligence.) Second, and more importantly, the fact that JOHNNIE may be an intelligent sequential machine is absolutely no support for sentential AI. In fact, if JOHNNIE were the *only* way of getting an intelligent sequential machine, that would mean that sentential AI could not succeed. Or, to put the point yet another way, the criticisms of sentential AI were not directly criticisms of the abilities of sequential hardware; they were criticisms of a certain strategy for using that hardware. You do not rescue that strategy by pointing out that you might get flexibility by using a completely different strategy that rests on having first designed a completely different kind of machine.

Notice now that we have, in a sense, gotten ahead of ourselves. We have, just now, been asking a SO WHAT question, so what if we got PDP to work and then got a sequential machine to imitate it? But we have not answered the COULD THERE BE question that we have been pursuing in the last few chapters. We want to know: Could there really be a PDP machine that would pass the Turing test? We cannot know what we should say about this until we have looked at problems that have been raised for PDP. It is now time to do this.

Chapter 10

New Doubts and New Prospects

Not everyone is equally enthusiastic about PDP research, and we will begin this chapter by seeing why. When we have introduced some difficulties, we will look at some conclusions that have been drawn from them and some proposals for overcoming them. Some of the questions that will naturally occur to us in this chapter are scientific ones for whose resolution we must await further research. A different sort of question asks what we are entitled to say about the prospects for artificial intelligence on the basis of present evidence. I shall try to be very clear about this at the end of the chapter.

Some Difficulties for PDP

No one can reasonably object to trying to discover the properties of things, whether they be natural objects or newly designed machines. The project of PDP research, however, has had the wider aim of studying networks in order to develop those that can either be intelligent or at least help us to understand how intelligence may be possible. There are five difficulties for this wider project that I will talk about in this section. These are not all the doubts that critics have had about the project of PDP, but they are quite serious and they are representative of the kinds of problems PDP encounters.

Similarity Is Everywhere

Intelligence often involves generalization, and PDP networks, we saw, can provide a way of generalizing. They can give the same or similar outputs for a range of similar inputs. Unfortunately, however, in one respect or another, everything is similar to everything else. To take one illustrative example, an acorn is similar to a walnut in one way, to a head covered by a beret in another way, and to an oak tree in a third way. Any of these might be a relevant similarity in some context, but probably not all of them in any one context. The fact that similarity is everywhere may sound wonderful but in fact it is fatal. It would be contrary to intelligence to respond in the same way to everything; indeed, that would just be perfect *inflexibility*. Intelligence requires responding in the same way to *relevantly* similar inputs. You cannot, however, get relevant similarity out of just similarity alone. So, the generalizing property that PDP networks have cannot by itself explain the useful ability of generalizing to relevantly similar cases.

It may be tempting to suppose that this problem can be overcome by attending to *degrees* of similarity. That is, we might think that relevant similarities can be found just by allowing generalization to inputs that are highly similar, but not to those that are only distantly similar. Unfortunately, however, this will not work. Part of the reason is that there can be no standard measure of degrees of similarity. To see why, let us ask how we should measure the degree of similarity of musical tones. Should we use closeness of frequency? This would make D, for example, closely similar to C, while C′ (the note one octave higher than C) would be far away. Yet, from some points of view, C′ is more similar to C than is D. Moreover, even if we should come to some decision about similarity of sounds, how would we apply it to colors? There does not seem to be anything like the phenomenon of octaves in the color spectrum. Of course, we might suggest closeness of frequency for both, but then, this criterion will make no sense when we try to estimate degrees of similarity of dogs or vegetables.

Mistakes Need Correction

In Chapter 9, I discussed an example that involved chimpanzees, bananas, and gorillas. I said that I did not know whether gorillas really like bananas or not. I still have not found out about this, but I am going to suppose, as an example, that we are going to discover that gorillas do not like bananas. If we discover this, we can remember it, and that presumably will change the way that we answer questions about gorillas and bananas. If we think of this kind of change in terms of PDP networks, we will have to think of resetting some weights, so that the pattern for bananas is no longer activated by the pattern for gorillas. But we do *not* want to do this in such a way as to lose the connection between the gorilla pattern and the chimpanzee pattern in general. That is, it will still be a good idea for the network to generalize from properties of chimpanzees to properties of the similar gorillas; so, we want the network to preserve such generalization for future cases, while removing the particular connection to bananas. This kind of weight change can indeed be done for particular cases. We would, however, like it to be done in general, that is, whenever we learn of a mistaken generalization that we have made. We would like to have a scheme that makes the change automatically, without having to know in advance which changes will be made. Finally, we would like to have such changes made in an efficient way, that is, without requiring too many cycles of retraining of the network. Designing a large network that will have these desirable characteristics is, however, a formidable problem.

Backpropagation

In Chapter 9, we saw that in some cases the creation of a set of associations between patterns requires the use of hidden units. To keep the illustration of this point simple, I used the XOR problem and I assumed weights for the connections in the network without saying anything about how they were found. As in the case of the first PDP network we examined, I had calculated this set of weights by hand. This is easy to do for such a simple network, but it is unfeasible for larger networks. If networks with hidden units are to be of

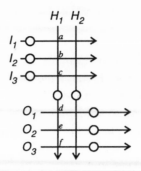

FIGURE 10.1

general utility, therefore, there must be a general method for finding appropriate weights. Fortunately, there is such a method; it is called "backpropagation".

Backpropagation is often referred to as a generalization of the delta rule. The delta rule tells us that the weight of a unit onto an output unit should be changed in a way that depends on how far and in what direction the activity of the output unit differs from what it should be. The generalization tells us how to change a weight between an input unit, say I_2, and a hidden unit, say H_1, onto which it projects (see connection b in Figure 10.1). The central idea is the same: We must increase this weight if the output of H_1 is less than it should be and decrease it if the output of H_1 is more than it should be.

How do we tell whether the output of H_1 is more or less than it should be? If the outputs of the output units (that is, O_1, O_2, and O_3) were exactly what they should be, we would not want to change anything, so the output of H_1 would be what it should be. If the output units were on the whole too active, we would want to decrease the output of H_1; if the output units were on the whole less active than they should be, we would want to increase the output of H_1. The amounts for these adjustments depend on a rather complex calculation. Fortunately, it will be sufficient for our purposes to give a rough outline of what is involved. First, we must find the error in the output of O_1, that is, the difference between its target output and its actual output. Next, we multiply this by the weight at connection d (and also by another factor whose description I omit). Then, we have to do the same thing for the error in the output of O_2 and the weight at connection e, and the error in the output of O_3 and the weight at connection f. Then, we must add these products together. This will enable us to generate an *error signal*, which corresponds to the error contribution of H_1. We can now propagate this error signal backward in the system—that is, we can use it as the measure of the difference between the desired output of H_1 and its actual output in an application of the delta rule (described in Chapter 9). Multiplication of the error signal by the activity in I_2 will tell us what change to make at connection b, and similar applications of the delta rule to the same error signal will tell us what changes we should make at connections a and c. Repetition of the whole calculation for H_2 will enable us to calculate the changes to be made at the connections between that unit and the input units.

Backpropagation is a systematic way to find weight adjustments onto hidden units. Because many applications of PDP depend on having such a method, backpropagation solves a key problem for this approach. Unfortunately, it also raises a difficulty for the attractiveness of PDP. We saw that simple applications of the delta rule can be claimed to be *local:* All the information required to make a weight change at a connection is present at that connection within a short time frame. It is plausible to suppose that synapses might be able to change in an analogous way, and this suggests that simple pattern associators might be somewhat brainlike. This appearance of brain-likeness, however, is completely lost in backpropagation. The calculations in the previous paragraph are not local. There is no evidence that there is anything in the brain analogous to devices that could add up error-times-weight products for several different synapses and then feed the result back to synapses that occur earlier in the system. The more we have to rely on networks with hidden units, therefore, the weaker becomes the connection between PDP research and the project of understanding how our brains can account for our intelligence.

Principles of Network Order

One idea that may seem to help with the problem just outlined is that of *systems* of networks. A bit of special terminology will be helpful in explaining why, so let us introduce it. (We shall also need it later in the chapter.) When we have a system of networks, both the parts and the whole system are networks. In order not to be confused about whether we are referring to the whole system or to one of the constituent parts, let us use "network" for the whole and "(sub)network" for a network that is only part of the whole system.

If we have several (sub)networks that are richly connected within themselves, and only sparsely connected between themselves, we could regard each one as operating almost independently and only contributing its output to the others. We could then say that each (sub)network would have to store only relatively few associations. Similarity in different respects could be "recognized" by different (sub)networks, which might be activated by different sets of inputs to the whole system. Corrections, when needed, could be made by resetting relatively few weights, because only one of the (sub)networks would have to be adjusted.

Unfortunately, the advantages of a system of (sub)networks can be purchased only at a considerable price. This is because, in such a system, everything would depend on how the different (sub)networks are connected. We would be back with a severe problem that you should remember from our discussion of sentential AI, namely, the problem of how relevant information comes to be found and used on appropriate occasions. In PDP terms, the problem would be how it comes about that a (sub)network that stores a relevant association contributes significant output to *the right* (that is, useful on a particular occasion) other (sub)network. I am not saying that we could not find solutions to this kind of problem for a small set of (sub)networks that we want to perform a limited set of tasks. In order to have a general solution that would apply to large sets of associations, however, we would have to understand some principles of how (sub)networks can be ordered—that is, how they can be connected to each other—that would explain how they can contribute their outputs to the right places on the right occasions. We do not yet have these principles.

The problem just described is analogous to the problem about classification schemes for animals that we described in Chapter 8. If we are given a problem (or set of problems) we can find a useful classification scheme. This scheme may be counterproductive, however, if a different kind of problem is presented. Similarly, one set of connections among (sub)networks may provide an elegant solution to one kind of problem. If we are given the problem in advance, we may be able to find such a useful set of connections. The same set of connections, however, may not help at all with a different problem. If we are not already given the range of problems to be dealt with, we will not know what set of connections would be useful. What we would like to have but do not have yet are principles that would guide us in this situation, or give us the design for a system that would operate competently (but not elegantly) over a very wide range.

If systems of (sub)networks seem to point us back to old problems, maybe we should avoid them and design only large, single networks. The problem is that we will *still* need some principles of network order. That is, if we are going to build large, successful networks, we will have to first understand or be able to explain how they can work. We will have to explain how we can make corrections without either destroying valuable connections or spending an excessive effort in retraining. More exactly, we will have to have some principles that explain how a large network can do this, without having to be told from outside which strengthenings of weights would cause those associations to be most highly activated that would be useful or relevant on each particular occasion. As before, these principles seem difficult to find and they are not yet known.

Rules and Regularities

We saw that one of the advantages claimed for PDP networks is that they can find rules and behave in accordance with them, without having to be told which ones are appropriate. Some authors, however, dispute that PDP networks can really do this.[1] They hold that PDP networks can act in ways that are regular, that is, ways that associate the same output pattern with every presentation of the same input pattern, but they also hold that exhibiting such regularity is not the same as following rules.

We can understand the problem about rules by thinking about games. If you play chess or almost any card game or any board game like *Monopoly*, you will know some rules that you can follow to tell whether a move is legal. Other rules may tell you what is a *good* move in a game, but for the moment let us focus just on the rules for legal moves. Now, at a particular point in a game of any complexity, there will be many moves that you know to be legal ones, *even though you have never seen this hand of cards or this board position before.* Since you have not seen this position before, you *cannot* have associated it with a set of legal moves. (It is actually even worse than this. If you have played some chess, you have seen many board positions, but, apart from the opening and some special end game cases, there is almost certainly no board position for which you have actually seen or even thought of all the possible legal moves.) You must apply what you know about rules in order to figure out what you cannot have learned by seeing the pattern for the present position and the patterns for legal moves presented one after the other.

PDP networks are good at associating patterns. But if applying rules is not the same thing as associating patterns, then their associating ability may not enable them to follow genuine rules. The explanation that I gave under "rule generation" in the last chapter may only describe how associations can give an illusion of an ability to generate rules.

The issue about rules is extremely important, because rules are not limited to games. The meaning of what we say is not dependent only on the meanings of the words we use, for much depends on grammatical construction. Think, for example, of the difference between "The cat is on the mat" and "The mat is on the cat." But grammatical construction depends on rules. So, every time we speak, and every time we understand what another speaker has said, we seem to be applying rules. If PDP networks do not explain how to apply rules, then they do not explain something that is absolutely central to our intelligent performances. This issue is, in fact, so important that we shall have to return to it in the next section.

The problems I have been describing form a strong case against what I shall call "simple PDP". By this term, I mean the view that an adequate account of intelligence will arise directly from the properties of PDP networks described in Chapter 9. It is the view that we will eventually be able to explain intelligence entirely at the level of networks, without considering larger-scale principles of network organization. To doubt the success of simple PDP is not by itself to doubt that PDP research has something important to offer. We still have much to learn about what we can do by using multiple layers of hidden units, and about what kinds of lateral and feedback connections may be most useful. Work on these questions is ongoing and should (and will) continue. At the same time, however, we should expect that we will need higher-level principles of organization in order to fully understand how intelligence is possible. In the following sections, I will explain what I mean by "higher level" principles as a part of my discussion of examples of views that propose them.

Mere Implementation

Some philosophers and scientists believe that PDP research has only a minor contribution to make in the understanding of intelligence. They hold that PDP networks are essentially pattern associators that cannot explain the things we do by using rules.[2] They believe that sentential AI correctly identifies the principles that can ultimately explain intelligence, both in us and in machines.

We might wonder what the defenders of sentential AI think about the fact that the brain seems to be a network of neurons connected by variable-strength synapses. Their answer is that networks of this kind can be used to form the symbols and sentences required by sentential AI. The networks are, so to speak, the material out of which sentential AI is made, and the organization that explains how intelligence can work is the organization that is described by the principles of sentential AI. PDP networks, they believe, may be useful, but only in so far as they are made to be *mere implementations* of principles of sentential AI.

This view will be clearer if we call to mind some other examples in which we speak of implementations. One case is policies. The National Institutes of Health (NIH), for example, have a policy that medical research should include both men and women. They have recently been accused of poor implementation of the policy, because they criticize violators after the fact, instead of reviewing choice of subject populations before experiments are done. We also speak of implementing designs. A refrigerator must have a pump to move the coolant around. But a pump may use a piston, or it may work more like a fan; each would be an implementation of the design that specifies only that a pump should go at a certain place in the cooling system. Again, we speak of implementing ideas of a very general kind. Conserving energy, for example, is a good idea when supplies are short. Implementing this idea can involve many aspects, for example, legislating requirements for automobile fuel efficiency and lowering thermostats.

The common pattern in all these cases is this. First, what we implement can be described in general terms. Relative to this description, the implementations are more specific or more detailed. Second, there are always several possible implementations. Third, what we implement explains why we have the implementation. We have a pump in the refrigerator in order to move fluid. This job is required by the design and that is the explanation of why the pump is there, no matter what kind of pump we use. Again, the reason for the NIH policy is gender equity, and that will be the explanation of why they have a more specific rule for its implementation, whichever rule they have.

When we apply this pattern to the present case, we get the following view. The principles of sentential AI can be implemented in several ways, for example, in a brain, in a sequentially designed machine, and possibly in a PDP machine too. But, however they are implemented, the *explanation* of intelligence will be found only through the principles of sentential AI. These principles, which we described in Chapter 7, require that intelligence is the result of formal operations on elements that can be regarded as symbols. These elements may actually be patterns of activation of the units in a network, but the *explanation* of intelligence will be found in the formal operations, which could also be implemented in other ways.

At the end of Chapter 7, I considered what I called "the picture-processing myth" and I explained why proponents of sentential AI would not be impressed. We can give the reason for this in terms that we have introduced in this chapter. According to the proponents of sentential AI that we imagined, the picture-processing myth was a mere implementation of sentential AI. It used pictures for words instead of arbitrary signs, but it worked only because the pictures could be operated upon with the same rules that could be applied to any kind of sign. Many proponents of sentential AI will want to apply this lesson to PDP networks. Patterns of activation are often called

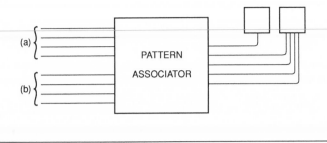

FIGURE 10.2

"representations" and they can be regarded as analogous to "pictures" of whatever is imagined to cause them. It is true that such "pictures" cause new pictures, that is, new patterns of activation, in a way that does not apply rules of calculation. Proponents of sentential AI, however, can say that the results of this kind of processing will be intelligent only if the pattern that is a representation of one thing causes the patterns that are representations of other things that they "should" cause, that is, that they should cause according to the principles of sentential AI.

Let us make this view a little more concrete by looking at the network diagrammed in Figure 10.2. The pattern associator in this figure is a (sub)network that associates each of 100 patterns on its eight input units with one of 19 patterns on its five output units. All the units are either ON (represented, let us say, by "1") or OFF (represented by "0"). Thus, inputs can be represented by strings of eight 1s and 0s, outputs by strings of five 1s and 0s. We may suppose that there are hidden units in the pattern associator, but the precise structure of the (sub)network is of no interest here, so long as it is clear that it is parallel and distributed throughout.

What we do want to focus on is the question of what this (sub)network does. I am going to suppose that we have trained the pattern associator so that the following description is true. First, divide the input units into two sets of four (labeled "(a)" and "(b)" in Figure 10.2). The patterns on each of these sets can be regarded as representations of single-digit numbers from 0 to 9. (For those who know binary notation, there is an obvious representational scheme, but any set of ten patterns out of the sixteen that are possible on four units will do, as long as we use the same scheme throughout.) The pattern on the eight input units can thus be regarded as representing two numbers. The output pattern represents the sum of these numbers, but according to a different scheme of representation. The top output unit is ON when the sum of the inputs is ten or more, and OFF when the sum is less than ten. The window to which it is attached reads either "1" or "0" accordingly. The remaining four output units represent the correct digit for units, according to the same representational scheme that is used for the inputs. These four output units drive the right-hand window, which contains the correct digit 0 through 9. For example, using the binary table

0000 = 0	0101 = 5
0001 = 1	0110 = 6
0010 = 2	0111 = 7
0011 = 3	1000 = 8
0100 = 4	1001 = 9

the input pattern 10010011 would produce the output pattern 10010, which would drive the windows to show 1 and 2. These, read as 12, give the correct answer to what the input represents, that is, 9 + 3.

The device in Figure 10.2 is indeed a PDP network, but it is not making use of any of the advantages of PDP that we described in the previous chapter. Instead, the pattern associator is used to store elementary addition facts, and to perform the function of carrying (that is, carrying a 1 over into the tens column, represented by the left-hand window). This function could be done just as well in other ways, and in particular by non-PDP devices. If the device in Figure 10.2 were to contribute to correct outcomes in a larger network, the *explanation* of the correct outcomes would refer only to its correct addition and not to the parallel distributed character of its pattern associator. The essential logic of the result, we might say, is arithmetical; the method used here to get it is merely accidental.

The mere implementation view is the view that PDP networks are always nonessential in the way that this example illustrates. It holds that the real explanation of how a mechanical device or a brain manages to produce intelligent output lies in the fact that it follows sentential AI rules. It holds that the patterns of activation on PDP (sub)networks function, in the economy of the brain, merely as symbols that must be operated upon in accordance with rules in order to produce any intelligent results. It offers an answer to the problem of network organizing principles, namely, that (sub)networks provide the symbols and connections that generate just those new symbols (patterns of activation in (sub)networks) that rules of sentential AI would dictate.

What should we think of the mere implementation view? In order to properly evaluate it, we must distinguish several different claims that are implied by my description of it.

> 1. We sometimes consciously follow rules. When we
> do so, parts of our brain go through processes that
> implement those rules. For example, successive
> activations of (sub)networks correspond to
> successive stages of application of the rules.
> Processes occur that would have produced different
> results if conditions had been different, in a way that
> parallels the different outcomes of applying rules to
> different situations.

By merely considering a particular example, we can see that this claim is extremely plausible. Thus, suppose you are using the long form for figuring your taxes. You will find many rules in the instructions, of which many have the form illustrated by the following fragment. "Your child must be claimed as your dependent on line 6c. **Exception:** If you remarried and the child's other parent claimed the child as a dependent under the rules for **Children of Divorced or Separated Parents** (see page 8), you can take the [earned-income] credit if you meet all of the other conditions listed above."[3] It is extremely plausible to suppose that people who encounter this instruction (and who resist the temptation to give up in disgust because of the bureaucratese) go through a process in which they (a) recognize whether or not they have remarried, (b) if so, ask themselves whether the child's other parent claimed the child as a dependent, and (c) if so, identify which conditions are meant by those "listed above", and (d) ask themselves whether they meet all of them. Moreover, they do these things in order, since there would be no point in continuing after (a) or (b) if they had not remarried or if the child's other parent did not claim the child as a dependent. Finally, the process that people go through in reading this instruction would normally have different outcomes in different cases, depending on what they decided at each step in the process.

> 2. We sometimes follow rules unconsciously, by going through a series of brain processes that fit the conditions described in 1. In these cases, unlike those in Claim 1, we are not conscious of the completion of steps in the process, but only of the input and the results.

This claim is also extremely plausible. Consider, for example, some facts about our linguistic abilities. When I listen to what you say, I am not aware of any grammatical processing. There is not anything like a conscious decision about what is the subject, the verb, or the direct object of your sentences. As far as consciousness goes, I hear you and I understand what you say. The study of linguistics, however, shows that in fact we must be applying grammatical rules in our understanding of language. The same point holds for our speaking. Suppose, for example, that I want to express the thought

Some people don't know what they want.

For many purposes, I might just as well express this by saying

Not everybody knows what he or she wants.

Although I might say either of these, it is most unlikely that I will say either "Some people don't knows what they want", or "Not everybody know what he or she wants." That is, if I express myself by starting out "Some people . . ." then I will use "know", but if I express virtually the same meaning by starting out "Not everybody . . ." then I will use "knows". Somehow, my sentence-producing processes follow the rule that an "s" is required after "know" in one case but not in the other. Yet, in everyday speech, I would just say what is on my mind, and would not be conscious at all of applying any such rule in composing my utterances.

We are at a point where the issue about PDP (sub)networks and rule-following becomes critical. There is no need for anyone to dispute Claim 1, that is, the obvious truth that we sometimes consciously follow step by step rules. With processes of which we are not conscious, however, nothing can be counted as obvious. The *results* of our language processing are obvious, and there is no doubt that they can be *described* by rules. For example, we can give a general rule that would explain the example of the last paragraph: Singular subjects add an "s" to the verb, plural subjects do not, and "everbody" is a singular subject (despite its meaning) while "people" is a plural subject. The fact that something can be *described* by a rule, however, does not prove that it is achieved by *applying* or following a rule. A simple case that illustrates this point is that of a thermostat. At a given setting, its behavior can be described by the rule: Turn the furnace on if the temperature falls below, say, 68 degrees, and turn it off if the temperature rises above 70 degrees. But satisfying this description depends only on the thermostat's setting and the fact that its electrical contact is mounted on a spring made of temperature-sensitive metal. So, the rule-satisfying description is not achieved by applying or following a rule. One important question that PDP research raises is whether some of our abilities that can be described by rules are achieved without following rules. Is the underlying process like that in Claim 1, only carried on unconsciously? Or does it resemble a thermostat in that, even though it is much more complicated, it does not get its results by following rules?

Although describability by rules does not *prove* that rules have been followed, our grammatical example is still persuasive evidence for rule following. It is true that we do not yet *know* just how far we can go in getting rulelike results without rule-following means. Certainly, further research on this question is warranted. We can see, however, that if we have results that are related in a complicated way to inputs, we are going to have complicated means of *some* kind to explain them. Simple devices will do for simple tasks like relating furnace running time to temperature, but not for more interesting tasks. Whenever we have more complicated devices, however, we have some new questions to answer: How are their parts connected? How are the outputs of different parts coordinated? On the one hand, Claim 2 gives a plausible, although schematic, answer. It says that we can behave in a way that satisfies many rules, some of which must be applied before others (for some of them depend on the results of applying others) because we actually do (unconsciously) follow such rules. On the other hand, we do not actually possess an alternative set of principles that explain how the behavior that fits grammatical rules could be generated. We should, of course, be open to the possibility of discovering principles of which we are now ignorant; but in the meantime we should count it as likely that the only explanatory idea we have will prove correct. We should also note that even if we could explain *some* cases of rule-fitting behavior without supposing that any rules are followed in producing it, that would not disprove Claim 2. Both kinds of process could perfectly well contribute to our abilities.

> 3. Implementing rules will prove to be the entire
>   explanation of all of our intelligent behavior.

Unlike the first two claims, this one is not plausible at all. We need not stop long to say why, since we have already given the reasons in Chapter 8. That is, the difficulties we raised for sentential AI are at the same time difficulties for the view that our intelligent behavior is all brought about by our implementing sentential AI rules. All we need to add here is that pointing to problems in PDP does nothing to answer the difficulties that were raised for sentential AI. Nor is the plausibility of Claims 1 and 2 any argument in favor of Claim 3.

It is not as if we knew that one of two views were correct. In that case, we could use problems encountered for one of them to support the other. (Even here, however, the fact that both sides have unresolved problems would suggest stalemate rather than victory for one side.) In the present case, however, there are obvious further possibilities. One of these is skepticism, the view that there simply cannot be any way in which the human mind (or the human brain) can understand itself, that is, understand how it manages to be intelligent. Another is that we can understand ourselves only through some theory that has not yet even been dreamed of. There are also

less obvious but more immediately interesting possibilities, two of
which we shall identify in the following sections.

Hybrid Views

The view I have just been discussing puts all the explanatory principles of intelligence on the side of sentential AI and uses PDP
(sub)networks only as means. It is, however, quite natural to respond
to the difficulties I described at the beginning of this chapter by cred-
iting PDP with genuine advantages and trying to combine them with
the strong points of sentential AI. I shall call such attempts "hybrid
views", and I shall use the term "hybrid systems" to refer to systems
that work in the ways these views describe.

There are several ways of developing hybrid views, but I shall
explain only one version.[4] The attractiveness of this version derives
from the fact that rules can be definite without being completely
specific. Juries, for example, are supposed to follow a definite rule in
obscenity cases: They must find appeal to prurient interest *and* viola-
tion of community standards *and* lack of artistic or political content.
Legal rules cannot, however, be completely specific about what
counts as satisfying such phrases as "violating community standards"
or "artistic content". Jury members may have to argue among themselves whether certain facts upon which they agree constitute such
violations or contents. Once these determinations are made they
have definite rules to follow, but the cases to which the rules will
apply are not specified in advance.

It is easy to see how a hybrid system can have rules that are
definite without being completely specific. All we need to do is to
make use of the generalization property of PDP (sub)networks. This,
let us recall, enables a class of similar inputs to result in the same
output pattern. The class need not be specified in advance.[5] The
output pattern of such a (sub)network can be treated as an element in
a system of definite rules. That is, there can be rules that perform
certain operations every time a particular output pattern occurs, or
every time that an output pattern occurs in conjunction with the
outputs of other (sub)networks. In this way, the rules can be definite,
and known in advance of their application, while the particular range

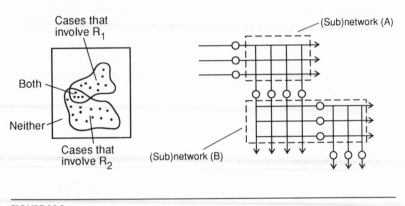

FIGURE 10.3

of inputs that will determine a certain result of their application is not specified in advance.

A variation of this idea would not require a (sub)network to yield the *same* output pattern. Connections could cause some operation to be performed whenever the output of a (sub)network is within a certain *range*. We could be completely explicit about fixing the boundaries of this range, without knowing what list of inputs to the (sub)network would cause the operation to be performed. A network that had been trained to connect certain input patterns to output patterns that are within the range might generalize so as to connect other similar (but not previously received) inputs to output patterns within the range.

Let us illustrate this idea in the context of a slightly more interesting system in which two rules are embodied. (Sub)network (A) of Figure 10.3 has four output lines to (sub)network (B). Suppose we have a rule, which we will call R_1, that states that a certain operation is to be performed if the output pattern of (A), that is, the input pattern to (B), is close enough to $(5,2,6,1)$. "Close enough" here means "within plus or minus one on each line". That is, R_1 will operate anytime the values put into (B) lie at or between $(6,3,7,2)$ and $(4,1,5,0)$. Similarly, a second rule, R_2 will operate anytime the values put into (B) are within plus or minus one of $(3,4,4,3)$, that is, when they are at or between $(4,5,5,4)$ and $(2,3,3,2)$. In this situation, any input to (A) that causes it to send the output $(4,3,5,2)$ to (B) will trigger the operations of *both* R_1 and R_2. By making the tolerances a little wider, for example, plus or minus 1.2, we will get a range of outputs that will trigger both rules.

The effect of such a network would be to "recognize" cases in which each of two rules apply singly, and cases in which they both apply. We may imagine that the network has been "trained" (its weights set) by error correction done on a number of cases, represented by the dots in the input classes. This training will result in certain relations being established between four classes of cases and the output of the whole network in Figure 10.3. That is, some cases will trigger or invoke R_1; some will invoke R_2; some will invoke both, and some will invoke neither. These relations can be understood as being established through a two-layer procedure. First, (sub)network (A) generalizes from training cases to those inputs that yield outputs in the given ranges; second, (sub)network (B) applies definite rules for what is to be done to the cases in each range.

This simple model is intended to illustrate how a hybrid view *might* work. Even in this simple case, there is a problem, namely, how to find the weights between units and the boundaries for rule operations that will produce useful results. This kind of question is being actively investigated, but it is not yet clear just how much we can expect to achieve by exploiting the properties of hybrid systems.

Action-Directed Views

The types into which I have divided the above views are generally recognized and each type includes well-developed examples. By contrast, the approach I describe in this section is new, less developed, and not yet generally recognized as distinctive. For this reason, my discussion here will be more speculative. It will aim to explain what the distinguishing features of this approach are, and why we should expect it to prove fruitful.

The approach I have in mind is structurally very similar to that of hybrid views. It holds that simple PDP is not enough and that higher-level organizing principles must be added. The additional principles, however, are not taken to be those of sentential AI. Since familiar hybrid views look to sentential AI for higher-level principles, we need the new term "action-directed views" to stand for views that look elsewhere for their additional principles. The common theme of these views is that explaining intelligence will require organizing principles for PDP (sub)networks that are linked closely to the needs of action. The motivation for this theme is the thought that intelligence must have something to do with survival. This connection requires the mechanisms of intelligence to be closely and directly connected with the mechanisms of action. The recommendation that flows from this observation is that we should try to understand the development of intelligence as the development of improvements in meeting requirements for useful (life-sustaining) action.

This description of action-directed views does not specify what set of principles will enable us to give a good account of intelligence. Different proposals for the right set of principles would yield different views of this type. It would be premature to try to actually identify such a set here. It is necessary, however, to illustrate the *kind* of principles that may in time provide understanding of intelligence.

Law of Effect

The most obvious principle that relates to action is the law of effect: The likelihood of repeating an action depends on the effect that doing the action has on the organism. That is, there will be a tendency for an organism to repeat actions that have beneficial results, and to avoid repeating actions that result in injuries or deprivations of beneficial things. The benefits and injuries are, of course, effects on the organism of the changes in the surrounding environment that its action brings about. To explain how the law of effect can work, however, it is not enough to say that an organism's actions react back upon it. It is further required that these reactions on the organism get connected to the "right" places. By the "right" places, I mean the brain parts that were responsible for producing the action in the first place. For example, suppose a puppy worries a porcupine and is stuck with quills as a result. This unfortunate consequence must get connected with at least some part of the mechanism that generated the behavior toward the porcupine. If it did not get connected in this way, the puppy would merely repeat the injurious action. Now, there are occasions on which the connections between actions and effects are not obvious, and on which *we* go through a process of figuring out what we should change in our behavior in order to avoid future injuries. This cannot, however, be the typical mechanism behind the law of effect, because that law applies in organisms to whom we do not credit any such degree of calculative ability. We must, therefore, suppose that there is a simpler method of connecting consequences to the organism with the mechanisms that produced them in the first place.

A natural suggestion here is to say that PDP networks associate, and that the mechanism of the law of effect involves associating circumstances and actions with benefits or injuries. I have no doubt that this is part of the story, but we must not forget the problem raised by the fact that similarity is everywhere. One way of putting this problem is to say that we need to associate benefits and injuries with actions in similar circumstances. (We do not want to repeat the grasping of the hot handle of a metal pan, but we do not want to achieve this result by blocking the grasping of anything at all!) But every circumstance is similar to every other in *some* respect. So, what we really need is to associate benefits and injuries with *relevantly* similar circumstances. To explain how this is possible we need some sort of principle that can show how different respects are singled out for association. As before, degree of similarity will not work. Grabbing a hot pan with an insulated handle can be enormously similar to grabbing one with a hot handle. Only the handle need be different.

I have no solution to this problem, but there is an intriguing case that suggests something that may prove useful. If rats taste something new and become nauseated within a few hours, the new food item (but not other novel features of its surroundings) will thereafter be avoided.[6] This useful result appears to be based on a direct and persisting connection among groups of neurons. Now, such a direct connection is not a mechanism of intelligence. Quite the contrary, it has no flexibility at all. If we bear in mind that useful thought must at least begin in close connection with action, however, we should expect that more interesting cases can be illuminated by this simple connection in rats. This connection in effect embodies a "judgment" that the new food item's taste or smell is relevant to avoidance behavior (and that other features of the situation are not thus relevant). If the new connection is stable then subsequent changes in different but connected parts of the rat's network will "respect" this "judgment"; that is, they will be influenced by the new connection, but will not influence (change or undo) it. Some of these subsequent changes may embody "judgments" of similarity, dissimilarity, or relevance. These "judgments" thus may depend (in part) on the new connection. If we now imagine that there may be several connections that are relatively stable, once they have been formed, we may suppose that there are several sources through which further "judgments" that govern actions can be influenced.

Approach-Avoidance

Approach-avoidance behavior sometimes occurs when a situation presents conflicting directions for action. A hungry animal that has to expose itself to danger in order to get to food may start for the food, then retreat, start again and retreat again several times. We sometimes do this kind of thing ourselves. I suppose many have had the experience of opening one's mouth to say something, and then thinking better of it. Sometimes this happens several times before we either speak out or become comfortable with being silent.

Approach-avoidance behavior reflects a competition of different parts of our neural networks for control of muscle activity. When this competition is expressed in actual movements, it is inefficient, that is, it wastes energy. For example, in the end, either the hungry animal's starting forward or its retreating (or both) were useless. It would therefore be beneficial if the competition could be carried out among neural (sub)networks without spilling over into action. Such a process would at least resemble a kind of thinking. Thus, if we could understand how approach-avoidance conflicts get pushed backward from overt behavior toward earlier resolution in (sub)network competition, we might understand something about the beginning of thinking. As in the case of the law of effect, it seems out of the question that the change from overt conflict to internal conflict is in general accomplished by anything resembling a calculation. We must look instead to the connections between innervating neurons and muscles, and how these might change in order to produce the internalizing effect.

Let us turn to a second point suggested by approach-avoidance situations. Sometimes, these get resolved because the external conditions change. The food is eaten by another animal, or the danger disappears. Someone else expresses what we wanted to say, or the discussion moves on and our utterance would no longer be appropriate. Sometimes, however, the conditions that give rise to the approach-avoidance situation last quite a while. In this case, some way of resolving the tension sooner rather than later would be useful. There is, therefore, reason to suspect that during an internal conflict, there is a tendency not to simply go over and over the same ground. There should be a tendency for the range of inputs to widen, so that if there is something relevant that will tip the balance decisively, it will be found. If we could understand how this process works, even in its beginnings, we might be started toward a theory of relevance, that is, a theory of how more time of neural processing can, sometimes, allow more and more relevant material to be brought to bear. It seems possible that we might understand how properties of networks help here, in a way that is quite unlike using classificatory schemes that are familiar to AI heuristics.[7]

Ordering

A well-adapted organism will improve its chances of obtaining benefits, but will not do so at the risk of immediate disaster. This is to say that there will be some ordering of importance of alternative actions that lie within its range of possibilities. We can notice in our own experience that the attention we devote to getting food rises with increasing hunger, and anyone who has spent a winter in the American Midwest will understand how extreme cold can force aside almost any thought except getting to shelter. Presumably, analogous ordering is at work in nonlinguistic animals. In any case, it is clear that the effects on our thinking of hunger and cold do not arise by our engaging in calculation. We should, therefore, expect to learn something about thinking by studying just how deprivations of food and warmth, and so on, affect our neural systems. We should not expect such study to tell us about calculational rules. Instead, we should expect it to tell us how (sub)networks interact so as to insure ordering among actions and high activity in (sub)networks that are relevant to high-priority needs. This, once again, will not by itself be an account of intelligence, but it may turn out to be the foundation of such an account, by explaining basic principles of relevance.[8]

Conclusions

We will return to the subject of requirements for action in the next chapter. I will describe a thought experiment that will give new emphasis to the importance of these requirements for our understanding of how intelligence is possible. Before doing that, however, I want to end this chapter by reviewing what we have done and drawing some conclusions. We must also return to our COULD THERE BE question and say what relevance our discussion has to it.

We began this chapter by raising some difficulties for simple PDP. We have mentioned that a possible response to these difficulties is skepticism regarding our ability to understand our intelligence in any way. We have described three kinds of nonskeptical response to the difficulties: mere implementation, hybrid views, and action-directed views. We saw that the mere implementation account answered to a need for broad organizational principles. From Chapter 8, however, we know that there are problems concerning sentential AI rules. So, the mere implementation account does not by itself give us a satisfying view of how intelligence is possible. This is so, despite the fact that on certain occasions—those in which we consciously follow rules—we may very well be using our neural (sub)networks to implement rules.

The fact that two leading approaches to the understanding of intelligence encounter serious difficulties may lead some to skepticism. Such a conclusion, however, would not be reasonable unless one also were persuaded that there is nothing one can add to simple PDP that would relieve its problems. One ought not to be persuaded of this. The purpose of describing hybrid views and action-directed views was to show that there is a wealth of possibilities now being explored that may provide understanding of how PDP (sub)networks are organized into intelligence-providing wholes.

In Chapter 1, I defended the Turing test as a test of intelligence. Since this test says nothing about the construction of the subjects that may pass it, it is automatically open to the possibility that there are several means of producing intelligence. So, the point of thinking about action, or of designing networks that are inspired by the brain, is certainly not that mimicking our structure is logically required for AI. The point of thinking about action and networks is instead to be understood as follows. Sentential AI approaches have run into difficulties that many find impressive. We saw (in Chapter 8) that we cannot argue that there must be a solution to the problems of sentential AI on the ground that *we* are such solutions. We *can* argue, however, that there must be some solution to how a thing can be intelligent, because we are examples of such a solution. So, a reasonable approach is to try to figure out how we manage to be intelligent, in the hope that if we can understand that, we can understand how to make a machine embody the same principles and also be intelligent. There is no guarantee that this will work. We do what we do with an organ of 10^{11}–10^{14} neurons and if all of them (or even a 1000th of them) are really necessary for intelligence, then it may never be practical to build a machine with enough elements. But there is no guarantee that it will not work. In calling something a *principle* of operation, we recognize that there may be more than one way of embodying the principle. If we do come to understand the principles of our own intelligence, it *may* be that we will also understand how to get a machine to make up in speed what it lacks in numbers of elements.

The answer to our COULD THERE BE (a machine that passed the Turing test) question is, therefore, that we do not now know. On the one hand, we have found no argument that shows that there *cannot* be artificial intelligence. We have, however, seen some of the questions we will have to answer if we are to succeed in making it. We can see that we are far from answering some of these questions. If we put several of the points made in this chapter together we will also see that we may need quite a few ideas in order to get a full understanding of intelligence. That is, we may find that we need:

> Mere Implementation for conscious rule following
>
> *plus*
>
> Mere Implementation for *some* unconscious rule following
>
> *plus*
>
> Hybrid Views for *some* unconscious rule following
>
> *plus*
>
> Action-directed Views for *some* unconscious rule following *and* for intelligent results that do not arise from rule following.

If we do need to think of our abilities in all these ways, we also have a further problem. Recall that introducing a plurality of (sub)networks requires us to introduce principles for their organization. Analogously, if we have several different kinds of principles at work in organizing (sub)networks, we will need to understand how they can all fit together.

In the case of our own intelligence, we will, ultimately, want to understand both how different kinds of organization fit together, and how this arrangement could have come about through the process of natural selection. This remark brings us back to the importance of action. We cannot, of course, describe the evolutionary course of a set of principles we do not yet understand. So we must merely keep our ultimate goal in the back of our minds while we work on more immediate problems that we know how to approach. It is in this spirit that I turn to the promised thought experiment.

Chapter 11

The Ill-Connected Robot

We often find it very natural to think of a robot as a computer mounted on the frame of a mobile unit and harnessed to mechanisms that are driven by its outputs. When we think of a robot in this way, it is also natural to put any intelligence we think the robot has on the side of the computer and to regard the robotic body as merely executing commands issued to it by its computer "brain". We also find it natural to apply the same division to ourselves. That is, we commonly think of our brains as the organs of intelligence and of our bodies as the machinery that carries out decisions produced in the brain. An exceptionally intelligent person, we often say, "has brains" or "has a good brain" and we criticize bunglers for not using their brains. We distinguish between brain and brawn, and we try to develop the first by study and the second by exercise.

If we understand this division properly, there can be no objection to it. If we misunderstand the division, however, it will be easy to overlook certain problems. In this chapter, I will describe a robot in a way that is very explicit about the relations between its central intelligence agency and its motors. The way I shall set this robot up seems very natural in some ways, but it leads to some surprises. Once we have seen these, we will want to ask what exactly they show us about the possibilities for our organization, and the organization of possible robots.

Historical Note: We think of robots as purely electromechanical, and we may think of our bodies (including our brains) as purely physical things. It is, therefore, interesting to note that the division between an intelligent computer-brain and a body that merely executes its orders parallels a division that occurs in Descartes's dualistic philosophy. Descartes placed intelligent activity in a nonphysical mind, which communicated with the body through the pineal gland. (Unlike many brain structures, of which there are left and right symmetrically placed pairs, there is only one pineal gland, corresponding to the fact that normally we have only one mind.) The rest of the body was connected to the pineal gland through nerves, and the state of the nerves at their pineal gland ends determined what the rest of the body would do. All the intelligence was in the mind and the pineal gland and nervous system merely carried out the decisions made there.

Robot RIt

Our imaginary robot—Robot RIt—is to have a computer that we will refer to as its brain. This brain is connected to what we shall call Robot RIt's body. The movements of this body are to be under the control of Robot RIt's brain. A key restriction that we shall rigidly observe is this: All of Robot RIt's intelligence derives solely from its brain. We should recall from Chapter 1 that a key property of intelligence is flexibility. So, I am laying it down that Robot RIt has only one source that is able to provide flexible responses to inputs, and that is its brain.

Although I have been restrictive about the *source* of Robot RIt's intelligence, I shall be very liberal about the degree of that intelligence. I shall assume that Robot RIt's brain is some sort of computer that we could have put to use in a Turing test situation. I shall assume that if we had done this, Robot RIt's brain would have succeeded wonderfully. This means, let us recall, that interrogators would have obtained no useful information from the test and so would have been equally likely to guess wrong as to guess right about which subject is the person and which is the computer. I am not assuming that Robot Rlt's brain is a computer of a familiar kind, nor that it is not. I am not asserting that the problems we have seen in strategies for AI can be solved, nor am I asserting that they cannot be solved. I am just going to *suppose* that by some means or other, we have got a computer that does well in the Turing test and that we are using this computer as Robot Rlt's brain.

The next restriction that Robot Rlt must satisfy depends on the idea of a *channel* that I shall now introduce. The term is familiar from its use in connection with television sets and has approximately the same sense here. Channels are conduits through which communications may pass. We can use a single wire as a channel, and using different wires that are insulated from each other is a convenient and familiar way of having several distinct channels travel over almost the same route. But a single channel need not be a single wire. If our message consists of patterns of signals in, say, five wires, then those five wires constitute one channel. We must, however, be a little careful. If I get five telephone calls from different places and then make one decision based on all the information I received, I still get messages over five different channels. I can divide up the total information I received into five messages. If we want to consider five wires as composing one channel, then our method of communication must not count the output of any four wires as an intelligible message. That is, the minimum usable output must be a pattern that is defined by the signals arriving over all five wires. Such a situation is not hard to imagine. We might have a row of five lights that are either on or off. When all are off, no employee has to go see the boss, but for each of the 31 patterns that have at least one light on, there is an employee for whom that pattern is a command to go see the boss. Partially obstructed vision of the five lights would mean that the message was not fully usable. If everyone could see only four lights, there would always be two employees who did not know whether they were or were not supposed to go.

When you watch TV, the image you receive is caused by what is put out from the broadcasting antenna. That is characteristic of channels, and we may require as part of their definition that conditions that occur later and farther away in a channel are effects of events in that channel that occur earlier and nearer. Similarly, your television would be unusable if the channels interfered with each

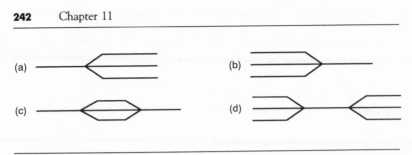

FIGURE 11.1

other, that is, if the images in the different channels did not depend on *different* causes. We can generalize this to the requirement that events in different channels must be causally independent of each other.

A single channel can divide into several, as in part (a) of Figure 11.1. This means that a signal in one channel causes events in several channels that are causally independent of each other after the division. So long as nothing happens to one of the channels that does not happen to all of them, the message in each will, of course, be the same. That is because they are all caused by the same earlier event, not because they affect each other. Conversely, several channels may merge into a single one, as in part (b) of Figure 11.1. This means that before they merge, the messages they pass are causally independent of each other, but that after they join, the messages are no longer independent. That is, the message after the point where they join is causally dependent, not on just what is in one or two of the contributing channels, but on what is in all of them.

Part (c) of Figure 11.1 represents a case where a channel divides and then rejoins. While it is divided, the message in each division is the same. Yet, these are several channels before they merge, because they are causally independent. That is, something *could have* affected one without affecting the others, even though no case of this has been depicted. In part (d) of Figure 11.1, things are a bit more interesting. At the left there are three channels, which may be assumed to be independent. These merge into a single channel whose message will in general be different from the one in any of the contributing channels, because it depends on all of them. This channel then divides into three that have the same message, but which may join with different other channels later on.

With this background, we can understand what I mean by saying that the output of a computer in the Turing test situation is a *single channel* output. The communication channel that is ordinarily thought of in the Turing test situation connects the computer to a typewriter that types one letter at a time. It has its effect by sending a series of signals over one channel. (In general, it would be natural to conceive of this channel as one wire, although, as we have seen, there is no necessary connection between the number of channels and the number of wires.) Now, I am going to lay it down that *Robot Rlt's brain has a single channel output*. Its production of that output may involve parallel processing (that is, multiple-channel processing) or it may not, but the output itself comes over a single channel. It is this output that contains, so to speak, all the intelligence that Robot Rlt's actions will have, and that will drive Robot Rlt's movements.

The point of the phrase "ill-connected robot" is to remind us of this restriction. An ill-connected robot's source of intelligence is indeed connected to its mechanisms of action, but the connection is a "narrow" one, that is, one with a "width" of only one channel. The contrasting term "well-connected robot" would refer to a robot that was connected throughout by many channels. It would be one whose intelligent action was produced by a process that was always parallel.

We need one further stipulation about our robot, namely that it must not be too simple. It must have several different parts, each of which can move in several ways. For definiteness, I shall assume that Robot Rlt has a head, a torso, two arms, two legs, and two hands that each have two fingers. I shall assume that there are joints at the analogues of neck, shoulder, hip, wrist, and knuckle. I shall assume that these joints are movable and that Robot Rlt can move its head and limbs to positions roughly analogous to all the positions to which we can move our corresponding parts. Simpler robots would be enough to illustrate the reasoning I am about to present. We are, however, imagining that Robot Rlt's brain does well in the Turing test, so it will be convenient to provide it with a body that is physically capable of carrying out all the actions that correspond to advice that its brain might provide.

Robot Rlt, we may say, has a very capable body and a very intelligent brain. What we want in a robot, however, is intelligent *action*.

We can begin our discussion of how we might get intelligent action by noting that there is one obvious requirement for which we have not yet made any provision. No matter how clever you are, you will act stupidly if you do not know what situation you are in. To act intelligently, you must have some way of getting to know what is going on around you. The same point exactly holds for Robot Rlt. So, let us provide it with a TV eye, a microphone ear, some pressure sensors, and some gas detectors.

Let us also make the vast assumption that the signals that these sensors produce are converted into useful inputs for Robot Rlt's brain. What I have in mind is this. Because Robot Rlt's brain would do well on the Turing test, we can assume that it gives credible answers to questions about what it should do in various situations. For example, if an interrogator were to ask it what it should do if it smells smoke and does not know of any explanation for it other than some unseen fire, Robot Rlt's brain might produce something along the lines of "Look for a benign cause (one that presents no danger) and if you do not find one, call the fire department and leave." If the interrogator were to follow up by asking for examples of benign causes of smoke, Robot Rlt's brain might mention frying food or fireplace smoke from another room.[1] Now, if Robot Rlt is to use its brain's ability to give these satisfactory outputs in order to act intelligently, it must be able to tell when it is in a situation in which there is smoke but it cannot find a benign cause. This is going to require a lot more than just a smoke detector and a TV camera. There will have to be something that gets the signals from these devices hooked into the same part of Robot Rlt's brain that was activated by the interrogator's question about what to do if one smells smoke. We can explain how Robot Rlt's brain's intelligent answer to the interrogator is connected with Robot Rlt's intelligent action only if we suppose that the input from the sensors is made to stimulate the same capacities that are activated by the input from the interrogator.

The problems involved in making this connection are interesting and enormous. Moreover, thinking about them raises some of the same complications that come out of the reasoning I am about to present. Nonetheless, I am going to assume that somehow we have solved them. My purpose in making this assumption is to enable us to focus on a problem that concerns what we may call the output side of

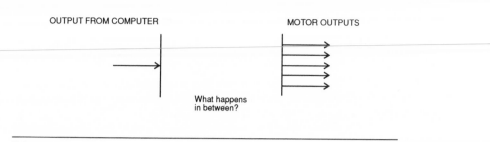

OUTPUT FROM COMPUTER   MOTOR OUTPUTS

What happens
in between?

FIGURE 11.2

Robot Rlt's brain. I want to make it very clear that *even if* we solved all the problems on the input side, we would still have a problem to cope with on the output side. Let us now try to understand this problem.

Dividing Outputs

Robot Rlt, we have supposed, has a body with several parts that can move in many ways. Having such a body will require Robot Rlt to have several motors that move these parts. If Robot Rlt's actions are to reflect the intelligence of its computer-brain output, these motors must be able to produce a wide variety of actions. Each of these actions *may*, of course, be regarded as a single output (of the robot, not of its brain). Since they are the resultant of the outputs of Robot Rlt's several motors, however, it is always open to us to regard Robot Rlt's output as consisting of the activity of each of its motors. Actions regarded in this way will involve *multiple* channels. We are supposing, however, that all of Robot Rlt's motors are under the control of its brain's single-channel output. What we must now do, therefore, is to think about how signals in a single channel might be converted into a multiple-channel output. This problem is schematized in Figure 11.2.

There is one possibility for single to multiple-channel conversion that is very simple—so simple, in fact, that it may give the impression that the general problem is trivial. This is the case in which one channel feeds several identical devices (see the schematic diagram in Figure 11.3). An example is a house with many telephone extensions. One signal comes in, but it is divided (or, multiplied) in the manner of a tree, and thus produces the same result in several

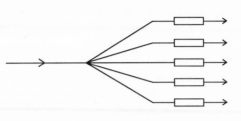

FIGURE 11.3

places at once. The arrangement in Figure 11.3 cannot, however, adequately represent what is going on in Robot Rlt. This is because its motors have to do *different* things. Some will have to be running while others are off, and those that are running will not always be going at the same speed. For example, when looking for a source of smoke, Robot Rlt's head may be turning while its legs are moving back and forth and its arms hanging still. We can put the point generally by saying that the output of Robot Rlt's motors is not only multiple but *independent*. Correspondingly, our problem is not just to get multiple-channel output out of the signal in a single channel but to get independent outputs in multiple channels out of such a signal.

Let us turn to a somewhat more complicated arrangement. As before, the signal in the output channel of Robot Rlt's brain is divided into several branches, each of which carries the same signal. These branches, however, end in *different* devices, which therefore give rise to different effects. Figure 11.4 gives a schematic representation of this arrangement. We can imagine an example by starting with automatic garage doors. These are operated by one-channel signals sent from approaching cars. Opening a door is almost all that these signals do. It would, however, be easy to arrange for the same signal to unlock the front door, start cooking dinner, and activate a recording that would boom out a welcoming salutation. These results would be obtained just because the devices that received the signal are different devices and react differently to it.

Before asking whether this structure might be suitable for Robot Rlt, let us consider two variants. Some garage-door openers do one thing besides raising the door: They may also turn on a light. This need not happen at the same time that the door starts to go up, and we may imagine two possible arrangements for producing a delay.

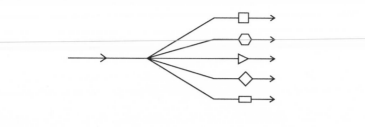

FIGURE 11.4

First, it may be that a switch for the light is activated by the same signal that opens the door, but that it is an inefficient mechanical switch. This would mean that it would take some noticeable time to make the electrical connection that turns on the light. Alternatively, it may be that the signal from the car turns on only the motor for the door, and then the door trips the switch for the light at some point on its way up. We should notice that either of these strategies could be used to introduce a considerable amount of sequencing into the response of a set of different devices that are all activated in one way or another by the same single-channel signal.

Garage-door openers with lights or with other imagined gadgets have provided a familiar and simple way of introducing one solution to the problem of getting multiple independent outputs from a single channel. There are two respects, however, in which these devices are too simple for use in constructing Robot Rlt. One is that, in addition to having only one channel, they can send only one signal in that channel, namely, Move![2] Robot Rlt's brain, however, can transmit a wide variety of signals through its single channel. It may transmit as many signals as may be required in order to do well on the Turing test. Second, a garage door motor either runs or does not. Robot Rlt's motors, however, may run faster or slower, continuously or intermittently.

Let us now ask what the minimum alteration to Figure 11.4 would be that would allow us to take account of the complexities just mentioned. The answer is schematized in Figure 11.5. Let us focus for a moment on just one of Robot Rlt's motors, which we will call M_1 and which we will take to be represented schematically by the top entry in Figure 11.5. This motor, we shall suppose, can do more than one thing. It may be on or off, and if it is on it may be in various

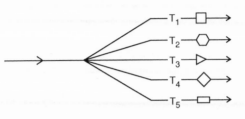

FIGURE 11.5

states of speed. Let us represent these different states schematically as A, B, C, D, and E. Now let us also schematically represent the possible messages that may be outputs of Robot Rlt's brain and therefore inputs that come down the branch channel that connects to M_1. We can do this simply by imagining that we have numbered the possible outputs, 1, 2, 3, n. Finally, the Ts in Figure 11.5 are tables, each constructed like the example given in Table 11.1. When a message comes down the branch line from Robot Rlt's brain, there is a device that looks up the message in the table, notes the corresponding state, and sends a command to the motor to get into that state.

Let us now ask whether the strategy summarized in Figure 11.5 is one that we can use to construct Robot Rlt. The answer is that although this strategy is logically possible, it comes at a prohibitive price. Since the number of messages can be taken to be finite, there is no formal contradiction in imagining having our robotics engineers work out tables of connections like Table 11.1.[3] But the number of possible messages has been assumed to be very, very large. The

Messages		States
2, 3, 16, 19, . . .	⟶	A
1, 5, 8, 12, . . .	⟶	B
4, 9, 11, 17, . . .	⟶	C
7, 13, 15, 20, . . .	⟶	D
6, 10, 14, 18, . . .	⟶	E

TABLE 11.1

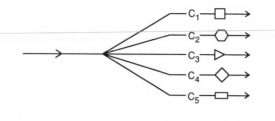

FIGURE 11.6

specter of the Block machine (see Chapter 1) looms over the project of making such tables. Our engineers will have to be up all night, night after night, calculating the right motor outputs for each of the directives to action that Robot Rlt's brain might produce. They will, of course, have to do the same for all of Robot Rlt's motors. Then they will have to add to each motor a device that implements the table.

Let us sum up by saying that the project of building Robot Rlt according to the strategy of Figure 11.5 is *unfeasible*. Since we would like a feasible method, not just a logically possible one, we must look for alternative strategies. Figure 11.6 schematizes a strategy that seems to be suggested naturally by the problem we have just described. Instead of having our engineers work out the tables that connect inputs from Robot Rlt's brain to motor outputs, let us put a computer on each branch channel to work this out as needed when a message actually arrives. Whether we might build some robot in this way, I shall not say. What is clear is that we cannot build *Robot Rlt* in this way. Robot Rlt, let us recall, has *only one* source of intelligence, its brain. A robot built according to the strategy of Figure 11.6, however, has many sources of intelligence, namely, each one of the little computers on the separate branches. Why is this so? We can indicate the point briefly by remarking that these computers have to accomplish the same task as our engineers did in our previous try. More carefully, let us recall that the hallmark of intelligence is flexibility. The little computers in Figure 11.6 must have this property. Even though they need to give only one of five outputs, they must be able to figure out which is the *appropriate* one, given their input. The

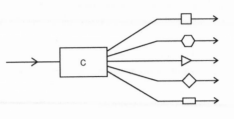

FIGURE 11.7

inputs, however, are in general new ones. That is, there may some-times be a repeated message, but each computer is going to have to be prepared to find an appropriate output for any of the large number of messages it may receive. So, in general, it must have the flexibility that is required to find appropriate responses to new input situations.

The same objection applies to the configuration represented in Figure 11.7. Here, the conversion of the signal in the single-channel output of Robot Rlt's brain to independent multiple outputs is accomplished by a single computer that calculates the results for all the branches to the motors. This gets the number of sources of intelligence down to two, but this remains one too many for compliance with the specifications for Robot Rlt.

Action Kernels

We seem to be approaching a dead end. We must turn a single channel output into independent, multiple-channel output. Doing this by table proved unfeasible; doing it any other way violates our constraint that there be only one source of intelligence. Perhaps it is just not possible to build Robot Rlt according to the constraints we have set down. We shall indeed want to keep this possibility in mind. Our ultimate conclusion must, however, be somewhat more complicated. In this section, I will introduce the background that we will need in order to see why.

Let us begin by reminding ourselves that there are *only two* assumptions about the output of Robot Rlt's brain that we have used in the foregoing argument: The output of Robot Rlt's brain comes through a single channel, and there can be very, very many different output signals. Nothing about the *form* of the outputs mattered to the argument. In particular, we need not assume that they are given in a natural language. Since Robot Rlt's brain was introduced as one that can pass the Turing test, we may have found it easy to think of the outputs as linguistic, but this was never assumed as part of any of the arguments in the preceding section.

Attending closely to this point may lead the reader to suggest a way of removing an obstacle to Robot Rlt's construction. Perhaps, after all, there need not be so very many output signals that come from Robot Rlt's brain. If there were, say, only a few hundred commands for actions that this brain ever needed to issue, then it would become feasible for us to work out in advance the tables that listed the appropriate motor states for each command.

In order to see whether such a proposal could be made to work, let us develop it in somewhat more detail. The first thing we must do is to deal with a problem I glossed over when I discussed the strategy represented by Figure 11.5. The difficulty I did call attention to (namely, a prohibitively large number of different signals) was sufficient to dismiss that strategy, so I did not need to talk about other problems. If, however, we want to provisionally accept that strategy (because we think we may be able to keep the different signals down to a feasible number) we must now mention the following complication. How motors must be operated in order to do an action depends on where a robot is and how its parts are positioned in relation to surrounding objects. "Pick up the broom", for example, will require one motion if the broom is two feet away and another if it is ten feet away, one motion if it is on the floor, another if it is standing up, one motion if Robot Rlt is lying on the floor and another if it is standing up. There can be no such thing as a set of motor states (or, a set of movements) for a given action. At best, there might be a set of motor states given an action *plus* a location *plus* a set of positions of a robot's parts. If we are to base Robot Rlt's intelligent action on the strategy represented in Figure 11.5, we will have to add something that will enable it to react to these additional factors.

It is not hard to imagine how these additions might be made, as long as we do not press for details. Positions of parts can be described in terms of angles of rotation from some baseline position. Perhaps we could arrange things so that the distance traveled by, say, an arm is reduced proportionately to the angle it has already traveled in the right direction. So, for example, a command to raise its arm might move one of Robot Rlt's arm-motors for three seconds at medium speed, if the arm was hanging straight down to begin with. Perhaps the same command will run that motor for only one and a half seconds if the arm is already extended straight forward, and three-quarters of a second if the arm is already 45 degrees above horizontal. Differences of location (of things, like the broom in our example) can be handled by having Robot Rlt's brain issue a command like "Go forward" or "Turn" together with an indication of time, so that longer times yield greater distances or rotations. Or, perhaps it issues a series of commands, "Go forward", "Go forward", . . . , with more members corresponding to greater distances.

We must notice that these problems must be solved, but we must not get bogged down in them. Let us help ourselves to remember them by giving them a name, "orientation problems". Let us put them aside, however, by simply *assuming* that they can be solved. Let us, moreover, assume that they can be solved without adding a second source of intelligence to Robot Rlt. If this seems like giving away too much, I can only ask the reader to wait and see where we end up after making these assumptions. I do, in fact, think that the assumptions are plausible. The modifications of motor activity can be proportional to the amount of prior displacement of parts or distance from objects to be acted upon. This means that there is nothing complicated to figure out about what modifications to make. (This is emphatically not to say anything about the actual engineering complications of the devices that make those modifications.) It would seem that they could be accomplished by feedback control mechanisms of a type that no one would credit with intelligence. This is, however, to be taken only as a plausibility argument, to make us feel good about the assumptions we are making.

Let us recall that we are developing the suggestion that we can succeed in building Robot Rlt if the number of commands for actions that its brain ever has to issue is in the range of only a few hundred. It is now time to turn to the main question for this proposal: How can we suppose that the number of action commands can be so few? After all, we did lay it down that Robot Rlt has a capable body and that it can act out the intelligent advice it gives. If it gives advice about what to do when smoke is detected, it can proceed to act on it when its smoke detector is stimulated. If it can tell you how to get to the electrical repair shop, it can get there itself when its brushes are due for replacement. If there is no end to the things it may advise, there is no end to the things it might do.

If we can make the suggestion we are investigating work, we must find a way of "reducing" the many actions that Robot Rlt might do to a relative few. The key to doing this is to notice that we can get a lot of variety out of *series* of commands. To make the point very simply, the commands "go forward one foot", "left face", and "right face" can be used to get a robot to any place, by appropriate ordering and repetitions. Perhaps, then, we can envisage Robot Rlt's brain as using its intelligence to figure out how it can get done what needs doing. This will have to mean that it does more than just figure out some general description of an action. It must figure out how that action can be accomplished by a series of appropriately sequenced and repeated actions drawn from a repertoire of a few hundred "simple" or "basic" actions. Each of the commands for these few hundred actions can be feasibly listed in tables that associate them with motor states. The instructions for motor states can then be supposed to be modified by whatever we use to solve orientation problems.

Let us have some terminology that will help us remember this somewhat complicated situation. We have imagined that everything we would count as an action done by Robot Rlt may be "composed" of some comparatively small number of actions. By "composed" I mean that you get the composed action by going through some series of the actions in the small set. I propose to call the actions in the small set "action *kernels*" or just "kernels". Actions that are kernels are associated directly with motor states in the tables (of Figure 11.5). Actions that are not kernels I shall sometimes call "gross actions". Gross actions are products of the kernels that compose them and the associations in the tables between those kernels and motor states. The association given by the tables is, as always, subject to modifications that solve orientation problems.

I shall call the kind of account I have just described an "action kernel theory", or AKT for short. When I say that AKT *applies* to something, I shall mean that an action kernel theory is true of that thing.

There is one kind of "action" in which the idea of an AKT is extremely plausible and we can use this case to give a transparent illustration of the essential idea. This is the production of language. There are very many sentences that we might utter and saying them can be thought of as gross actions. The vast number of sentences that we might produce are, however, all composed of a relatively small set of syllables. It is at least plausible to suppose that our brains produce not only what content we wish to convey but also a series of syllables that will convey it. There may then be the equivalent of a "table" that gets the right set of larynx and mouth muscles operating for each syllable. There will be an additional factor concerning how loud we intend to speak and there is the fact that the production of one syllable depends partly on the syllables that come before and after it. We can think of these complications as analogous to orientation problems in the production of nonlinguistic actions. We can then think of AKT as proposing that nonlinguistic actions are decomposable into "syllables" (kernels) whose proper sequencing in a "language of (nonlinguistic) action" results in our familiar (gross) actions.

Is there any alternative way that we can solve the problem that led us to introduce AKT? I do not see how there can be. There can, of course, be different action kernel theories. That is, there can be different proposals as to what the kernels are, and how many are required. To take one of the very simplest cases, we do not really need three orders, right face, left face, and forward, to get a robot to any spot, since "right face" can be "composed" out of three "left face" orders in a row. Still, an actual theory might propose either that there are just two orders, or that there are in fact all three as distinct brain outputs. There might be different views about how "atomistic" a decomposition is required. For example, one theory might treat extending a jointed arm as a kernel, while another might compose this out of one action for the upper arm and another for the forearm. But to avail oneself of the strategy of trying to build Robot Rlt by reducing the number of commands that need to be listed in the tables of Figure 11.5 is to commit oneself to the claim that all that Robot Rlt does can be brought about by (series of) commands that lie within a relatively small set; and that is to adopt AKT.

What Is the Significance of the Ill-Connected Robot?

It is time to draw some conclusions from our thought experiment. The simplest way I can think of to state its result is this: If we can build Robot Rlt at all, an AKT must apply to it. The argument for this can be summarized as follows. So long as we supposed the number of commands for action that might arrive from Robot Rlt's brain to be very, very large, there was no way to build it, that is, no feasible way to satisfy all the constraints we laid down. So, we had to make the number of commands for action small. But the only way we could find to do this was to accept AKT.

We can restate our conclusion in the following way. If we want to build a robot—any robot—that can match the flexibility of action that we have attributed to Robot Rlt, then we must either accept that an AKT applies to it, or we must violate at least one constraint of Robot Rlt's construction. The key constraints are the limitation to just one source of intelligence, and the limitation of the output of this source to just one channel. So, if we want to build a robot that has the capabilities we imagined for Robot Rlt, then *either* an AKT applies to it *or* it has more than one source of intelligence *or* its source of intelligence gives multiple-channel output. It will help us to remember these alternatives if we have names for them. I shall say that we can get the capabilities we imagined for Robot Rlt only through AKT or through *homuncularism* (a term I shall explain below) or through *well-connected systems*.

This conclusion was derived from assumptions that mention hardly anything about the details of robotic construction. It was forced upon us by considering what was needed for intelligent action by an agent whose body has several parts that can move independently of one another. This description, however, fits human beings. Our set of three alternatives applies, therefore, not only to robots, but to ourselves.

At this point, it would certainly be desirable to eliminate two of the three alternatives as candidates for an account of how human action should be conceived. Unfortunately, I do not believe I can produce an argument that will do this. Since my sympathies probably will be evident anyway, I should perhaps say that they lie with the third alternative. Nothing that follows, however, should be mis-

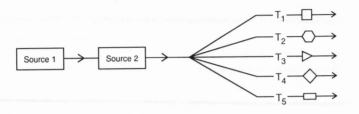

FIGURE 11.8

construed as a claim to proving that this is the correct alternative for describing us. Despite the fact that we must remain tentative, there is something of interest to be learned by considering each of the accounts.

AKT

Anyone who proposes that an AKT applies to us is committed to the existence of some definite set of action kernels. These can be allowed to vary somewhat from person to person, but one would expect that there would be a lot of overlap between one person's set of kernels and another's. If one adopts this alternative, there is a clearly suggested research project of trying to identify the kernel actions.

A full account of this kind ought to address itself to two further questions. One of these asks why it is that we should have to do *research* here. Why should we not be conscious of the actions from which all we do is composed? These actions, according to AKT, must be repeated very often, so it seems odd that they should escape our notice. The other question asks about the relations between our conscious reasoning about actions and the process of producing commands for our kernel actions.

A possible way of responding to both these questions begins with the arrangement represented in Figure 11.8. When a new situation presents itself, a part of our brain (Source 1) engages in some processing that gives an instruction for a gross action as a single-channel output. This output drives a second source of intelligence that figures out which series of kernel actions is required to get the gross action performed. The outputs of this source are then connected through tables to independently operating motors. If one adopts this division of sources of intelligence, one may also find it plausible to hypothesize that we are conscious of the results of Source 1, but unconscious of the results of Source 2.

We can get a better understanding of this response by asking what would happen if we allowed multiple outputs from Source 1. The result would be to remove the motivation for holding an AKT. An AKT is needed only if you have to convert a single-channel output into multiple, independent signals; and multiple outputs from Source 1 would make this unnecessary. We can make the same point in this way: Allowing multiple-channel output from Source 1 results in a view that is indistinguishable from one that denies the applicability of an AKT to us and proposes a thoroughly well-connected structure throughout our processing. Still another way of making the point is to say that if we suppose multiple outputs from Source 1, there will be little or nothing for Source 2 to do.

Although there is nothing contradictory about the view represented in Figure 11.8, it seems to me extremely unlikely that it is true of us. The reason is that it doesn't make evolutionary sense. Source 2 is useless without Source 1 and the tables, T_1 through T_5. But each of these will be useless to an organism without the other one and Source 2. It is very hard to swallow the idea that we have evolved a set of distinct, complex structures each of which is useless until the whole mechanism is in place.

A natural response here is to move away from the idea that there are so many distinct structures. If we do this by absorbing both Source 2 and the tables into Source 1, we will have a device with multiple-channel output. This, we have seen, removes the motivation for having an AKT at all. What if we suppose only that the functions of Source 1 and Source 2 are done by a brain part that cannot be analyzed into two units connected by a single channel? (We would suppose its output to be series of kernel actions.) This seems to be the best way of understanding how an AKT might apply to us. Again, however, it has a tendency to undercut the reason for believing in the applicability of an AKT. This is because we must now allow for at least some parallel distributed processing. If the processing in our source of intelligence is never squeezed down to a single channel, then at every stage of processing between input to our source of intelligence and output of series of kernel actions, there must be at least two channels such that the pattern of signals in both, and not just one of them, is the minimal unit relevant to producing appropriate outcomes. It is *possible* that we might have to admit just this much parallelism and no more. If we have to admit this much, however, then we have to allow that parallel distributed processing *can* produce intelligent results; and if we have to allow this, it seems ill-motivated to suppose that it can make only a very limited contribution to our intelligence.

I believe these remarks will explain why I am doubtful that an AKT applies to us. Ill-motivation, however, is not contradiction, so perhaps such a theory will prove true of us after all. Our discussion should in any case lead those who doubt PDP approaches to work on developing an AKT.

Homuncularism

Homunculus means "little human". Since intelligence is a human characteristic, a little intelligent thing of any kind is like a little human and may be called a homunculus. The second of our alternative views regards people as composed of distinct units that are intelligent and connected among each other by single channels. Since each of several parts must be smaller than the whole they compose, such a view regards people as composed of homunculi.[4]

It is important to conceive of a plurality of units when thinking about homuncularism. Proposing that *one* homunculus resides within an intelligent thing cannot give any *explanation* of that thing's intelligence; it merely shifts the problem to explaining the intelligence of the homunculus. A plurality of homunculi, however, can be more stupid individually than the whole to whose intelligence they are supposed to contribute through their activities and connections. We can even suppose that there are homunculi within homunculi, so long as each part-homunculus is more stupid than the whole homunculus of which it is a part.

Homuncularism is an attractive approach to AI, because it responds to a good principle of engineering. Designing things from scratch can involve an expense that can be avoided if we can use advances already made. If we can take a bunch of parts that we already have and do something new by connecting them, we may find an easy, even if somewhat messy, solution to a problem.

Unfortunately, what makes sense for engineering may not make much sense from an evolutionary point of view. We know how devices that we invented came to be made, but we must wonder how brain-parts that might be thought to do particular intelligent jobs happened to come into existence. If they have a lot of intelligence, then their having come into existence before connection with other brain-parts does not seem plausible at all. This is, of course, a point that we made in reference to the view represented in Figure 11.8, which can indeed be regarded as a two-homunculus view.

We can go some way toward relieving this problem by supposing that there are many units of intelligence, each one of which does not do very much. Perhaps rather simple units could make some small contribution to survival, and evolution could increase their number and "experiment" with various ways of connecting them. This is a fascinating possibility. Those who pursue it must, however, recognize that we ultimately will want to have some organizing principles for homunculi. To see what we need, let us first notice that we cannot have an evolutionarily plausible view if the usefulness of each homunculus depends on its being connected to all the others in some special and precise way. It must, on the contrary, be useful in many different contexts of connection. So, if we pursue homuncularism, we must hope to find a theory that (a) tells us what relatively simple and not-too-richly connected units can contribute to survival, (b) offers principles that explain how or why connecting these in ways that are not unrealistically precise can increase survival value, and (c) explains how evolutionarily possible refinements of connections eventually can produce human intelligence.

As before, I have no argument that shows that there cannot be a theory of this kind. Nonetheless, I am doubtful. The more intelligent we must suppose individual homunculi to be, and the more carefully connected, the harder it will be to square homuncularism with evolution. So, it looks as if we should suppose a successful homuncularism to have many homunculi that do not depend on precise wiring connections to make their contribution. The obvious way to decrease dependence on precise connections is to be very liberal with them and have everything multiply connected. A device with lots of units that are multiply connected, however, will begin to look very like a well-connected PDP system. So, it seems that the more plausible we make our version of homuncularism, the harder it will be to distinguish it from the "alternative" of PDP.

Well-Connected Systems

Our sensory inputs come to us over several channels—optical, auditory, olfactory, and so on. Most of these channels are themselves multiple-channel devices. The projections of our visual systems onto our brains preserve much of the spatial organization on our retinas. This means that even though there is some merging of different visual channels, a large multiplicity of channels is maintained deep into the visual processing system. Except under very special conditions, we also have multiple-channel output. That is, we typically act through innervating many muscles, each of which is served by bundles of innervating neurons. The view that we are well-connected systems is the view that this multiplicity of channels is, in general, *not* squeezed down to a single channel anywhere in the course of processing.

There is one of our outputs that can be regarded as involving a single channel, namely, our linguistic output. This fact is not in conflict with the view that we are well-connected systems, because the signal in the single channel here is an output, not a part of our processing. Similarly, language reception (whether by reading or listening) is a single-channel reception, but that is input, not processing. My hedging phrase "in general" allows for there to be *some* cases in which processing can be regarded as essentially taking place in a single channel. Perhaps there is some single-channel processing immediately prior to our production of words. (By "immediately" prior, I mean occurring as part of the process of language production that takes place *after* our thinking processes have arrived at the meaning to be expressed.) Arithmetical calculation appears to be another likely example. The view that we are well-connected systems regards such cases as very special exceptions to the general rule that the processing that lies behind our intelligence is done in multiple channels.

It implies that when the arithmetical calculation has been completed, the use of the result (for anything other than further calculation) will again involve several channels.

It is a consequence of the well-connected systems view that the "natural" way of looking at things with which we began this chapter is false. I am referring to the idea that we use our intelligence to arrive at a description of what should be done, and then feed the results of this intelligence to executing units. If the results of using intelligence are conceived, as I think is usual, as instructions, commands, or in any other quasilinguistic way, this conception has the consequence that our processing is squeezed down to one channel between intelligence and execution. If we deny this consequence, we must take a different view of the relation between language and action. We will have to think of (nonlinguistic) actions as our primary outputs. In their case, multiple motor-neuron outputs to muscles are merely the last stage of a processing of patterns that has been multiple-channel throughout. Language will then be regarded as an ability that has evolved as an addition to the processes that lead to (nonlinguistic) action.

One familiar experience might seem to be in conflict with the well-connected point of view. This is the fact that we often think to ourselves, in language. We "mull things over", that is to say, we *talk to ourselves*. This talking is silent, to be sure, but is nonetheless plainly linguistic in character. Moreover, silent soliloquy is often a prelude to action, and especially those actions we are likely to regard as particularly intelligent. How can we possibly square these facts with the idea that the processing behind intelligent performance is typically done in a multiple-channel way?

There is indeed something remarkable about talking to ourselves. We are, however, not entitled to take this phenomenon as showing that our intelligent processing is essentially linguistic. This is because there is an alternative view according to which what is remarkable about silent soliloquy is the fact that we can treat our own unvoiced output as if it were actual auditory input. We can, that is, produce inhibited single-channel output and then process it as if we had received it as single-channel input. Now, a view of this kind says nothing about the nature of the process that occurs between reception of linguistic input and production of our next linguistic output. Saying nothing, it does not, of course, prove that the processing is not single channel. But it is *compatible* with the well-connected point of view.

So far, I have been explaining and to some extent defending the well-connected point of view. I must now mention—or, rather, give a reminder—that this view is not without some problems. They are those that we saw in the last chapter, and which we can summarize in this way: The criticisms of simple PDP show that we need some organizing principles in order to explain how a collection of PDP (sub)networks could give rise to intelligence. The well-connected system view that we have just been describing proposes that we are a collection of PDP (sub)networks, and so it requires such organizing principles. We do not, however, know what these principles are. We have (in Chapter 10) looked at some ideas that may pan out, and we have seen some suggestions about what principles of action might look like. We do not, however, actually have a theory that explains how a well-connected system can work. Even if one is sympathetic to my leanings in the direction of the well-connected view, one must admit that there is an enormous amount of work that remains to be done.

Concluding Remarks

The ill-connected robot brings to our attention a problem that arises when we try to think carefully about thought and action. It does not provide the solution, but it does give some structure to the field of possible solutions. It shows us that certain proposals for providing the solution must meet certain challenges.

The relation of the ill-connected robot to our COULD THERE BE question is this. We do not at present have a theory that shows us how to make a computer that passes the Turing test. We saw in earlier chapters that we could not prove that sentential AI will work. We saw that we cannot legitimately argue that it must work because we are intelligent. We get a much stronger argument, however, if we say that there is *some* way by which a thing can be intelligent, because *we* are intelligent. This cannot *disprove* skepticism, of course: It is not inconsistent to say that intelligence is simply mysterious. It is not inconsistent to say that there can be no understanding of ourselves if this means having a theory about how our parts work so as to produce intelligence. It would, however, be unreasonable to accept this view unless all attempts to find a way of having a theory of intelligence had come to a dead end. The difficulties of sentential AI do not put us in this position, for there are many ideas yet to be pursued. The ill-connected robot helps to make it clear that there are indeed interesting questions that still need to be investigated.

Some readers may be inclined to draw a different conclusion from our discussion. Our original question, after all, was COULD THERE BE a *computer* that passes the *Turing test?* This says nothing about robots or about action. If we *have* to bring in robots and action in order to have a theory of intelligence, perhaps this shows that we *cannot* have a computer that passes the Turing test.

This, however, is not the right conclusion to draw. We act and we speak. I have been arguing, in effect, that we cannot understand how we act intelligently by first understanding how we speak intelligently. On the contrary, I have been explaining why I incline to the approximately opposite view that we must understand how we can act intelligently as a necessary part of understanding how we can speak intelligently. But this does not imply that we must be able to act in order to be able to speak. It implies only that the organizing principles of an intelligent speaker must be those suitable for an intelligent agent. This requires the possibility of having a capacity for action, but it does not require actual possession of that capacity. Our friends from Chapter 3, the paralytic Akinetia and Robot Esh (when disconnected), are again useful here. They cannot act, but their organizing principles are those of agents. None of the foregoing arguments rules out the possibility of Robot Esh; and none of them shows any inappropriateness in my use (see p. 46) of "computer" as a label for one of its parts.

Some readers may draw a despairing conclusion from our discussion: All this effort on AI and still no actual working theory! My hope, however, is that these last two chapters will leave the reader with quite a different attitude. The human brain is a marvelously complex organ and the exploration of its operations will be a fascinating part of the project of understanding ourselves for a very long time. The pursuit of artificial intelligence will be both partner in and beneficiary of this project. There are many opportunities here for creative work, many ideas about computer organization to be tried out, and many models of robotic design to be investigated.

Chapter 1

1. Alan Turing, "Computing Machinery and Intelligence", *Mind* 59 (1950): 433–60. Reprinted in Alan Ross Anderson, *Minds and Machines* (Englewood Cliffs, N.J.: Prentice-Hall, 1964), pp. 4–30. Parenthetical numbers in the text refer to the latter source.

2. Joseph Weizenbaum, *Computer Power and Human Reason: From Judgment to Calculation* (San Francisco: W. H. Freeman, 1976), pp. 3–8 and 188–91.

3. This objection is inspired by Keith Gunderson. See his "The Imitation Game", *Mind* 73 (1964): 234–45. Reprinted in Anderson, *Minds and Machines*, pp. 60–71.

4. I have changed the example for the sake of realism, but the point is intended to capture one aspect of Keith Gunderson's discussion of his rock box example in "The Imitation Game".

5. Ned Block, "Psychologism and Behaviorism", *The Philosophical Review* 90 (1981): 5–43.

6. We can suppose things are arranged so that in the unlikely event of the same opener being used in two different games, the second branch will be read. This idea can be put in force at each subsequent level of contestants' responses.

7. Views similar to several of those in this chapter can be found in James Moor, "An Analysis of the Turing Test", *Philosophical Studies* 30 (1976): 249–58, and Daniel C. Dennett, "Can Machines Think?" in Michael Shafto, ed., *How We Know* (San Francisco: Harper & Row, 1985), pp. 121–45.

Chapter 2

1. John R. Searle, "Minds, Brains, and Programs", *The Behavioral and Brain Sciences* 3 (1980): 417–24. Parenthetical numbers in text refer to this source. Searle's article is followed by several interesting "Open Peer Commentaries".

2. Searle refers to R. C. Schank and R. P. Abelson, *Scripts, Plans, Goals, and Understanding* (Hillsdale, N.J.: Erlbaum, 1977).

3. In the discussion of the systems reply in "Minds, Brains, and Programs", esp. p. 419, Searle often refers to the understanding of *subsystems*. This unfortunately directs our attention away from the absolutely essential point of the systems reply, which is quite clear when Searle *introduces* it, namely, that the boundary of a subject of understanding includes the whole *person*, not some *part* of a person. It has the effect of making some of Searle's remarks inapplicable to the systems reply as correctly understood. In the following discussion, I shall resolutely hold to the person as the (putative) subject of understanding.

4. This point was brought to my attention by my student Brian Tiffany.

5. "Split brain" patients have had the corpus callosum (a band of fibers that connects the two sides of the brain) severed in order to prevent epileptic seizures. For a discussion of these fascinating cases see Michael S. Gazzaniga and Joseph E. LeDoux, *The Integrated Mind* (New York: Plenum, 1978).

6. Searle is not very explicit about distinguishing this reason from others, but I take it that he is giving this reason when he says, "Whereas the English subsystem knows that 'hamburgers' refers to hamburgers, the Chinese subsystem knows only that 'squiggle squiggle' is followed by 'squoggle squoggle'" (Searle, "Minds, Brains, and Programs", p. 419).

Chapter 3

1. Strictly, I should say connections to the *rest of* the body, since a computer will be part of a robot's body in the same way that a brain is part of a human being's body. I do not think, however, that anyone would have a problem with understanding a remark like "Akinetia's brain works fine, it's her body that's giving her a problem"; so no one should misunderstand analogous remarks about robots.

Chapter 4

1. Daniel C. Dennett, "Why You Can't Make a Computer That Feels Pain", in *Brainstorms* (Montgomery, Vt.: Bradford Books, 1978), pp. 190–229.

2. Dennett describes the morphine patients as "bearing all the usual earmarks of belief that one is in pain" (ibid., p. 227). This is, however, plainly false. Presumably, Dennett has in mind the striking fact that, when you ask these patients whether they have a pain, they answer yes. But they do not ask for

(further) pain killer and they say that they do not mind whatever it is they are having. These tendencies clearly differentiate their dispositions from the usual dispositions of people who claim to be in pain.

3. Ronald Melzack and P. D. Wall, "Pain Mechanisms: A New Theory", *Science* 150 (1965): 971–79; and *The Challenge of Pain* (Harmondsworth: Penguin Books, 1982), chap. 9.

4. Some of the boxes in Figure 4.2 are not reflections of physiological knowledge or even of serious physiological speculation. For example, Dennett notes that if we have a pain, we ordinarily believe we have it and remember that we had it. He forthwith puts a memory and belief box in his diagram (see Dennett, *Brainstorms*, pp. 203–4), which thereafter appears in his diagrams as a separate box with definite connections to other boxes. One might get the impression that if we are going to have a pain-feeling robot, we should have one whose innards instantiate this diagram. But wait: the position of the memory and belief box is merely the projection of the *external* function (that when we get anvil on foot, for example, we answer yes to "Does it hurt bad?" and likewise to "Did it hurt bad?" asked a few weeks later). Any plausible mechanism that gets this function performed would have served about as well as any other. (A similar point holds with respect to some boxes that are *partly* based on physiological research: Their precise position in the diagram is merely one among many that would have got the job of performing the "external" function accomplished.) What we are entitled to learn from such parts of the diagram is thus *only* that the "external" function is subserved *somehow* by an internal mechanism. The diagrammatic presentation suggests, however, that we are actually representing a definite requirement on the internal construction.

5. It has been objected by Mark Bowes that we would not need to model our reactions to drugs perfectly in order to be entitled to claim to have created the causal conditions of pain. After all, there is variability among people. If an animal, or an alien, had a structure of drug reactions more or less like ours, but differing in the chemicals that were effective, we would probably still regard it as a strong candidate for a feeler of pain. This seems right, but it is not an objection to the view being taken here. For, a complex structure of drug reactions, analogous to ours, will still require an organic internal structure. To the extent that one moves away from such organic structure, one will inevitably move away from the structure of drug reactions that provides the support for thinking that the causes of pains have been provided.

Chapter 5

1. For an excellent and highly readable review of the history and status of Church's Thesis, see Richard L. Epstein and Walter A. Carnielli, *Computability: Computable Functions, Logic, and the Foundations of Mathematics* (Pacific Grove, Calif.: Wadsworth & Brooks/Cole, 1989), chaps. 10 and 25.

2. Daniel Dennett, "Why the Law of Effect Will Not Go Away", in *Brainstorms* (Montgomery, Vt.: Bradford Books), pp. 71–89. See esp. pp. 82–83.

3. Notice that I do not say "every *possible* artwork". No description we could give would rule out the possibility of someone (other than Picasso) making an artwork that satisfied that description. Even specifying exact likeness would not be enough to divide the Picassos from all possible non-Picassos: A perfect forgery would still not be a Picasso.

Chapter 6

1. J. R. Lucas, "Minds, Machines and Gödel", Philosophy 36 (1961); reprinted in A. R. Anderson, *Minds and Machines* (Englewood Cliffs, N.J.: Prentice-Hall, 1964), pp. 43–59. An argument similar to Lucas's has recently been advanced by Roger Penrose in *The Emperor's New Mind* (Oxford: Oxford University Press, 1989), pp. 416–18. I have chosen to discuss Lucas's formulation, however, because it is far clearer and more convincing. The criticisms of Lucas that we shall discuss later in the chapter can be tailored to apply to Penrose's version.

2. To make this quite general, we should note that one kind of rule allows any of the axioms to be written down after any other expression in a proof.

3. There is, indeed, a purely formal criterion derivable from the work of Emil Post, which says that a system is consistent if there is any wff that is not a theorem. (See "Introduction to a General Theory of Elementary Propositions", *American Journal of Mathematics* 43 [1921]: 163–85.) This criterion, however, cannot be motivated within the present system (or in any system that lacks the resources to derive every wff from any contradiction). Thus, the present way of approaching consistency is the only one that makes sense at this stage. We shall say a little more about this criterion when the matter comes up naturally again in the discussion of Lucas's argument.

4. Automata can be probabilistic when considered at a level of meaningful operations above the physical level. Discussion of this, however, would complicate matters without affecting points relevant to Lucas's argument. This is because, at the level of arithmetic, we are not probabilistic in our answers. However much we might vary in our preferences for styles of expression or branches to try in a search problem, we do not answer $2 + 2 = ?$ sometimes one way and sometimes another (unless we make *mistakes*, which is different from normal but probabilistic operation).

5. Operations done in parallel (simultaneously in different parts of the robot) correspond to parts of a proof that do not depend on each other, and so can be written down in any order.

6. Kurt Gödel, "Über Formal Unentscheidbare Sätze der *Principia Mathematica* und Verwandter Systeme, I", *Monatshefte für Mathematik und Physik* 38 (1931): 173–98. My presentation of Gödel's result does not hew strictly to the 1931 paper but reflects simplifications developed in later work by Gödel, Turing,

and J. B. Rosser. This combining of results is now standard practice in all but technical works and is evidently made use of by Lucas, and his critics. None of the critical discussion of Lucas's argument essentially depends on the simplifications, although the statement of them would be considerably more complicated without them.

7. W. V. Quine, *The Ways of Paradox and Other Essays* (New York: Random House, 1966), p. 35.

8. This is the formulation that is most helpful in understanding Lucas's argument. But what about incompleteness according to the formal definition? Here too we have the same result. If PAT is consistent but incomplete in the formal sense, then adding [5FE] to the set of theorems must not produce inconsistency. Now, it *would* produce inconsistency if the negation of [5FE] were a theorem (and vice versa, although we have not given any argument for that). Gödel showed, however, that the negations of statements like [5FE] also are not theorems of consistent systems for arithmetic. Informally, you can think of the matter this way: Suppose "[5FE] is false" (strictly, the fully expressed version of this) were a theorem. That would say that it is false that *i* is not a member of PAT-THEOREMNOS, which is a long-winded way of saying that *i* *is* a member of PATTHEOREMNOS. But *i* is the Gödel number of [5FE]; so to say it is a member of PATTHEOREMNOS is to say that [5FE] is a theorem after all. Thus, just as a proof of [5FE] would imply that it could not be proved, a proof that [5FE] is false would imply that it could be proved. If your system is consistent, you are not going to be able to get *either* kind of proof; so adding either [5FE] or its negation (not both, of course) will not produce inconsistency; so your system will be incomplete.

9. More detailed discussions of Gödel's theorem and its background can be found in Ernest Nagel and James R. Newman, *Gödel's Proof* (New York: NYU Press, 1958), and in Douglas Hofstader, *Gödel, Escher, Bach* (New York: Basic Books, 1979).

10. These are described by Daniel Dennett in "The Abilities of Men and Machines", in *Brainstorms* (Montgomery, Vt.: Bradford Books, 1978), pp. 256–66. We shall be following out and commenting on the line of argument developed in that essay.

11. See Amelie Rorty, ed., *The Identities of Persons* (Berkeley: The University of California Press, 1976).

12. The restriction of S_x to well-formed formulas comes through the fact that, in our representation of the pattern, "S_2" had to be a sentence, and the analogue of sentences in formal proofs is wffs.

13. Turning this around, we get the consistency criterion derived from Emil Post: A system is consistent if there is a wff that is not a theorem. (See esp. p. 177 of reference in note 3 of this chapter.) The advantage of this criterion is that wff-hood and theorem-hood are purely formal notions. In systems that contain rules corresponding to our two arguments (or rules that give the same results)— that is to say, all really interesting systems—we can thus have a very simple and elegant formulation of consistency. This simplicity does, however, rest on know-

ing that the system has a certain richness. A very simple system can have wffs that are not theorems, and yet be inconsistent according to any familiar understanding of this term. To see this, consider the ABIN+ system, which is the ABIN system together with the further axiom scheme NNxII (x subject to the same proviso as the one that applies to the first axiom scheme). This enlarged system permits the derivation of many, many inconsistent pairs of theorems (e.g., NBII and NNBII) but you still cannot get the wff NANBB.

14. See Anderson, *Minds and Machines*, pp. 53–55.

15. Hilary Putnam, Review of Nagel and Newman, *Gödel's Proof*, in *Philosophy of Science* 27 (1960): 205–7. The quotation is from p. 207. Note that Nagel and Newman's book precedes the publication of Lucas's article. Lucas's article is the one generally discussed, however, because it contains the more explicit and detailed statement of the modeling argument.

16. Ernest Nagel and James R. Newman, "Putnam's Review of *Gödel's Proof*", *Philosophy of Science* 28 (1961): 209–11.

Chapter 7

1. See, for example, Allen Newell and Herbert A. Simon, "Computer Science as Empirical Inquiry: Symbols and Search", *Communications of the Association for Computing Machinery* 19 (1976): 113–26; Zenon Pylyshyn, *Computation and Cognition* (Cambridge, Mass.: The MIT Press, 1984); and Jerry Fodor, "Why There Still Has to Be a Language of Thought", in his *Psychosemantics* (Cambridge, Mass.: The MIT Press, 1987). For a divergent theory that still recognizes the appeal of the sentence-processing view, see Terence Horgan and John Tienson, "Settling Into a New Paradigm", *Southern Journal of Philosophy* 26 (1987), Supplementary Spindel Conference volume, pp. 97–113.

2. See Ludwig Wittgenstein, *Philosophical Investigations* (New York: Macmillan, 1953), esp. pt. 1, pp. 11 and 54, and sects. 139–41.

3. This alternative should be understood to include the case in which the relevant units of our operation are groups of cells (perhaps numbering in the hundreds) rather than individual cells, and so we imagine that our machines simulate the operation of groups of cells. The justification for this inclusion is that the difference between the individual cell case and the groups of cells case is trivial in this context. The problems we shall soon raise are the same for both.

Chapter 8

1. Hubert L. Dreyfus, *What Computers Can't Do* (New York: Harper & Row, 1972); Hubert L. Dreyfus and Stuart E. Dreyfus, "Making a Mind Versus Modeling a Brain: Artificial Intelligence Back at a Branchpoint", in Stephen Graubard, ed., *The Artificial Intelligence Debate* (Cambridge, Mass.: The MIT Press, 1988; originally published as an issue of *Daedalus*, Winter 1988); and *Mind*

over Matter (New York: The Free Press, 1986). See also Hilary Putnam's article, "Much Ado About Not Very Much", in Graubard, *The Artificial Intelligence Debate*.

2. See Drew McDermott, "Artificial Intelligence Meets Natural Stupidity", in J. Haugeland, *Mind Design* (Montgomery, Vt.: Bradford Books, 1981), pp. 143–60. The examples in the text can be found here.

3. Numbers given in this section are taken mainly from David F. Lindsley and J. Eric Holmes, *Basic Human Neurophysiology* (New York: Elsevier, 1984). Other interesting discussions, from which some numbers have been used, can be found in J. T. Schwartz, "The New Connectionism", in Graubard, *The Artificial Intelligence Debate*, pp. 123–41; and Patricia Churchland, *Neurophilosophy* (Cambridge, Mass.: The MIT Press, 1986).

4. This has become known as "Feldman's 100 step rule" after J. A. Feldman, who made this point in his "Connectionist Models and Their Applications: Introduction", *Cognitive Science* 9 (1985): 1–2.

5. Of course, if you take matters down to individual ions, you can find discrete operations of neurons. But this is not the effective level of operation. To think so is as misguided as arguing that we must suppose degrees of sweetness of coffee to come in discrete units because, after all, sugar comes (usually) in discrete granules, and some definite number of granules has been added to the coffee. These premises are true, but irrelevant, since we are not aware of any difference in coffee solutions that differ only by one granule (and so, our taste mechanism is not effectively operating on one-granule differences).

Chapter 9

1. Pioneering work on the machines discussed in this chapter was done by Frank Rosenblatt (see *Problems of Neurodynamics: Perceptrons and the Theory of Brain Mechanisms* [Washington, D.C.: Spartan Books, 1962]). The primary source for the material in this chapter is David E. Rumelhart, James L. McClelland, and the PDP Research Group, *Parallel Distributed Processing: Explorations in the Microstructure of Cognition*, vols. 1 and 2 (Cambridge, Mass.: The MIT Press, 1986). The interested reader should proceed to the papers in this collection, which include introductory and summary overviews as well as detailed experiments, or to William Bechtel and Adele Abrahamsen, *Connectionism and the Mind: An Introduction to Parallel Processing in Networks* (Cambridge, Mass.: Basil Blackwell, 1991). Use also has been made of papers in G. E. Hinton and J. A. Anderson, *Parallel Models of Associative Memory* (Hillsdale, N.J.: Erlbaum, 1981).

2. There are some cases in which activity at a synapse between, say, neurons A and B is affected by activity in a third neuron, C. These cases may be exceptions to the point about locality that will shortly be made in the text. Although such cases complicate the view that we must have of brain operations, they do not seem to be frequent enough to undercut the usefulness of a general

assumption of locality. They are even compatible with a version of it; for a synapse between A and B can be affected by C only insofar as C delivers impulses at (or very close to) the synapse.

3. A simple version of this view is that if neurons have their firing rates raised at the same times, the synaptic connection will tend to become strong. The standard reference for this idea is D. O. Hebb, *The Organization of Behavior* (New York: Wiley, 1949). W. R. Uttal, in his *The Psychobiology of Mind* (Hillsdale, N.J.: Erlbaum, 1978), p. 613, puts the idea that synaptic connectivity underlies learning as far back as 1893.

4. The pattern associator described here is a model that illustrates several points typical of pattern associators described in Rumelhart and McClelland, *Parallel Distributed Processing*, and Hinton and Anderson, *Parallel Models*. The diagram is closest to that of T. Kohonen, P. Lethio, and E. Oja, "Storage and Processing of Information in Distributed Associative Memory Systems", in Hinton and Anderson, *Parallel Models*, p. 110.

5. The diagram in Figure 9.6 is topologically equivalent to one given by J. A. Anderson and Michael C. Mozer in "Categorization and Selective Neurons", in Hinton and Anderson, *Parallel Models*. Compare Rumelhart and McClelland, *Parallel Distributed Processing*, 2: 174. The latter model uses a form of the delta rule to calculate weight changes, while the former uses a Hebbian scheme that makes the change proportional to the product of activations in the connected elements.

6. See Kohonen, Lethio, and Oja, "Storage and Processing of Information", p. 124.

7. Frank Rosenblatt, *Problems of Neurodynamics: Perceptrons and the Theory of Brain Mechanisms* (Washington, D.C.: Spartan Books, 1962), p. 403.

8. Strictly, a machine that is equivalent to some Turing machine.

Chapter 10

1. For a well-known and thorough investigation of this kind of difficulty for the wider project of PDP, see Steven Pinker and Alan Prince, "On Language and Connectionism: Analysis of a Parallel Distributed Model of Language Acquisition", in Steven Pinker and Jacques Mehler, eds., *Connections and Symbols* (Cambridge, Mass.: The MIT Press, 1988), pp. 73–193.

2. See ibid. for an example. A paper by two leading critics of PDP, Jerry Fodor and Zenon Pylyshyn, can be found on pp. 3–71 of the same volume, under the title, "Connectionism and Cognitive Architecture: A Critical Analysis".

3. See p. 20 of the instructions for the 1989 U.S. 1040 income tax form.

4. My discussion owes something to Andy Clark, *Microcognition* (Cambridge, Mass.: The MIT Press, 1989), but I am aiming to represent one clear idea about why hybridization is plausible, and not the details of anyone's developed view. See also Paul Smolensky, "On the Proper Treatment of Connectionism", *Behavioral and Brain Sciences* 11 (1988): 1–74.

5. There is a trivial sense in which the class of inputs that will result in a given output is specifiable in advance of putting a system to work; for one way to refer to this class is "the class of inputs that will result in output O". The point here is that we need not have investigated what the members of this class actually are in any nontrivial sense. If the system effectively admits only finite sets of inputs (as would be the case, for example, with digital input devices no matter how small the difference between distinct inputs), then the members of the class will be calcul*able*; but they need not have been calculated.

6. See J. Garcia and R. A. Koelling, "Relation of Cue to Consequence in Avoidance Learning", *Psychonomic Science* 4 (1966): 123–24. Compare I. L. Bernstein, "Learned Taste Aversions in Children Receiving Chemotherapy", *Science* 200 (1978): 1302–3.

7. One mechanism of this kind is described in Bruce L. McNaughton and Lynn Nadel, "Hebb-Marr Networks and the Neurobiological Representation of Action in Space", in M. A. Gluck and D. E. Rumelhart, *Neuroscience and Connectionist Theory* (Hillsdale, N.J.: Erlbaum, 1990), pp. 1–63, esp. p. 21.

8. Readers who found the foregoing section interesting may wish to read Valentino Braitenberg's fascinating book *Vehicles* (Cambridge, Mass.: The MIT Press, 1984). More detailed related material can be found in chapter 10 of Patricia S. Churchland's *Neurophilosophy* (Cambridge, Mass.: The MIT Press, 1986), and in C. R. Gallistel's *The Organization of Action: A New Synthesis* (Hillsdale, N.J.: Erlbaum, 1980).

Chapter 11

1. Remember that intelligence does not require the *best* response, only a reasonable one, and that there can be many of these. I am not suggesting that the stated responses are the only ones an intelligent subject might give, just that giving them would not reveal their producer to be nonintelligent.

2. You may, if you insist, count the same physical signal as *move up* or *move down* depending on where the door is; and you may get a third signal by counting absence of any signal as an instruction to stay put. These choices will not affect the argument.

3. Two technical points are in order. First, the length of an English sentence has no theoretical upper limit. To do well on the Turing test, however, Robot Rlt will probably never have to process a sentence of more than forty words. (I doubt that this book contains one that is that long.) So, we can assume a finite maximum length for its brain's output. Since vocabularies also are finite, we will have a finite (though very large) number of possible messages.

Second, what a robot must do to leave a room, for example, varies with where it is and which way it is faced when it starts. So, we could not really have a table of the kind described in the text. At best, we could have something like it, where present position was factored in by some means. This shows that the problem for the strategy schematized in Figure 11.4 is *worse* than I say it is in the text. That is fine with me. The problem in the text is *bad enough*, and that is the point that I want to bring out most clearly. I shall say a little more about all this later on.

4. Some of the remarks I will make here apply to versions of homuncularism that have been arrived at in ways quite different from the approach taken here. See, for example, Daniel Dennett, *Brainstorms* (Montgomery, Vt.: Bradford Books, 1978), and William Lycan, *Consciousness* (Cambridge, Mass.: The MIT Press, 1987).

Index of Robots

Numbers below indicate the pages at which each robot is introduced and described.

Index